# NO ONE GOT CRACKED OVER THE HEAD FOR NO REASON

# NO ONE GOT CRACKED OVER THE HEAD FOR NO REASON

## DISPATCHES FROM A CRIME REPORTER

MARTIN BRUNT

Biteback Publishing

First published in Great Britain in 2023 by
Biteback Publishing Ltd, London
Copyright © Martin Brunt 2023

ISBN 978-1-78590-778-4

10 9 8 7 6 5 4 3 2 1

A CIP catalogue record for this book is available from the British Library.

Set in Minion Pro

Printed and bound in Great Britain by
CPI Group (UK) Ltd, Croydon CR0 4YY

FSC
www.fsc.org
MIX
Paper | Supporting
responsible forestry
FSC® C171272

*For Tom, Jolyon and Ella*

# CONTENTS

# PREFACE

I'm in a pub near Scotland Yard where coppers and crime reporters meet to discuss subjects of mutual interest. I walk steadily
from the bar and place two pints of lager on a corner table. It's
around midday. Head down, Detective Inspector Will O'Reilly
rummages in the battered brown leather briefcase at his feet and
brings up a folded sheet of paper. He slides it across the table. He
has something he's keen to show me, but he's being careful not to
reveal it to anyone nearby.

Inside is a small, creased and grainy photograph. There are six
black men standing close together, side by side in a group. They
are casually dressed, except for the man on the far left who has
his hands behind his back and is wearing what looks like a black
police uniform. The men are obviously posing for the camera but
appear relaxed, neither gloating nor self-conscious. None of them
is smiling.

On the grubby floor at their feet sits a small, naked black child
who may be three or four years old. If I peer closely, I can just make

out it's a boy. His arms hang loose, his thin legs stretched out in front of him. It's impossible to tell his expression. Why? Because the picture is blurred and the lighting is poor, but mostly because the boy's head is missing. Well, not missing entirely: when I look again more closely, I can see the man standing directly behind him is holding it.

It's impossible to look at the picture without imagining the terror and pain of the little victim and the depravity of those who killed him. Was he still alive when they cut off his head? Was his murder a sacrifice to some ancient god? The lunchtime drinkers gathering around us are completely unaware of the grim nature of our business. If they notice us at all, they may think we are sharing memories of an old family photograph.

For DI O'Reilly, unfortunately – and that hardly seems the appropriate word – the decapitated boy in the picture is not the one he is looking for. This isn't the child whose butchered body was found floating in the River Thames months earlier and whose murder he is struggling to solve. But the photograph, found barely a mile from where we are sitting, does fuel his theory that his own troubling case may not be the first voodoo killing with a British connection.

That episode in a London pub says so much about the relationship between a detective and a crime reporter. Or how it used to be: trust, a shared confidence, a beer, no press officer to monitor our discussion and a meeting O'Reilly's bosses at Scotland Yard probably knew nothing about. It wasn't just an excuse for a cop and a hack to have a drink and tut-tut over a shocking photograph. There was a serious purpose.

In the hour we spent together, O'Reilly reignited my interest in his own frustrated investigation, the murder of a young African boy whose headless, limbless torso had been fished out of the river a year earlier. And I promised him I would do a story, offering him renewed publicity that might just prompt a witness to call him with the vital clue to solve the mystery. That's how things once were. Journalists used to say: 'That's how the world goes around.' Our world at least. Today that world turns on a different axis.

# INTRODUCTION

*Well, I didn't say: 'Darling, I'm just off to stick up Barclays.' I told her*
*I was going out to do a bit of work and see you later*
– Retired gangster Freddie Foreman

Not every day of a crime reporter's life is filled with such horror. And sitting in a pub, sipping beer with a friendly detective, isn't something I do a lot. But it's not a bad way to earn a living. Some reporters do still enjoy a regular boozy lunch with their contacts, especially those who work for newspapers where we developed bad habits in secret drinking dens that were open all day long before pubs were allowed extended hours.

When I joined Sky News after a dozen years as a newspaper hack, I soon discovered that alcohol and live television don't mix, although TV producers have since seized on the cocktail as a vital ingredient of prurient reality shows, where contestants are encouraged to have sex in front of the cameras. I like to think that news, for now at least, is a rather more serious business, though I've had my light-hearted and much-ridiculed moments on screen, and not all of them were intentional.

My world changed when newspaper reporters at the Sunday tabloid *News of the World* discovered a simple way of hacking into the mobile phones of royal aides, celebrities and politicians and finding out what they were up to. Scotland Yard's initial, half-hearted pursuit of the journalists – and the hacking of a murdered schoolgirl's phone – prompted a high-profile police investigation, more official scrutiny and the closure of Britain's best-selling newspaper. That all culminated in the Leveson judicial inquiry into the media's relationship with police and politicians. There was always going to be only one loser. The job of being a crime reporter, whether on TV, newspapers or the internet, changed for ever.

Leveson effectively brought an end to the way in which reporters got exclusive stories from their police contacts. Sir Brian Leveson, a senior judge, acknowledged the media had a vital role in certain functions, but he didn't believe that some journalists should be given special access to information held by a public body such as the police service. From then on, he said, police should record all contact with journalists.

If he'd known about it, Leveson would have frowned on my pub meeting with DI O'Reilly to discuss the Thames torso case. The judge wrote in his report: 'If a police officer tips off a member of the press, the perception may well be that he or she has done so in exchange for past favours or the expectation of some future benefit.'

There was no such edge to my meeting with the detective. All O'Reilly wanted was help in solving a troubling murder. Maybe that was the future benefit Leveson meant, but what was wrong with that? The police wouldn't bother talking to journalists at all if they didn't believe there would be some kind of benefit, which in most cases is the public's help in solving a crime. Surely, catching criminals is to the public's benefit, isn't it?

O'Reilly had retired by the time of the Leveson Report – he'd been promoted to chief inspector but hadn't solved the torso case – but plenty of my contacts were still investigating major crimes, and after Leveson my calls and texts to them went largely unanswered. I got used to seeing them only at press conferences, where we were spoon fed limited information about current cases and given little chance to probe behind the official version. At least my bar bills went down.

If my job has become harder, it's even tougher now to be a villain and get away with it, though recent Home Office revelations of falling crime detection rates suggested a temporary shift in the balance between good and evil. The increasingly detailed analysis of DNA, mobile phone tracking, the spread of CCTV, new money-laundering laws, the growth of home-security and car-dashboard cameras, the use of drones and the development of facial and vehicle recognition technology: all have been added to police capability in the war on crime. And law enforcers are always looking for new ideas.

A detective involved in a complicated corruption case once complained to me, over a coffee near my Westminster office, that his suspects were too clever to be caught out by listening devices hidden in their phones and cars. He asked if my employers at Sky would put a bug inside a suspect's satellite TV system. It would involve our technical department creating a 'fault' and then sending round a technician to 'correct it'. I passed on the request, but I already knew the answer would be a firm no and not even a polite one.

Criminals, like the rest of us, use the latest communications systems. It's almost impossible for them to avoid leaving a digital footprint that can provide prosecution evidence as damning as a fingerprint. Some villains do fight back in the technology war, with cheap, disposable and unregistered 'burner' mobile phones bought for cash, encrypted messaging systems and all sorts of signal blockers and jammers. But a lot of villains still don't get it and think gloves and a balaclava will prevent them being identified.

I asked the Flying Squad commander Peter Spindler how the ageing Hatton Garden heist gang – the 'diamond wheezers' as a *Sun* headline brilliantly put it – were caught, so soon after they escaped with their £14 million loot. He summed it up succinctly: 'They were analogue villains operating in a digital world.' Among the gang's stupid mistakes: the getaway driver used his own car, another bought a drill and gave his home address, and they failed to turn off a security camera. In court the key evidence against them was digital data from their mobile phones, their computers and CCTV, rather than old-fashioned witnesses.

I've interviewed many criminals because it's interesting to hear their stories. I'm not sure it sheds much light on their motives, which are usually greed and idleness or, as I heard a lawyer describe it rather poetically: 'The prospect of dishonest gain almost beyond the dreams of avarice.'

I asked Freddie Foreman, once one of Britain's most-feared gangsters and a figure much respected in the underworld, what he told his wife when he left home to commit an armed robbery. 'Well, I didn't say: "Darling, I'm just off to stick up Barclays." I told her I was going out to do a bit of work and see you later.' How much later Mrs Foreman saw Fred rather depended on the success of the robbery.

On my grim beat, many of the characters I encounter are as

seemingly humdrum as the rest of us but sometimes, by their actions and ambitions, the most captivating individuals. They can hold your attention rapt and at the same time send a shiver down your spine. At a sunny beach cafe beside the Adriatic Sea, Italian gangster Valerio Viccei had me gripped with tales of his £60 million diamond heist.

Viccei was educated, charming and articulate, not your everyday robber with his traditional lifestyle of 'birds, booze and betting.' I knew my audience would be thrilled by a glimpse into a world forbidden to most of them, imagining perhaps what they might do with just one of the ten Fabergé eggs he stole. My own fascination with Viccei dipped a bit when he threatened to kill me.

These are some of the characters in this book, along with the stories behind the stories, which are often more interesting than the headline-grabbing crimes themselves. Sometimes they're quite bizarre. In a Spanish jail, conman Mark Acklom asked me if Sky would pay his €30,000 bail money. Before you ask, we didn't.

Tales like that break up the monotony of the day-to-day crime stories we get from the police. Membership of the Crime Reporters' Association gives us access to special background briefings by detectives but, since Leveson, they don't happen as often as they did. We used to have monthly gatherings in the press room at Scotland Yard, the headquarters of the Metropolitan Police in London, with the commissioner. In theory at least, nothing was off-limits, and we could expect a candid response to a probing question.

We got most out of those meetings when Sir John Stevens – now Lord Stevens – was commissioner. He was a tall, imposing figure who was forthright in his views, understood the media and knew a good headline. One day, his officers were accused of overreacting during a pro-fox-hunting demonstration outside Parliament. This wasn't your average rally, but a gathering of largely conservative, land-owning individuals, many dressed in waxed Barbour coats, whose natural instincts were to support the police. The explorer Sir Ranulph Fiennes and the TV cook Clarissa Dickson Wright were among the posh protestors.

The demonstration had started peacefully enough but turned angry. Before long police had drawn their batons and were exchanging blows with a section of the crowd. Bottles were thrown and some officers had their helmets knocked off. More than a dozen protestors and two police officers were injured, though none seriously. The Independent Police Complaints Commission launched an investigation into allegations of police brutality. The next day we asked the commissioner why his officers had lashed out. He paused before answering: 'No one got cracked over the head for no reason.' It was a mangled way of putting it, unusually for him, but we knew what he meant. *No One Got Cracked Over the Head for No Reason.* One day, I thought, I'll use that for the title of a book.

Sir John had a good relationship with crime reporters, once telling us to ring up his major crime investigators and go and visit them if we wanted to know what they were up to. It was long before the Leveson Report. It sounded promising, but it didn't always result in open access and good stories. 'You're fucking joking! He said *what*?' was the response from one of his overworked detectives. But they had to talk to us because the boss said so. We haven't always felt so respected. It's usually quite the opposite, a feeling reinforced by the portrayal of reporters in most Hollywood movies and TV dramas, with only a few notable exceptions, as sleazy, dirt-digging scumbags who would sell their grandmother for a good story. Well, I don't have a grandmother to sell anymore. I do have an ageing mother, though.

Our stock rose remarkably, if briefly, during the coronavirus pandemic of 2020–22 when the government declared journalists to be essential workers. We were hardly up there on a pedestal with doctors and nurses, but it acknowledged at least that we had a message to deliver, even if it was mostly one of doom. In the early days of the pandemic, crime slipped down the news agenda, until the introduction of emergency Covid lockdown laws to stop the virus spreading. Police got into terrible muddles trying to interpret rules that they resented having to enforce anyway. None more so than the Metropolitan Police, who compounded their shame over the kidnap, rape and murder by one of their own officers of a young woman, Sarah Everard… by wrestling to the ground a young woman protesting about police failing to protect young women.

The force later triggered another huge row by ignoring, and then being pressed into investigating, Covid lockdown breaches at 10 Downing Street. It raised the intriguing prospect of the Prime Minister, Boris Johnson, being arrested, but he managed to escape with only a £50 fine. The policing of the pandemic lockdown was an interesting diversion from my regular beat. I reported on people being fined for meeting others, for travelling too far, for staying too long in a pub. Eventually I got back to more traditional and interesting crimes.

The ruthless exploits of murderers, diamond thieves and fraudsters are the staple diet of crime reporters and have inspired fiction writers from William Shakespeare to… well, I was going to say John

Grisham, but in terms of huge book sales I think I'll go with Richard Osman, the new crime-writing phenomenon. All crime, true or imagined, continues to fascinate. The biggest-selling fiction books of all time are often said to be the detective novels of Agatha Christie. In Fleet Street, the age-old mantra occasionally still applies to the choice of front-page news: if it bleeds it leads. The criminals in this book are real, and most of them are still alive and have paid their debt to society. But beware, a few may not have changed their ways. Some haven't even been caught yet.

What follows is, I hope, an insight into the life of a crime reporter as I navigate the various changes in policing and the upheaval in the relationship between cops and hacks. It's best illustrated by some of the stories I've reported, but especially the untold tales that sparked them off; how rumours, snippets, gossip and tip-offs are turned into the news that feeds the public's seemingly never-ending appetite for true crime.

That fascination was one of the reasons for writing this book. I explore the phenomenon with various specialists: the criminologist who believes we have a subconscious need to learn about violent crime, to be able to avoid it; the author whose female readers tell him they get a secret thrill from the gory details; and the museum curator who exhibits videos of jihadi beheadings, because he feels people have a right to know the full horror of the threat to British citizens.

For all the changes over the years, the cast of characters in the real crime world remains the same. The names may alter, but they are still people who believe, despite advances in science and technology, that they can kill, kidnap, rape, rob, steal or deceive without getting found out. There are still those dedicated to the job of catching them, others to punishing them. And there are still the innocent victims, some of whom are plunged into extraordinary events that bring them to the usually unwelcome attention of a crime reporter.

# CHAPTER 1

# THE PAPERBOY

*The force should avoid warm cuddly community stories. The public
wants crime fighters, not street dancers*
– FORMER COMMANDER ROY RAMM

If I want to get away from the post-Leveson chill and catch a
glimpse of how things used to be, a time when nobody minded
cops and journalists having a drink together and dark humour was
acceptable, I drop in on the Association of Ex-CID Officers of the
Metropolitan Police. There's an air of 'the good old days', usually
happily acknowledged, and no one is listening out for inappropriate
language. But even veteran members have had to accept inevitable
change. Gone are the black-tie dinners with their Masonic over-
tones where, for many years, the only women I saw there were serving the men or washing up their dirty plates. Now, there's equality,
inclusiveness and informality, but they love to poke fun at political
correctness.

Roy Ramm, a former commander of specialist operations, is the regular star turn at the association's twice-yearly lunches, welcoming guests with a mix of charm and irreverence. In a recent speech, he began with his take on the controversial issue of gender identification:

> Mr President, members of the Association, honoured and distinguished guests... with a penis, honoured and distinguished guests without a penis, guests without a penis but who would like to have a penis, guests with an unwanted penis, guests who can't make their mind up whether they want a penis or not, guests who pretend either to have or not to have a penis depending on how they dress, guests who see the penis as an existential threat and occasional penis users of all genders. And, most importantly of all, those of you who simply don't give a toss about the relevance of your own genitalia or those of others. You are all most welcome.

Ramm is a respected commentator on policing, urging a return to pride and discipline and an end to woke behaviour and excessive community engagement. He told me: 'The force should avoid warm cuddly community stories. The public wants crime fighters, not street dancers.' I'm sure Ramm is happiest when he's addressing the 'ex-tecs' lunches. He once welcomed Commissioner Dame Cressida Dick by observing she wasn't the first 'dick' to lead the force. She appeared to enjoy the joke. The association often invites along journalists and makes a particular fuss of broadcasters. I drew the raffle once and was slightly alarmed to find myself handing out prizes of envelopes of cash to police officers.

At a recent event, the award-winning LBC radio host Nick Ferrari was on my table. The same night, he was a guest at the Albert Hall for the Royal Variety Performance, an annual charity show of comedians, musicians, dancers and magicians. He said afterwards that none of the professionals had been any more entertaining than Roy Ramm. Ferrari's career and mine have sometimes mirrored each other. We worked on the same local newspaper group in Kent, and I joined the Ferrari Press Agency, which his father Lino founded. I later followed Nick to *The Sun* and the *Sunday Mirror*. When Sky News began, he was appointed launch editor and invited me to leave Fleet Street and join him at the new channel. He went on to do many and greater things, while I'm still a crime reporter, but he still speaks to me.

As well as his father, who became a *Daily Mirror* executive, Ferrari's brothers were journalists, but I have no such links to the profession. I'm not sure what set me on the same path, but I'm grateful that something did because without it I would have had to get a proper job. It may have been my early teenage days at Burrows newsagents in Ely in Cambridgeshire, where I was one of thirty or so young boys, on bone-shaker bikes, delivering morning papers before school. The shop was opened in 1899 by journalist and printer James Burrows. It has since relocated twice, but it has always stood in the shadow of the imposing medieval cathedral that dominates the centre of the small Fenland city.

In my early teens, I often accompanied James's son Percy, who had inherited the business, to Ely Station to meet the 6.40 a.m. train from London Liverpool Street. Percy, a stickler for punctuality, jotted down the time of the train's arrival each morning in a diary published by the Marylebone Cricket Club. I don't know why he did that, because he couldn't claim compensation for delays as we commuters do today.

Together, the boss and I heaved around 3,000 papers, in string-tied bundles, off the goods wagon onto wooden trolleys and then tossed them into the back of our green Austin van. The papers were literally hot off the press, still warm by the time they reached Ely and all the more welcomed for that on cold, dark winter mornings. The current owner, Jeff 'Bud' Burrows, ruddy-cheeked like his dad, has worked in the business since his schooldays and still enjoys it at the age of seventy-four. 'The papers were so warm that on freezing mornings we used to stick our hands in the middle of the bundles to thaw out,' he recalled over coffee in the Lamb Hotel next door to the shop. 'Of course, in those days the ink came off, so your hands were always black.'

Black hands apart, the sweet smell of the newsprint, the whis-tle and steam of the old locomotives that were being replaced by diesel trains, and the bold front-page headlines, created a romantic image of an exciting world that was only eighty miles up the track. It seemed much further. The news of global events at that time – Martin Luther King's assassination, the Moon landing, Vietnam War protests – may have triggered a subconscious desire in me to play a part in telling such stories.

But it was a grim story, much closer to home, that fascinated me and was front-page news for days: the kidnap of Muriel McKay, the wife of newspaper executive Alick McKay. She was abducted from her home in Wimbledon, south London, just after Christmas in 1969, by two brothers, Arthur and Nizamodeen Hosein. They mistook her for Anna, the wife of Alick's millionaire boss Rupert

Murdoch who had just bought the *News of the World* and *The Sun* newspapers. They held Muriel, who was fifty-five, at their rundown Rooks Farm in Stocking Pelham, Hertfordshire. They demanded a £1 million ransom, playing a cat and mouse game with Scotland Yard over several weeks.

At one stage, detectives left a suitcase of mostly fake cash at an arranged location, only to see a curious passer-by pick it up and call the nearest police station. The puzzled local force had no idea what was going on because the Yard hadn't told them. The Hosein brothers were later arrested and convicted of Muriel's murder. It was one of the first successful prosecutions without the discovery of the victim's body. The kidnappers refused to say what happened to Muriel. It was a tragic but gripping story, told in banner headlines across the morning papers that were crammed into my bike's wicker basket. The case captured the public's imagination and mine.

Fifty-three years later, long after I had forgotten all about it, the story excited me again. I got to know Muriel's daughter Dianne, by then eighty-two years old, and her grandson Mark Dyer, during a period of renewed activity to locate Muriel's remains. Mark, a corporate investor, kept me informed of what was going on while his mother Dianne became the official family spokesperson. I interviewed Dianne several times at her house, fifteen miles from my home, and I discovered she was best friends with two of my neighbours. I had socialised with the neighbours for years, without ever knowing of their connection to this extraordinary crime story. Now, as well as local gossip and our efforts to combat tomato blight, my neighbours and I could discuss the latest astonishing twists in a gripping murder mystery.

After all those years, the McKay family had fresh clues. They persuaded police to excavate farmland where they believed Muriel was buried, but they found nothing. The publicity prompted more new information, suggesting her body had been left at a rubbish dump. The landowner resisted a search. Then an author discovered an old letter from the solicitor for one of the kidnappers, claiming Muriel's body had been hidden on an Essex beach. But the sand dunes were vast, too extensive to search, said the detective in charge, so nothing happened. The whereabouts of Muriel's last resting place remained a mystery.

My old newsagent Percy Burrows must have followed the McKay kidnap story. He read the papers avidly every day, when customers in his bustling shop allowed him a moment's break. 'Even when we went on holiday, Dad would read the news and always bought the local paper as well,' said his son Jeff. 'I remember the Muriel McKay murder and other big crime stories, there were so many of them in those days.' They filled the papers that Jeff and his father sold every day in huge numbers: 2,200 delivered to readers' doors and another 800 bought over the counter.

The local paper, the *Ely Standard*, has had big crime stories to cover, too. Schoolgirls Holly Wells and Jessica Chapman were murdered in Soham, seven miles away, in 2002. Their killer Ian Huntley was the caretaker at my old secondary school. I spent weeks covering the case. I even accompanied the trial jury around the school building, where Huntley burned the girls' distinctive Manchester United football shirts and left the charred remains in a bin. It was a strange feeling after an absence of thirty years, hardly the happy reunion that takes most pupils back to their old classrooms. A few years later, when I did return for a Soham Grammarians old boys' lunch, nobody mentioned the murders at all. It taught me that people's fascination with true crime goes only so far. It stops abruptly when the crime gets too close to home. That wasn't the only example.

At the Ely junior school, I knew a boy called Andrew Kostiuk. He was a year older than me, a troubled loner who was shunned by his classmates. When I tried to befriend him in the playground, out of sympathy and concern, he resisted. He never joined in our kickabouts. He was a big boy, with cropped hair and an odd, smiley face. He was often tense and seemed ready to explode. In 1979, when I was just starting out in my newspaper career, Kostiuk used a poker to batter to death his 46-year-old neighbour, mother-of-three Mary Scarff, in front of her children. He'd had a row with her about something in the street the day before. He was twenty-six. He had left school at fifteen, done a series of odd jobs and had a string of convictions, some for violence. He was diagnosed with schizophrenia and had spells in a local mental hospital.

Kostiuk's mother Edith spoke to the *Cambridge Evening News* about her only son. It was clear his life had not been easy, and she was bitter:

> Nobody wanted to help him. Society cast him aside and look what has happened. If these people – the magistrates, the police and the social workers – are as intelligent as they are supposed to be, then surely they should have seen he needed something different to prisons, probation hostels and borstals.

Kostiuk pleaded guilty to manslaughter with diminished responsibility and was ordered to be detained indefinitely at a secure hospital.

I discovered he died, aged fifty-four, in 2008, when I found

Kostiuk's name in a register of unclaimed estates. It seemed such a sad end to a miserable, wasted existence in which he had even taken someone else's life. When I tried to research more about the murder, on a Facebook community site, I received a lot of replies, but then my own post was suddenly removed. When I asked why, I got this message: 'Martin the victim's daughter saw the thread and was very upset. She asked for it to be stopped. While it's a topic of interest to you, it's a raw reality that has caused much pain to some people.'

Today, Burrows newsagents sells a quarter of the *Ely Standard* and other papers it once did. The *Cambridge Evening News* no longer exists. It's remarkable the shop has survived, especially with local competition from a WHSmith store, supermarkets, petrol stations, corner shops and free newspapers. Jeff's niece Annabel Reddick, who grew up three doors away on the same street as me, says the shop's survival is due to loyalty to its customers. It's the only news-agent in the area that has continued with deliveries and still has thirty-eight individual rounds. Annabel, who helps out in the shop as her mum Ann did before her, said:

> The only day we've ever let down the customers was the Millennium New Year's Day when we just didn't have any paperboys, they were all partying or had gone away. We warned our regulars, but it was still mental in the shop with everyone ringing up to complain. Mum was working here, and we were so busy she nearly had a heart attack.

No one has to get up before dawn anymore and collect papers from Ely Station. They are delivered to the shop in lorries, from a whole-saler in nearby Newmarket. There are no warm, sweet-smelling bundles of newsprint to inspire another generation of reporters.

Neither Annabel nor her brother Jeff's own two daughters are keen to take over the business, so its future is as uncertain as the newspaper industry's. The invention of a certain 24-hour TV news channel hastened the decline of the traditional press, but that world, my world, is changing rapidly, too. Much of our audience gave up reading newspapers, preferring to watch round-the-clock television news. Today, the same viewers get their news, increasingly, from their mobile telephone and computer screens. Now, they are giving up the telly in the corner of the lounge. But whatever their chosen delivery system, I'd like to think they still want crime stories. And those crime stories can come from anywhere. Just ask Paul McCartney.

# CHAPTER 2

# THE ROCK STAR

*Any talk of a kidnap plot is bound to give ideas to all sorts of nutters*
– ROCK STAR PAUL MCCARTNEY

The day was chilly, and the fields and hedgerows were glimmering in the autumn sun. For a multi-millionaire rock star who guarded his family privacy, the medieval landscape of the High Weald of south-east England seemed a perfect place to live. Unless a local nutter and his friends were planning to kidnap your wife and hold her prisoner in a woodland lair until the payment of a £10 million ransom. That was the story I wanted to discuss with Paul McCartney, the greatest songwriter of the twentieth century whose old band The Beatles practically invented British pop music.

It was just after nine o'clock on a Saturday morning, not too early I thought to call and discuss bad news with someone, famous or not. If he wasn't up yet, I could wait. I steered my shabby Austin Montego off the country lane and down a long drive towards a modern, brick-built farmhouse and parked behind it. As I got out, a young farmhand in gumboots and a donkey jacket emerged from a barn thirty yards away and walked quickly towards me. I was relieved to see he wasn't carrying a shotgun.

'Can I help you?' he asked, with only a faint hint of menace. Before I could answer, the back door of the house opened and a familiar Liverpudlian voice called out: 'It's OK, he's a reporter.' How did he know that? I turned round to see an unsmiling McCartney standing in the doorway. It may have been the first time he had greeted a hack in his pyjamas (he was wearing the pyjamas, not me). The musician was also wearing an expensive dressing gown and a pair of those awful gold-crested, black velvet slippers beloved by men with too much money. He was forty-two and should have known better.

He didn't seem pleased to see me, but I went over and introduced myself as a *Sunday Mirror* reporter, as I was then, and shook what I thought was the hand that penned the soundtrack to my formative years. I was disappointed to learn later that although he greets visitors with a traditional shake of the right hand he writes left-handed, in the same way he plays guitar. I got straight to the point. So did McCartney. 'It's bullshit,' he insisted, after I'd explained the kidnap plot. But I knew it was true because a policeman had told me it was. The story had been leaked to me from a police source twenty-four hours earlier, but before confronting McCartney I had needed to make sure what I'd been told was accurate. It's the sort of story that a police press officer might initially deny, or not know about or at least play for time and make me miss my deadline, so I didn't bother with an official request for information through the normal channel: a call to the Sussex Police press office.

Instead, the previous night I had walked into Newhaven Police Station, where the investigating detectives were actually based, and announced at the front desk: 'I'm a reporter from the *Sunday Mirror* and I'd like to talk to the officer dealing with the McCartney kidnap plot.' Instead of showing surprise or claiming he didn't know what I was talking about, the desk sergeant told me to wait. He said: 'I'll try and contact the officer dealing with the case,' and when he made a phone call in front of me, he referred to 'the Paul McCartney job'. Without realising it, he had just confirmed my story was true. When I headed up McCartney's drive the next morning, I was ready for his anticipated denial.

It was 1984 and the story illustrates how some aspects of crime reporting have changed, especially the access to police. A local police station was actually open to the public in the evening and the front-desk officer was prepared to help a reporter he'd never met. Recently, Newhaven Police Station was moved to a new building, which it has to share with the town's fire service. It's a one-stop shop that's handy today if your home gets burgled and set on fire at the same time, but only if it happens between its restricted weekday opening hours of 10 a.m. to 2 p.m. The residents of Newhaven should count themselves lucky to still have their own police station. In the past decade more than 600 of them have been closed in budget cuts.

I knew my way around police stations. It's where cub reporters once learned the skills of dealing with cops. Every morning I would visit the local station, chat to the duty sergeant and get a list of the latest crimes recorded, by hand, in a logbook. For big crimes a detective would often join us to give more information, and relationships would build up.

The most extraordinary thing about my meeting with McCartney was that I was able to drive all the way to his back door and, not only did he open it himself, he was ready to chat to a reporter about something so sensitive. This was less than four years after a deranged fan had shot dead fellow ex-Beatle John Lennon outside his New York apartment. I couldn't believe McCartney's own security was so lax. The only warning I saw as I drove through the open farm gate was a wooden sign nailed to a tree that read: 'Please drive slowly – children playing.' I thought I'd be turned back by a security guard or stopped by an inner barrier long before I got near his house. I certainly didn't expect to be standing at his kitchen door listening to my boyhood hero talk. And boy could he talk.

He denied the kidnap plot was true and then started talking about his family life. 'I try to lead a normal life with Linda and the kids. I don't like talking about my security measures. Any talk of a kidnap plot is bound to give ideas to all sorts of nutters.' I couldn't help but sympathise. He was a mega-rich star who was trying to live like an ordinary person, invited his neighbours round for drinks, went shopping in the village and was happy for his daughter to work behind the bar of the local pub. I admired all that and for a few moments was a little embarrassed by my intrusion. I would much rather have been asking him to show me the chord structure and finger-picking pattern of his beautiful guitar ballad *Blackbird*. I'd been playing it badly since I was twelve.

When a soft New Yorker's voice called out from the kitchen and asked who he was talking to, McCartney responded over his shoulder to his wife Linda: 'It's just a reporter with some bullshit story.' I knew for a fact that the suspect had been arrested for some other crime and it was during a search of his home that police had discovered the kidnap plot. The young man had apparently built a lair in woods near Newhaven where he planned to hide Linda while he issued a ransom demand for £10 million. Linda was to be

14

snatched on one of the country lanes near the farm while Paul was kept prisoner in their home until the ransom was paid. She would be released as the gang fled the country.

I had also been told that police had revealed the plot to McCartney recently, but I wasn't sure if Linda had been informed. It seems ridiculous to think, as the intended victim, she wouldn't have been told, but it was the feeling I got. Her husband insisted my story wasn't true but said he expected me to write it anyway, whatever his concerns about protecting his family. I was a little disappointed by his lack of faith in my journalistic integrity. He may have occupied the moral high ground, but I had the facts on my side.

The conversation then took a bizarre twist. He went on to talk about his days on the road with The Beatles and told me about a former colleague of mine from the *Daily Mirror*. 'Don Short, the *Mirror*'s showbiz guy, used to come on tour with us,' he said. 'He came everywhere with us, and we treated him very well. We thought he was our friend, but in the end, he wrote bad things about us like everyone else. We realised eventually we couldn't trust him.' Now, much as I was spellbound by his reminiscing, I had a deadline to meet and if I was to write up and phone in my story I had to get away. After a few more minutes of listening to him moaning I made my excuses and left.

In the village I stopped and scribbled down what McCartney had told me. I found a phone box that hadn't been vandalised, called my news editor and was put through to 'copy'. In those days before mobile phones and computers I had to dictate a story to a copy-taker who would type it out, often in bored silence, sometimes with harsh comments on my grammar, occasionally with a word of praise.

As I drove back to London it crossed my mind that McCartney

could still keep my story out of the paper. All he had to do was ring my new proprietor Robert Maxwell who I believed would be both flattered and sympathetic and could be persuaded to drop the story. Perhaps I should have suggested that to McCartney. Maybe, in return for me scuppering the scoop of my career, he would hire me as his media advisor. He could finally show me how to play *Blackbird*. And maybe we could have done something about those slippers.

But I was a fledgling Fleet Street hack who was aiming to fly high. The story was published the next day under the headline 'McCA-RTNEY KIDNAP PLOT', alongside a picture of the rock star with his arm around his smiling wife and a 'world exclusive' tagline. In those days a great scoop trumped the sort of privacy concerns that would one day loom over many stories I offered my news editors. A spokesman for McCartney's company confirmed that police had spoken to him about the plot and said: 'They called and advised Paul. They said they were questioning two men but there have so far been no charges.' The kidnap plot had been 'nipped in the bud in the very early stages', the spokesman added and stressed: 'High security surrounds Paul and the rest of the family.' Really?

When I look back at the faded *Sunday Mirror* newspaper cutting, I'm surprised to read some of the words I wrote, because I included the line:

Since the murder of fellow ex-Beatle John Lennon four years earlier, McCartney – said to be worth £400 million – has spent a fortune on protecting his homes in Britain and the US. His Sussex farm is like a mini-fortress. It nestles in a network of sophisticated devices, with security guards and a six-foot high fence. A 60-ft watchtower dominates the grounds and bullet-proof windows protect the farmhouse.

And I added, for good measure: 'Locals have dubbed the McCartney residence "Paul-ditz".' To understand that rather forced play on words, younger readers may have to google Colditz, the infamous and supposedly impenetrable German castle that was used to house Allied military officers captured in World War Two. While they're at it, they should probably google World War Two as well.

I can only think that, despite the ease with which I arrived on McCartney's doorstep, my editor agreed to the fib that he and his family were surrounded by security so that other would-be kidnappers would be deterred. It seemed a reasonable compromise in return for McCartney finally acknowledging the story was true. Shortly afterwards he did ramp up his protection and later hired as a personal publicist Geoff Baker, a reporter from the *Daily Star*. He became the musician's friend and guided him through the media pitfalls and bear traps for the next fifteen years. Eventually McCartney fired him, apparently for tipping off a photographer that he was making an impromptu visit to see US magician David Blaine attempt to survive without food while suspended in a Perspex box near London's Tower Bridge. That's showbiz.

Today Sir Paul McCartney is worth a lot more than £400 million, is happily married to his third wife and is still performing brilliantly. In the summer of 2022, a week after his eightieth birthday, he and his band were the headline act at the Glastonbury festival where the rock superstar showed that he can still thrill a crowd of 100,000 fans, among which many youngsters could be seen mouthing every word of his lyrics. In between the songs McCartney also demonstrated that he still talks too much, rambling on when his audience just wanted more music. He played *Blackbird* beautifully. I'm still struggling with it.

Three years later I confronted another celebrity, family favourite and all-round entertainer Max Bygraves, who was caught up in a very different problem and managed, initially at least, to wriggle out of it. Through a former colleague on a local paper, a man contacted me and said he wanted to sell an astonishing story about the most scandal-free star in show business: Max had a secret love child called Stephen, who was by then twenty-six years old.

I spent a couple of weeks tracking down and speaking to the main characters, including Stephen. Late on a Friday night I drove out of London and knocked on the door of Bygraves's secluded cliff-top home, which overlooked the sea in Bournemouth. He didn't have much to say, but his obvious shock and the speed with which he shut the door in my face confirmed the story. Bygraves was a hugely popular showbiz legend and had appeared at twenty Royal Variety performances, singing, dancing and telling jokes to the delight of the Queen Mother and other royals. His image was of a happily married family man. My story would have shattered his reputation and perhaps cost him a fortune in lost bookings.

Unknown to his adoring fans, Max was a serial philanderer and many years earlier had a brief affair with Stephen's mother, a dancer called Pat Marlowe. They often had sex in his dressing room during breaks between shows at the London Palladium. In a deal thrashed out between her solicitor and his manager he paid Pat £10,000 – a huge sum in the early 1960s – to bring up Stephen and keep his father's identity secret. Sixteen months after Stephen's birth his mother killed herself. Max had refused ever since to acknowledge

Stephen was his son and had rejected the boy's efforts to contact him. My informant was a member of Pat Marlowe's family who told me the story in a bid to embarrass the star into accepting responsibility. I saw Stephen only briefly. He didn't want to talk and he and his partner fled their home. He looked like his father, the same shock of black hair, the large nose and the wide smile, though that vanished soon after he opened his front door to me.

Bygraves persuaded my deputy editor, who was running the paper in the editor's absence, to drop the story because of the effect it would have on his wife Blossom and their own three children. I was annoyed because it was my own scoop, I had spent a lot of time on it and I believed it exposed a public figure's hypocrisy. My deputy editor saw the bigger picture of a shattered family and was prepared to pass up a story that would have captivated our readers. He was ahead of his time. A fortnight later my story was a front-page 'world exclusive' in the rival *News of the World*, under the headline 'TV MAX LOVE CHILD SENSATION'. A week after that Max got over his shame and bared his soul in a personal article for the same newspaper, for which I heard he was paid £8,000. In the paper, the entertainer described me as 'a tough-looking character' who turned up on his doorstep and blurted out his dark secret in front of his wife. She was apparently standing behind him in the shadows of their hallway as he opened the door to me.

Tough-looking? It must have been the dark, stormy night and the upturned collar of my reporter's trench coat. I was trying to offer Max a warm smile and a sympathetic ear, but all he saw was a dodgy guy straight from the pages of a Raymond Chandler novel. Ever the trouper, Bygraves used his confessional article to get in a plug for his 'new one-man show I Wanna Tell You A Story which opens in Brighton in June'. When Max died twenty-five years later it was revealed he had two other secret children his wife knew nothing about. My Max Bygraves scoop wasn't a crime story, but there was certainly more than one dodgy character involved.

Were either of the McCartney and Bygraves stories important? They felt so at the time and I'm sure were read with interest by millions. Certainly, the McCartney story was a double whammy with its combination of crime and celebrity, offering a glimpse into two worlds far removed from the lives of most people. The two subjects still jostle for prominence in today's news agenda.

But both reports were highly intrusive into the private lives not just of the celebrities but of their families, too. Any editor would hesitate to run either story in these more restrained times. Most likely, they would be spiked and, with some regret, eventually forgotten. There are other stories whose details we would all be quite happy to forget. If only we could.

# CHAPTER 3

# THE HOUSE OF HORRORS

*We opened another hatch and dropped down on to the landing and*
*suddenly we were inside the House of Horrors*

– Anonymous TV cameraman

It still gives my colleague the chills when he thinks about what I
asked him to do, but that hasn't stopped him regaling his friends
with the story of the night I suggested he break into the House of
Horrors. It was the grubby Edwardian townhouse where odd-job
man Fred West and his prostitute wife Rose tied up, tortured, raped,
murdered and buried nine young female victims, including their
own teenage daughter Heather. It wasn't a job for the faint-hearted.

I say broke in, but it wasn't quite like that, and I don't suppose
we would have done it if it had involved any criminality. But the
opportunity to be the first journalists inside 25 Cromwell Street,
Gloucester, was too good to pass up, especially since the police had
by then finished their forensic work and all the bodies had gone.

The scoop cost us £300. Not a fine, but the fee for the scallywag who found a way to get my cameraman in.

I'm not sure we would do it now because media lawyers have become risk averse and, to avoid stirring up trouble, would rather say no to something that might possibly prompt a complaint, attract a legal writ or, heaven forbid, offend someone. Of course, it's not the lawyer who has the final say in editorial decisions, but today if the legal specialist urges 'don't do it' it's a brave and increasingly rare news executive who will ignore the advice. To frustrated reporters, certain in-house media lawyers have become known as News Prevention Officers. But on this occasion in 1994 the company lawyer didn't object, though I can't say for certain that he was ever asked for his opinion.

The shabby, semi-detached house at the north end of Cromwell Street stood not far from Gloucester Cathedral, but it was a world away from the stained-glassed cloisters that were to feature, years later, as the corridors of the fictional Hogwarts School of Witchcraft and Wizardry in the *Harry Potter* movies. The neighbourhood around Cromwell Street was home to many poor, sad individuals who had drifted to its bedsit land over the years. Some I met were alcoholics, some drug dependent, some were both and they all may have been down on their luck, but when the world's media beat a path to their doorsteps a few of them rose to the occasion. They reckoned their local knowledge could earn them money.

One young man, let's call him Jim, introduced me to a dozen people who claimed to have known the Wests and had sexual relations with one or both of them. Normally a reporter has to sift through such claims to identify who's trying to con you for money or attention, but it eventually became clear that a lot of them were telling the truth, because Fred and Rose were sex maniacs. Jim's biggest coup, though, was to discover a way into No. 25 to let us film the interior of the House of Horrors, fast becoming a notorious building whose exterior had filled front pages around the world but whose interior had never been seen by anyone other than official investigators. It was sometime after the police had left it boarded up, but long before a courtroom jury was to hear the shocking details of what happened there.

I had just spent another week in Gloucester looking for more stories on the Wests, it was late and I was almost home, 140 miles away, when Jim rang to say he could get us inside the house with our camera. I guessed that if we hesitated, he would offer the scoop to a rival, so I told the head of home news Simon Cole we should do it as soon as possible and he agreed. I was desperate to be involved but was too knackered to drive back to Gloucester, so instead I arranged for a cameraman and a colleague to meet Jim that night. The three of them gathered at 1 a.m. in neighbouring Wellington Street where £300 cash was handed over. After making sure a police constable was no longer guarding the entrance to 25 Cromwell Street, the raiding party crept in silence up to No. 23, the adjoining house.

My cameraman, who wants to remain anonymous even now, picks up the story:

We walked up to the front door and went straight in. I didn't see if he had a key or if it was unlocked, but he certainly didn't force it. I knew the house was empty, because it was made up of bedsits and everyone had been moved out weeks before when the police started taking No. 25 apart. We had torches and I had the camera light and we climbed the stairs to the top landing and then hauled ourselves up through the hatch into the attic. It was a big space and there was no wall or anything to stop us getting into the attic of No. 25.

We just walked across, being careful to step on the wooden joists. We opened another hatch and dropped down on to the landing and suddenly we were inside the House of Horrors. It was surreal, beyond belief really, but we knew we had to be quick, so I just got on with the filming, shooting each room as we went down the stairs, top floor, first floor and ground floor, then the cellar. I didn't have time to think too much about whether we should be there.

I woke up the next morning eager to look at the footage the camer-aman had sent to Sky HQ. His 23-minute video of the inside of the Wests' home was every bit as macabre and compelling as I thought it would be. It was £300 well spent, cheap when we considered that no one other than the police, forensics teams and the pathologist had been inside the building since the couple's arrest.

The first thing the cameraman filmed was a discarded white rubber glove, left near the loft hatch presumably by a detective or scenes-of-crime officer. I watched as the invaders made their way down the two upper floors, via a narrow staircase with its oddly colourless patterned wallpaper. Then came spartan lodgers' rooms, a bathroom and a kitchen stripped bare of almost all fittings and furniture. The cameraman kept rolling from room to room, his harsh light creating shadows that added to the eeriness. On a wall on the first floor was a photographic mural of impossibly blue seas and a glorious sunny coastline scattered with palms and exotic bird-of-paradise flowers. It was a tantalising glimpse of a better life, far away from the miserable existence of the occupants of No. 25.

The stairwell door to the ground floor was covered in another blown-up photograph, this one of a beautiful, scantily-dressed and barefoot young woman with a provocative pose and an enticing smile. It was as if she was beckoning visitors towards the next room, where Rose West entertained her male clients and Fred watched through a peephole.

Finally, the camera swept along the ground floor to expose the entrance and a ladder down to the cellar. It appeared that the staircase had been removed during the investigation. The camera was switched off as my colleague negotiated an unsteady descent into the basement of the house, where the police had made their most gruesome discoveries. The evidence of their excavation was clear to see. There were five patches on the concrete floor where they had dug up the remains of five victims, filled in the holes and laid a rough screed on top. 'It was certainly creepy,' said my cameraman with some understatement, 'especially when you thought of what the victims had gone through. I shot it all very quickly because Jim didn't want to hang around and get caught.'

I discovered much later a more likely reason why Jim the guide was in such a hurry – we weren't the only TV crew he took into the House of Horrors. He probably had one of our rivals lined up waiting for the 2 a.m. tour. So much for our exclusive, but I could hardly blame him for seizing a rare opportunity to make some cash.

There were various drawings, paintings and childish scribblings on the cellar walls, including a declaration of young love that must have been written by Tara, one of Rose's three children by other men. It read 'Tar 4 Ian' and was accompanied by a heart sign. It would be wrong to describe Tara as one of the lucky ones, but she appeared to have a better life than her siblings. She later suggested that, although her mother regularly hit her, she was spared the sadistic sex attacks inflicted on her sisters because she was not one of Fred's daughters. Fred seemed to reserve the worst for his own children, telling a friend: 'I made them, I can do what I like with them.'

The most vivid of the wall paintings was of a cartoon cowboy, hands on hips and wearing a waistcoat, boots and a Stetson, with a gun on his belt and a cheroot hanging from his lips. It was one of several images drawn by the West children. What was extraordinary, if not a little spooky, was how much the cowboy resembled Woody, the star of the animated Pixar movie *Toy Story*, which was released later that year, the same month as Rose West's eventual conviction for ten murders. I was disappointed that the footage wasn't broadcast straight away because my bosses thought it would prejudice the trial. It was shown only after her conviction. By that time, everyone else had filmed inside the house, too.

Because the House of Horrors was such a big story, I was given virtual free rein to explore the Wests' background for as long as I needed. From the start of the Gloucestershire Police investigation, Fred and Rose's arrests and the discovery of the first bodies, I spent weeks at a time in the area tracking down surviving victims, the Wests' family and friends and anyone else who might offer an insight into the couple's life. It was, and still is, rare for me to get such freedom to pursue my own leads over such a long time, but it was driven by the huge interest the story created and the public's thirst for the specifics of horrific crimes as they unfold. It's easy but wrong to think that such stories appeal only to the readers of sensational tabloid newspapers, because journalists from the posher papers such as *The Times*, *Guardian* and *Telegraph* compete just as fiercely for information and, in their broadsheet days, published much more of it.

Readers of those upmarket publications may consider themselves more interested in the law, politics and issues around crime, but they still pore transfixed over the details of the grimmest cases. *The Times* still has two crime correspondents to meet the demand. The *Telegraph*'s page three once had a reputation for carrying longer reports of the most harrowing courtroom dramas than any other paper. The stories were known as 'marmalade droppers'. The notion being that breakfast-time readers froze in shock as they transferred marmalade from the jar to their toast, letting it drop from the knife into their lap.

The extraordinary pull of the West case was brought home to me when I bumped into a white-haired and slightly stooped figure I recognised, an unlikely visitor to the crime scene. The author and poet Laurie Lee had slipped unnoticed into Gloucester, to find out for himself what was going on. We met in the chilly gents toilet of the Wellington Arms, just around the corner from Cromwell Street.

He had read about Fred's local pub in *The Times* and wanted to meet the colourful characters who drank there. I was looking for the same people, for stories about Fred and Rose, but we had both chosen a bad day: all the regulars had gone off in a charabanc to the Cheltenham races. In the warmth of the deserted bar, I bought Lee a whisky and we chatted for nearly an hour. He was seventy-nine at the time and admitted he'd had to persuade his wife to drive him the fourteen miles from his home at Slad, the Cotswold village he made famous in his best-selling memoir *Cider with Rosie*. He had been drawn to the House of Horrors, where so many young people had been murdered in a world so different from his own idyllic childhood.

He asked me about the Wests, eager to hear what I had learned so far, and grimaced when I described some of the couple's vulnerable acquaintances I had interviewed: the young woman with no teeth, the old man with one leg, the cross-eyed bisexual who craved attention, all of whom had sorry tales to tell of misfortune, poor health or simple bad luck.

It was a brief, chance meeting that didn't make it into any of my reports but is a rare fond memory from that extraordinarily bleak time. When I read his obituaries three years later, I was disappointed not to read of his fascination with the Cromwell Street murders.

On New Year's Eve, ten months before the trial and after confessing to twelve murders, Fred West hanged himself in his cell, much to the embarrassment of his jailers at Winson Green Prison in Birmingham. After admitting the killings, would he have given evidence to support his wife's claims of innocence? What an intriguing possibility. But even without him, the hearing was sensational enough.

To understand the couple's sheer depravity and what they did to their victims in the cellar you have only to read the courtroom testimony of Fred's daughter Anne Marie. I listened to it all over several days at Winchester Crown Court in the autumn of 1995, a long, painful session that was interrupted when Anne Marie tried to kill herself one night. It wasn't the first time she had attempted suicide. We learned she was distraught at the prospect of another day in the witness box, reliving the sexual and physical torture inflicted on her. She recovered quickly to resume testifying against her stepmother Rose. If Anne Marie felt fortunate to have survived, it was difficult to tell. She didn't seem to have had much luck throughout her life.

At the time of the trial Anne Marie was thirty-one years old, a mother of two young daughters and separated from her husband.

She had dark hair and had inherited something of her father's simian looks. Her mother was Rena West, Fred's first wife and first murder victim, killed when Anne Marie was seven. Anne Marie sat in the witness box of the vast Court Number Three, a few yards from her stepmother, occasionally glaring at Rose as she revealed her unimaginable, prolonged ordeal. It began when she was eight years old.

Speaking in a dull, monotonous voice Anne Marie described how Fred and Rose regularly led her down to the damp, ill-lit cellar, promising that what they were about to do to her was for her own good. She told the jury:

> I was told I should be very grateful and I was very lucky that I had such caring parents and they were going to help me make sure that when I got married I would be able to satisfy my husband … I was led to believe that all loving parents were the same.

Anne Marie told jurors how she was stripped, tied up and raped by her father while her stepmother held her down and watched, laughing. She said the pain was unbearable and for the first of many times she wished she was dead. On other occasions they would tie her to a weird metal contraption that Fred had built. He would rape her, and her stepmother would abuse her with a vibrator, all the time telling her they were doing this because they were good parents and loved her. It went on for years.

Throughout her stepdaughter's evidence, and for most of the trial, Rose West sat stone-like in the dock, blinking behind her large spectacles. After more than a year in jail she was still a roly-poly figure who, in looks at least, reminded me of the farmer's wife character

Ma Larkin from the TV series *The Darling Buds of May*. She showed no obvious emotion or response to Anne Marie's evidence.

What I found most heartbreaking was an almost-throwaway line that poor Anne Marie uttered towards the end of her time in the witness box. She said: 'I used to go to school each morning, meeting up with my friends and thinking that they must be going through the same experience with their parents who loved them.' It was gruesome stuff and none of us squeezed onto the packed press benches had heard anything quite like it before. Yet, it was also riveting because it was so grim, and to this day I feel a kind of privilege that I was there to witness the extraordinary case unfold. It wasn't just the journalists who were gripped by the courtroom drama. Seats in the public gallery were at a premium, too, and prompted queues that formed outside the building long before I and my colleagues were sitting down for breakfast nearby.

Like many of the reporters covering the trial, I stayed at a hotel in Winchester during the week to avoid the long trek from home to court and back each day. One of the benefits was the occasional socialising with the lawyers involved. I knew Rose's main barrister Richard Ferguson QC, a tall, fine-featured and engaging Northern Irishman, from his appearances at the Old Bailey and other London courts. I spent an evening in the company of him and his junior barrister Sasha Wass in the Wykeham Arms, a favourite eighteenth-century watering hole tucked away in a narrow street between the cathedral and Winchester College public school. We bought each other drinks, discussed some aspects of the case and forged a connection that lasted beyond the trial.

I can't say the same for Ferguson's courtroom adversary, a rather buttoned-up, strait-laced prosecutor who was friendly enough to nod hello to each morning, but there was never much chance of bumping into him propping up the snug bar of the Wykeham. His name was Brian Leveson. Yes, that one. Getting the jury to convict wicked Rose West probably wasn't his most difficult courtroom victory, but as Sir Brian Leveson, he was to go on to become a High Court judge, a Lord Justice of Appeal and later the ringmaster of the Leveson public inquiry into press ethics. As I explain elsewhere in this book, he was to prove no friend to crime reporters.

During the trial I caused a slight potential hiccup to Leveson's prosecution when I inadvertently gave some unexpected ammunition to Ferguson's defence of Rose. And he needed all the help he could get, because although the evidence against her was circumstantial, in that no one had seen her kill anyone and there was no forensic science to link her to the murders, her only explanation for the nine bodies buried in her house was that Fred did it and she had no idea what he'd been up to.

In my research for a documentary to be broadcast at the end of the case I had interviewed Kathryn Halliday, one of the oddball characters from the Wests' circle of acquaintances, who had an increasingly violent sexual relationship with both Fred and Rose. She was a prosecution witness in the trial, and I had agreed to pay her for an exclusive interview.

During a lunchtime meeting in a pub near the court, I mentioned this in passing and in confidence to an old friend, veteran crime reporter Jimmy Nicholson, known throughout Fleet Street as 'The Prince of Darkness' because of his rather Dickensian look and a black cape he wore. Jimmy was as sharp as a razor and asked me if other witnesses were getting paid. I told him as much as I knew: that various witnesses had contracts with national newspapers, and some had been promised a small fortune for interviews and photographs. It wasn't a secret.

He suddenly left his half-pint of Guinness on the bar, made his excuses and vanished, and when I sat down in court thirty minutes later, I discovered why: he had gone straight to his lawyer-pal Ferguson with my revelation about payments. The afternoon court session was about to get lively. When the court had broken for lunch, Ferguson had been midway through the cross-examination of a prosecution witness, and when the hearing resumed the first question that he asked was whether she was being paid for a media interview. She said she was, and from then on it was a question the barrister put to all those giving evidence against Rose.

Ferguson suggested to each witness that they had exaggerated their testimony to make their stories more valuable to the newspapers, one of which had offered £30,000 for an interview. They were huge sums and an indication of their readers' continuing grim fascination with the case. In court, the witnesses were limited in what they said by the questions they were asked. Many were also nervous, which further reduced their evidence. We all wanted to know more from people caught up in one of the most extraordinary crime stories ever, especially the Wests' own children. Life with Fred and Rose was unimaginable, but here were those who had shared it, could describe the reality of it and help us understand how they survived it. There were lessons for others in their experiences.

I couldn't compete with the sums offered to witnesses by my newspaper colleagues. When Ferguson asked Kathryn Halliday what Sky News was paying her, she replied sheepishly '£200' and beamed across the court at me. My colleagues reacted with horror. How could I have offered her so little?

The Press Complaints Commission, the media watchdog, later changed its code of conduct to ban witness payments in all but exceptional circumstances. If a payment had to be made all parties in a trial, including the jury, must be informed, said the PCC. It helped persuade the government that a new law wasn't necessary. We had already shown, in our delay in running the footage from inside No. 25 Cromwell Street, that self-regulation worked.

A key witness with a £20,000 newspaper deal was the Wests' former nanny Caroline Owens, an early victim and survivor who was tortured and raped by the couple. She reported them to the police but was so badly treated by the detective who interviewed her, she refused to give evidence in court. It had happened in the early 1970s and it wasn't uncommon in the days before enlightenment for police to disbelieve female victims of sexual assault, ask them highly personal questions about their sex life and mental health and generally treat them badly. Ten years later, a BBC fly-on-the-wall police TV documentary exposed a similar scandal in painful detail. This compelled police forces to treat victims much more sympathetically. Even today, many women have little confidence in police rape investigations, and the number of rapes that are prosecuted is shamefully low.

Caroline's refusal, many years earlier, to testify against Fred and Rose for rape meant they simply pleaded guilty to the lesser charge of indecent assault and walked free with a £100 fine, no doubt astonished to have got off so lightly and perhaps deciding that they could not allow their next victim to live. Caroline said years later in a television interview:

The detective that was brought in was not at all compassionate. He kept saying to me: 'You slept with this guy, then you slept with this guy, surely you were up for it, maybe it got a bit too rough.' He made me feel like it was all my fault. I felt so guilty about not getting them a prison sentence the first time round. If I'd got them a prison sentence probably none of these girls would have died.

On the twentieth anniversary of the Cromwell Street murders, I tracked down the detective involved. At his home on the edge of Gloucester I asked him about his treatment of Caroline. He agreed that he could have dealt with her more sympathetically and just about acknowledged that prosecuting the Wests with Caroline's support might have avoided the horror that followed their lucky escape.

During the trial, a handful of reporters and I were chosen to accompany the jury on a site visit to Cromwell Street. The prosecution had asked for jurors to see inside the Wests' home because the thrust of its case was that the building was so small that Rose, who blamed Fred alone for all the killings, must have known and been involved in what happened. The house was just as it had looked the night my rather nervous cameraman had wandered around and filmed it secretly many months before. As I climbed the stairs and peered into the rooms of the House of Horrors, I had to pretend these were images I'd never seen before.

When people ask me, as they often do: 'What's the worst case you've ever covered?' I don't hesitate. At the time it was the story of the Cromwell Street murders and it still is. I can't imagine anything will ever compete with it for such a dubious accolade.

The House of Horrors was my first big story since I became Sky's crime correspondent. It was a test to see if we could tell the story of an unfolding police investigation and subsequent trial to a new 24-hour television news audience in a way that was as compelling as a long, absorbing read in a newspaper. I had already discovered that TV and newspaper reporters were essentially after the same stories when I joined Sky News from Fleet Street five years earlier. But now I had to think more about the pictures. And I was expected to wear make-up.

# CHAPTER 4

# THE TV REPORTER

*We didn't know whether to call ourselves non-terrestrials*
*or extra-terrestrials, but I guess if we had looked like*
*E.T. we would not have passed the screen test*

– THE AUTHOR

I was one of six Fleet Street hacks hired by Sky News for the big experiment, the launch of Europe's first 24-hour news channel in early 1989. Only a couple of already-established local TV reporters were willing to take the same risk. There was a lot of hostility to the project, especially from left-wing politicians who hated my new billionaire boss Rupert Murdoch and feared that, because he already owned *The Sun*, the *News of the World*, *The Times* and the *Sunday Times* newspapers, he was building ownership of too large a share of the UK media.

I was lured away from the Street of Shame, as it's called by its detractors, where I was a relatively anonymous tabloid reporter hiding behind a by-line. I was now about to be launched on screen, warts and all, a hostage to the skills of the make-up department. What on earth had I got myself into? The portents for my new career were not good as I headed to an industrial estate in Osterley, a name I knew vaguely from its underground station towards the end of the Piccadilly line in west London.

A bitter January wind whipped at the collar of my sodden rain-coat as I picked my way unsteadily along the muddy duckboards that led to the Sky News studio. Builders were constructing my new workplace around me, literally. The screech of their drills and the bang of their hammers almost, but not quite, masked the dull drone of a jumbo jet on its final descent into nearby Heathrow Airport. Oh, and there wasn't a pub within a mile. I had just given up a well-paid job as the *Sunday Mirror*'s chief reporter and, as I leapt the final yard towards more solid ground at the flapping plastic reception door, two questions fought for an answer in my head. Why on earth had I taken this job? And was it too late to change my mind? Welcome to the glamorous world of television, I thought.

Inside the building, the path to the newsroom was drier, but no less tricky. I had to weave along the corridors, jumping across up-turned metal plates and gaping holes as workmen laid the labyrinth of cables that make television work. Until then all I'd needed to do my job was a notebook, a pen and a telephone. Now I had to learn about technology, cameras and microphones and stuff. Launch day was only a month away, 5 February, my birthday. Which would be the bigger celebration? As I gazed around the half-built nerve centre, with bare wires dangling from the open ceiling and untuned TV sets perched on dusty desks, the birthday party looked the better bet.

We were dubbed 'a new breed of reporter' in advertisements that were beginning to appear in national newspapers. Some time later, my young son Tom spotted a life-size, cardboard cut-out of me in the window of a TV rental shop. By the time his mum had gone back and asked if she could have it, the promotion was over and the image destroyed. Thank goodness. The adverts attracted a lot of leg-pulling and just a little barely disguised envy from those hacks who hadn't been invited to take part in the media revolution.

My fellow reporters on the *Sunday Mirror* had warned me I was mad to leave our comfort zone, where the new publisher Robert Maxwell was revitalising the group's newspapers. With Maxwell pouring money into the tabloid circulation battle with the rival *Sun*, my *Mirror* career and pension were assured, weren't they? What could possibly go wrong? One of my friends gave the new channel three months before it folded. But it wasn't long before some were wishing they had been offered the same opportunity as me, as the Fleet Street gravy train hit the buffers and began to derail. The days of big salaries, generous expenses and long lunches were coming to an end. By offering 24-hour rolling news, I guess Sky News and I had something to with that. If newspapermen had still worn hats with their trench coats, they would have been eating them, press cards and all.

A couple of years after Sky's launch one of my first foreign trips was to the Canary Islands to cover Maxwell's mysterious drowning after a fall from his yacht. Within days it was revealed he had plundered £460 million from the *Mirror* pension scheme. Fortunately, I had taken my *Mirror* pension with me when I left and invested it elsewhere, but that didn't stop me commiserating with my old, robbed colleagues.

From the moment the red light went on outside the Sky News

studio to indicate it had gone live, the long-established television system – ordinary telly – became known as 'terrestrial television', as opposed to the new satellite technology Sky used to beam our service into people's homes via a dish attached to their roofs. We didn't know whether to call ourselves non-terrestrials or extra-terrestrials, but I guess if we had looked like E.T. – the ugly, wrinkled alien from the Hollywood movie – we would not have passed the screen test. It took some of us longer than others to learn the ropes, and it soon became clear that the long process of filming and editing a TV news report often interfered with the journalism. So did those low-flying aircraft just up the road.

The tale I told for the first-ever bulletin was a crime story about the Moors murderer Myra Hindley, who, at the time, was Britain's most infamous female prisoner. She had been jailed for life for helping her psychopath lover Ian Brady murder three children, whose bodies they buried on Saddleworth Moor near Manchester. The couple later admitted two more child killings. In 1989 Hindley was in jail in Rochester, Kent, from where I learned she had been taken on occasional shopping outings to nearby Chatham as part of her rehabilitation and potential parole. Some people were outraged that Hindley should be given such treats.

I was living in Rochester at the time and, believe me, even if you were banged up for many hours a day, a trip to Chatham shopping centre was nothing to get worked up about. But exclusive footage of Hindley outside prison would be exciting and a great scoop for the Sky News launch. I called a former colleague on the local paper who knew a warder at the prison. Would his warder pal, I wondered, tip us off about Hindley's next outing? Would he hell. What he was prepared to do, though, was sit down with an artist and describe in grcat dctail what Myra looked like after more than two decades in jail.

So, Sky News viewers got the first real glimpse of how Hindley had changed from those demonising, scowling peroxide-blonde images from her arrest twenty-three years earlier into a benign, middle-aged woman who looked like someone's granny. Hindley died in 2002, fifteen years before the death of Brady, but their passing did not signal an end to news stories or books about them, and I still today report on their life and crimes.

Early on at Sky I got a sharp reminder of the anti-Murdoch sentiment when I approached Ken Livingstone, the left-wing Labour MP, for an interview. He was walking at the head of a march calling for the withdrawal of British troops from Northern Ireland, where they were controversially trying to keep the peace between warring paramilitary groups. Livingstone rather pompously told me he wouldn't talk to any reporter who worked for 'the pornographer Rupert Murdoch'. He didn't actually mention the Murdoch-owned *Sun*'s scantily clad page-three girls, but I got the message.

A year or so later Livingstone walked into our Westminster studio to be interviewed in the run-up to the general election, in which he was campaigning to be re-elected. My colleague Alex Crawford sitting next to me looked up as he strode past and said: 'Oh, Ken Livingstone, you wouldn't speak to Sky News a year ago. There must be an election on.' We chuckled and got back to our work, and he went on to be re-elected with a much bigger majority.

I spent my first four years at Sky News reporting on everything from the First Gulf War and the Balkan conflicts to the continuing Troubles in Northern Ireland and the contest to replace Tory leader and PM Margaret Thatcher. Between such momentous events were the kind of stories that kept me in touch with my tabloid past. There were no piano-playing parrots or skateboarding ducks, but it came close. I took a goldfish for a walk in a newly invented fish perambulator that was, basically, a golfing trolley with a metal ring to hold the glass bowl. I was filmed pulling the contraption around the streets of London's Soho including, to my great shame, a cobbled lane, which must have been a traumatic ride for the poor fish. I wasn't aware of any complaints but that's perhaps because we had barely any viewers at the time. I shudder to think of the reaction if I did something like that today, the outcry from animal lovers and others, and we would deserve it all.

When Sky's crime reporter Howard Foster left, I volunteered to replace him and got the approval of Sky's chief executive Kelvin MacKenzie, the former *Sun* editor, who I knew from my Fleet Street days. The head of news said MacKenzie had approved my change of role, but he then rather took the wind out of my sails by telling me his response was: 'Yeah, OK, let's have another crime reporter, but I don't care who does it.' In the course of various stories I had got to know a few police officers, and it struck me that our rolling news service, with hours and hours to fill, was tailor-made for the stereotype jack-the-lad detective to talk about his – mostly his – successful investigations. Though most cops were, and still are, wary of the media and fear being misquoted, many of them were flattered by the regular attention and expense account of a television reporter.

Their stories were generally not interesting enough to make it on to the short, fixed news bulletins of the BBC and ITV, so few people other than their own work colleagues would become aware of them. I offered detectives an international audience, though if they had asked me just how big it was in those early years, I'd have been embarrassed to tell them the truth. So, they were happy to boast to me of their triumphs, share documents and photographs and the occasional bit of video footage. And I lapped it up. All they asked was that I didn't 'verbal' them. They meant I shouldn't make up their words. I didn't point out that it was usually detectives who were accused of verballing: rewriting a suspect's statements to show their guilt.

Part of any reporter's brief is to hold authority to account, especially the police with all their powers, but what a crime reporter wants just as much is the chance to tell good detective stories, a point I make elsewhere in these pages. It's the same today as it has ever been. I set about encouraging officers of all ranks to help me reveal those stories. It took some time to win their trust, but slowly I was let into the various police squads and their investigations, sometimes unofficially.

A detective on a drugs investigation in Sunderland even let me and a cameraman film him meeting an informant on a canal towpath that ran underneath a railway bridge. It was dark, we were positioned a long way off and I had to agree to disguise the man's features. It added a vivid and unusual element to my report. I had never met the officer before, but he seemed impressed that I had travelled nearly 300 miles to cover his case. Of course, he could have been meeting anyone, and I had only his word for what we were recording. It involved trust on both sides.

It's astonishing how much access I got eventually, some of it official and some of it not. Another detective I got to know well took me to see one of his informants and later encouraged me to meet him on my own. In turn, the informant introduced me to several teenage drug dealers who, in a variety of small ways, helped me compile a number of news reports. Occasionally, after a wave of arrests, the detective warned me to avoid the informant for a while and, if I did bump into him in the street, to make sure I kept my distance from him. If the informant's role in the arrests had been discovered, the detective said he didn't want me caught up in a revenge attack.

It was another twenty years or so, with the Leveson Report into media ethics, before police were told they needed their senior officers' approval to talk to journalists and everything had to be noted and logged. It's still the same today. In terms of police and media relations, to slightly misquote the great journalist Charles Dickens (who also wrote a bit of fiction on the side): it was the best of times; it is the worst of times.

# CHAPTER 5

# THE JEWELLERY HEIST

*You are a prick and a cunt and if I ever see you again,*
*I'm gonna kill you*
– ROBBER VALERIO VICCEI

There's a basic principle in crime reporting that says that villains and their villainy should never be glamourised. But a judge, a detective and me, all three of us fell, in our own way, for the charms of Valerio Viccei. My interest in him eventually wore off when he threatened to kill me, but by then there were 1,000 miles between us, and he was in jail.

In his youth the dark and handsome Viccei was an egocentric, right-wing political activist, an educated lawyer's son who studied the philosopher Nietzsche and eventually adopted his doctrine to 'live dangerously'. He developed an addiction to crime, committed fifty robberies in Italy and fled as a fugitive to London, where he robbed the Queen's bank Coutts. Armed with pistols, he and a gang then pulled off what is still Britain's biggest heist, the raid on the

Knightsbridge safe deposit centre, where they smashed their way into 160 locked metal boxes and got away with £60 million worth of jewellery, gold, cash and drugs. Viccei had befriended the centre's debt-ridden manager Parvez Latif, plied him with cocaine and secured his insider help.

Viccei revelled in his playboy gangster image, later boasting that after dragging the loot in a dozen bags up to his top-floor rented flat in Hampstead, north London, he filled the bath with cash, something he'd seen done in an old crime movie. He chipped a fragment from a huge rock of cocaine and snorted it through a rolled 1,000-franc Swiss bank note, and as the rising sun burst through the curtains, he put on sunglasses to gaze at the dazzling pile of jewels on his lounge floor. He couldn't help indulging himself, even though he knew he shouldn't hang around for long.

He paid off his accomplices, a gang of petty villains he'd recruited in London, and sent them out of the country before he zipped around Europe depositing cash in various bank accounts. In the Belgian city of Antwerp he sold five diamonds for £1 million, a third of their true value. He was focused, organised and clever, but he left two bloody fingerprints in the Knightsbridge vault as he smashed open the safe deposit boxes, so he wasn't as clever as he should have been.

The judge at his Old Bailey trial, Common Serjeant Robert Lymbery, the second most senior judge of the Central Criminal Court, was the first of our trio of admirers to show him more respect than we should have done by telling him: 'In court I have seen a man of charm and courtesy, a man of substantial abilities.' He spoiled it a bit by adding: 'But these qualities combined with others serve to make you a very dangerous man.' Then he imprisoned him for twenty-two years. However, Lymbery later asked for a signed copy of the autobiography, modestly entitled *Knightsbridge: The Robbery of the Century*, that the robber wrote in the prison to which he had condemned him. The judge also sent a letter supporting Viccei's request for repatriation to complete his sentence back home in an Italian prison.

Four years after his conviction, Viccei swapped Parkhurst Prison on the Isle of Wight for jail in Pescara on Italy's Adriatic coast. And that's where I found him some years later, though he wasn't sitting languishing in his cell chalking up the days towards freedom. Far from it. He'd been allowed out of prison for the weekend. I caught up with him on a Friday night relaxing with his family and girl-friend in the plush seafront Carlton Hotel, living it up on good food and Krug champagne.

At dinner he sat at the head of the table in the dimly-lit, ochre-painted restaurant, dressed in a crimson Byblos jacket, sharply pressed black trousers and shoes by Ferragamo – hardly prison issue, even in Italy. A gold Rolex watch dangled loosely from his wrist. The raven hair, swept back from his widow's peak, was now flecked with grey and a little shorter since his face had grinned out from 100 front pages. The gold rope chain he wore in those photographs still hung around his neck.

There were classier restaurants in Pescara, but it was past the 9 p.m. curfew imposed on Viccei by the magistrate who agreed to his request for a five-day release from jail. Viccei and his entourage had booked two suites in the hotel because the court would not allow him to travel the sixty miles up the coast to his family home in Ascoli. I'd been tipped off that one of the UK's most notorious robbers was cocking a snook at the British criminal justice system

and living a lifestyle, albeit temporary, that officials had hardly en-
visaged when they agreed to his repatriation. He was dining on the
best of the day's catch from Pescara's fishing fleet when he should
have been eating porridge.

In his soft, high-pitched voice and mostly perfect English, Viccei
defended the brief freedom he'd been given less than halfway
through his original 22-year sentence. 'The legal system in Italy
may seem softer than yours, but it really is not,' he insisted. 'The
only difference is that here the rehabilitation programme does not
discriminate like in your country, where it is as if someone who
commits a serious crime cannot be rehabilitated. Everybody de-
serves a chance.'

Viccei was surrounded by the smiling, animated faces of his parents Marcello and Alba, brother Paolo and sister Raffa, his lawyer
Alfredo and his best pal Umberto. The generous host barely touched
his own food: he was too busy nuzzling his new girlfriend Anna
and looked ready to eat her. And he was paying for everyone's long
weekend with a gold Amex card. It wasn't difficult to see why Viccei
had wanted to finish his sentence in Italy. I wondered what His
Honour Judge Lymbery would say back at the Old Bailey, especially
if he knew that sitting among us at the dining table was the senior
Scotland Yard Flying Squad detective who caught Viccei.

Dick Leach is everything you might imagine of the tough robbery-
squad detectives immortalised in the TV police series *The Sweeney*:
he's old fashioned, big and loud with shoulders that could charge
down doors if the battering ram wasn't available, and he talks out of
the side of his mouth in a language that leaves no room for misun-
derstanding. At the time of our dinner, it was ten years since Leach's
surveillance team had ambushed Viccei's black Ferrari Testarossa at

Marble Arch in central London, not far from Buckingham Palace, and dragged him out after smashing his windscreen. Viccei was planning a new life in South America after spending what he could of the loot and hiding what he couldn't. His words to the arresting officers were: 'Right chaps, the game is up now and you have no need to be nasty.'

After the heist, the robber and the cop developed an unusual relationship, one I can't imagine would thrive today. It was based on a grudging respect for each other, but behind it lay a sort of cat-and-mouse game in which Viccei teased Leach about the missing loot and the detective badgered him from time to time to tell him where it was. Viccei described his adversary as 'the nearest thing to a fair cop'. He sent him postcards from jail addressed to 'Fred', as in Fred Basset, the newspaper comic-strip hound. A recent card was signed: 'Valerio, your penniless pal.' Leach used to write back to him in a humorously disparaging way.

'Don't underestimate him, though,' said Leach out of Viccei's hearing. 'He is very clever, manipulative and cunning. We arrested him just in time, within days of him leaving London for Colombia. It looked like a final exit, so I doubt he would have left anything behind. He paid off the rest of the gang straight away with £500,000, which was about half the cash from the robbery. Most of the other cash we got back: the £87,000 he bought the Ferrari with, money we found in the car and his own safe deposit box and various bank accounts. It's mostly jewels and gold that disappeared.'

The estimated value of the stolen loot has varied over the years. It was Viccei who claimed £60 million but he may well have inflated it because of his ambition to be the world's most famous robber. At the trial it was put at £40 million and only £10 million was recovered. The true value of such heists is never established because not all the victims are happy to report their losses, for a variety of reasons. Among the loot may be the proceeds of crime, illegal weapons, a drugs stash, laundered cash or simply valuables hidden from the taxman or a wife. A drug trafficker who foolishly made a claim for his stolen £200,000 was promptly unmasked, arrested and extradited to the United States where he was convicted of importing twenty tons of cannabis. Another box-holder was already serving a life sentence in Singapore's Changi jail for an international fraud conspiracy.

At the time of our Italian dinner, Leach had left the Flying Squad and moved on to investigating organised crime, principally drug trafficking, at the South-East Regional Crime Squad, but he felt he still had a duty to the victims of the Knightsbridge raid. 'I'm bound to follow up any new leads about what was never recovered, but how long do you go on looking?' he said, as we sat in the hotel lounge. 'Viccei was in complete control of all the stolen property and I believe he still is. He had to move the stuff quickly, sold some of the stones in bulk, but even allowing for that I reckon, rock bottom, he must have £5 million waiting for him, somewhere.'

Leach had one remarkable victory early on in the hunt for the missing loot when he recovered the five diamonds sold in Antwerp. As soon as he picked them up, he said, he wrapped them in tissue paper, stuffed them in an envelope and headed with colleagues to the airport. Their flight home was delayed and – this is most unlike British cops abroad – they ended up in a topless bar where a busty dancer was persuaded to put the gems in her cleavage and pose for a private photograph. The picture was captioned: 'Are these worth three million quid?'

Because he was still in pursuit of the missing loot, Scotland Yard, rather than his new employer the Regional Crime Squad, was paying for Leach's Italian trip. I wondered if either of his bosses would have any qualms about him sitting down to dinner with Viccei and his family. He was, after all, there on official business to question Viccei, even if it was on an informal basis. Wasn't there a danger that social-ising with the enemy might compromise his integrity?

'No,' said Leach, who is not a man with whom you would want to have a prolonged argument. 'My motive at all times was to get the money back, but to do that I had to communicate with Viccei. I'd met his Mum and Dad before and got on well with them and the whole family. It was quite natural for us all to be there together. It's a question of whether you talk to him or not and if you don't, you don't get anywhere. Sometimes you have to drink with the devil. I asked him if he was paying for the meal and he said no he wasn't, the Queen was.'

I still couldn't help wondering what the top brass at Scotland Yard would think if they knew a senior cop was being entertained by a villain he was there to interview – and all in front of a journalist. Thank goodness none of the snaps we took as mementoes of our trip were leaked to newspapers, because other detectives on foreign assignments have been exposed for less, pictured during down time relaxing by the pool and usually under the headline 'The Sunshine Squad'. In his Flying Squad days Leach was an intimidating figure, a demanding boss who worked and played hard, someone who in-spired great loyalty in his young detectives. He was naturally wary of journalists, but once you got to know him and showed some in-tegrity, he was prepared to trust you. He had unofficially approved my joining him on the trip to Italy.

The next morning Viccei went jet-skiing off Pescara beach. He was a prickly character and warned me that if my cameraman filmed him bouncing over the waves he would not sit down later for our interview. Clearly, there was a limit to how much he wanted to show off. 'I know the image you want to get, but I'm not going to play along with it,' he said. A couple of hours later Viccei and I sat facing each other across a shaded table on the terrace of a smart seafront cafe. Below us, the regimented rows of red-and-blue sun umbrellas stretched away into the heat haze. He had dressed down for the interview, wearing blue shorts, a white T-shirt and flip-flops, though he couldn't resist slipping on a vivid yellow Henri Lloyd gilet. And he'd swapped the gold Rolex watch for a silver one. Very restrained of him.

We chatted for a while about his life in prison, the arrangements for his weekend release and his hopes for parole. I knew that since his homecoming he had become an informant for the Anti-Mafia Group investigators in Rome, offering information which he believed would win his eventual freedom. I doubted it was something he would want to talk about, so I didn't ask him. I was afraid he might stand up and walk away. Sometimes there's a compromise to be made and, anyway, I had more pressing questions.

Like, where's the missing loot, the jewels and the gold that Leach and his team hadn't recovered? Viccei's relaxed manner suddenly changed and he snapped:

Ask the cops, they know. You say they haven't got all of it? Well, who knows how much money there was? I don't know. Was there £40 million, £50 million, or £60 million? What I'm saying is that it's impossible to know. Let me give you an example. There were ten eggs by Fabergé, each one worth £20,000 or £30,000, so that's maybe £300,000. You melt it down, which I know was a terrible thing to do, but it was done. So it became £3,000 but you still ask me where's the £300,000? You understand what I'm saying?

I did understand what he was saying, but I'm not sure I believed him. 'OK, you buy a chain in a shop with a few little stones, and you pay £2,000, you melt it down and it's worth £20. That money went. You don't believe me, do you? You are so sceptical.'

His mate Fred the Basset Hound, like a lot of others, didn't believe him either and thought it much more likely he had hidden treasure awaiting his release from prison. To spur him on, perhaps, the detective had hanging above his office desk in the UK an original JAK cartoon from the *Evening Standard*. It depicted a couple of villains outside a prison, shouting up to a cell window: 'Romeo, Romeo, wherefore art thou hiding the £20 million you took from our safety deposit box?'

Among the speculation was the thought that Viccei buried what was left of the stolen loot on Hampstead Heath, only a mile from his London flat. He laughed as the shouts of an ice-cream seller drifted up from the beach: 'If they want to help me dig it up, they can. Seriously, I cannot help you. Let's leave it. People's imaginations need this sort of thing. That's life.' I looked him in the eye, prolonged the dramatic pause and asked him if he was really telling me that it had all gone? 'Yeah,' he said and his answer hung in the air. 'You still don't believe me?' And a smile spread slowly across his suntanned face.

Leach had a much more likely theory: that an elderly Italian accomplice, who he knew had been staying in Viccei's flat at the time of the heist, had spirited away many of the jewels in a briefcase that he carried onto a train to Italy a few days later. The suspect was identified and pursued but was never charged because of a lack of evidence.

I was aware that two more Flying Squad detectives were in Pescara at the same time as Leach. They had come to question Viccei about his stolen loot and another matter, but they were waiting to do that more formally in the prison governor's office. They wanted to know more about Viccei's friendship in Parkhurst with a notorious killer called Wayne Hurren. Viccei had described Hurren as 'one of my best pals ever, a true and very lethal wolf'.

Hurren was in jail after a thirteen-year reign of terror across London in which he had committed a string of lucrative armed robberies and shot three police officers during a getaway chase. He was also charged with three execution-style gangland murders, but was eventually cleared of one and had the other cases dropped. The detectives were gathering intelligence on Hurren. They wanted to ask Viccei if Hurren had admitted anything to him about other crimes.

Whatever Viccei told them about Hurren, he still wasn't prepared to admit he had a Knightsbridge nest egg waiting for him somewhere. I don't know if Leach got any more out of Viccei than I did. He may have got much less. The detective was remarkably candid with me, but there was a limit to the operational details he was willing to share. By the time we were preparing to say goodbye to him, Viccei's happy mood was beginning to change: he seemed depressed and edgy, and not just at the prospect of his return to jail.

His mother had scolded him over breakfast about his lovemaking with his girlfriend Anna. It had kept her and his father awake in their adjoining second-floor suite. But what was annoying him more, as he paced the hotel foyer, was the local *Il Centro* newspaper he held in his hands. It had discovered he was in town and free. He slapped down the copy on a coffee table. The front-page headline was '*Pescara piace al boss*' – Pescara makes the boss happy. Inside was a snatched photograph of Viccei in shorts walking along the beach hand-in-hand with Anna under the headline '*Viccei, vacanze segrete*' – Viccei's secret holiday. 'This slippery bastard,' he hissed. 'Why do they do this? If they come and see me I will talk to them, but they are sneaky. They think they are clever and want to make a scoop. I tell you, they give me the fucking right hump.'

I waved him goodbye as he climbed on the back of a friend's moped and sped off into the busy seaside traffic to the fortress-like jail on the edge of town. He promised to keep in touch, though I wasn't sure how easy that would be for him. I shouldn't have worried. Four days later, I was sitting at my office desk when my mobile rang. The line from inside Pescara Prison was remarkably clear as a familiar, high-pitched voice whispered: 'Don't say too much, they think I'm calling my lawyer.' Viccei said he was expecting to get his partial parole soon, which would mean he would be free each day but have to return every night to sleep in jail. He was planning to launch a publishing company and told me: 'I just hope to make a little money if I can.'

Later still, an international telegram arrived from Italy. It read: 'Parole application successful. Stop. I will be out in a few days. Stop. All the best, Valerio.' I was beginning to think this was a fledging relationship that might last and provide me with future stories, but we fell out after I wrote an article about our trip for *GQ* magazine and perhaps included a little more detail than Valerio expected. I say fell out, but it was rather worse than that. When he received the copy of the magazine I sent him he called again. I don't know exactly what he objected to, but he didn't like what I'd written. 'You are a prick and a cunt and if I ever see you again, I'm gonna kill you,' he said in a quite measured tone, and all the more chilling for that, before slamming down the phone.

I didn't take the threat seriously, thinking that more than anything it was his ego I'd pricked, so to speak. Threats come with the territory I roam, though are seldom so stark. Within the UK crime reporting world there is very little evidence of anyone actually shooting the messenger, as journalists see themselves, though I wasn't sure how that worked in Italy. I wrote to Valerio in an attempt to placate him, but heard nothing more.

Three years later Viccei, forty-five years old by then, was out on day release and sitting in a parked, stolen Lancia with Antonio Malatesta, a known member of the Puglia mafia, when a police patrol car cruised past. As officer Enzo Baldini stopped, got out and approached the pair, Viccei opened fire with a .357 Magnum. He hit Baldini once in the leg, but the revolver was no match for the officer's sub-machine gun and a burst of fifteen rounds killed Viccei instantly. Police believed the two criminals were planning to ambush a bank cash van or kidnap for ransom a member of a wealthy industrialist's family who lived nearby.

I learned of Viccei's death the next day from an international news agency and couldn't believe he had acted so stupidly, almost as though he had a death wish. I can't say I was sad because I barely got to know him, but I knew the effect it would have on his close-knit family, all of whom had made me feel quite welcome. With Viccei's demise went Leach's best chance of finding the missing Knightsbridge loot. What also disappeared, of course, was my death threat. I was quite glad of that.

Did I glamourise Viccei? Yes, I probably did, briefly. He *was* glamorous, physically, handsome and debonair. The camera loved him. What I hope I didn't do, in my interview with him, was suggest for a moment that he had beaten the system, had chosen the easy path and was living a much better life than the rest of us. At times it may have felt like that to him: his heart pumping as he drove the loaded Renault getaway van unchallenged from the Knightsbridge vault, the ease with which he spread the cash around European banks, the smile on his smug face as he poured champagne for his family and friends – and me and the detective.

And, doubtless, many people considered the heist a 'victimless crime'. Their thinking: no one was physically hurt, and most of what he took from the safe deposit boxes probably belonged to other villains, or at least to the filthy rich who wouldn't really miss it. Almost a latter-day Robin Hood, some may have thought, though Viccei had no intention of giving any of it to the poor.

I made it clear in my reporting that Viccei was still a prisoner and, as I thought at the time, had many more years inside to go. He didn't cut quite the glamorous figure as he sped off in his baggy shorts and flip-flops, clinging to his pal on the back of the spluttering moped, in a rush to get back to his cell.

I'm sure his story satisfied a need for justice in other observers. For all his bravado, he got caught. What, I think, really fascinated people was the mystery of the missing loot. How much was left? Where was it? Would Dick Leach find it before Viccei's final prison release? That last question still lingers. Viccei is gone, but someone must know where his stolen treasure is.

Meeting Viccei provided a great boost to my career because I got a compelling, exclusive news story about a notorious criminal. We ran a special report, much longer than the usual news stories. It was the first TV interview he gave and, as it turned out, probably the last. It also helped me launch a side-line career as an occasional *GQ* feature writer, because the then editor of that male fashion bible was struck by Viccei's image.

None of it would have happened without the help of DI Leach and other officers who, all unofficially, trusted and encouraged me and helped me achieve what I wanted. I may have got more out of the trip than they did, but my bar bill was probably bigger than theirs. When Viccei was killed in the shootout with police, crime reporter Duncan Campbell wrote in *The Guardian* that his death had 'shaken Italy'. Around that time, however, Britain was still shaking from the shooting, in quite different circumstances, of a TV celebrity.

# CHAPTER 6

# THE CELEBRITY SHOOTING

*There is a lack of motive which troubles me and could indicate the lone stalker or obsessive, or something so deep in her life that it will take ages to emerge*

– FORMER DETECTIVE CHIEF SUPERINTENDENT
HAMISH CAMPBELL

The morning of Monday 26 April 1999 had been an unusually slow and boring start to my week. I'd already had two coffees as the newsroom clock ticked past midday and I was struggling to find anything to excite my news editor. Then the phone rang. 'Yeah, Brunty, I've got a good one for you,' said a familiar voice. No time for introductions or pleasantries.

'Go on,' I said.

'It's a belter,' he said. 'A woman's been stabbed in Fulham, Gowan Avenue. It could be Jill Dando and she might be dead.'

'*Whaaaat?*'

I called the news editor, told him the story and suddenly the boredom was gone. With the phone wedged between my shoulder and my jaw, my heart pumping, I tapped on my computer keyboard to check the much-loved TV presenter's name in the online electoral roll. I wanted to know if she lived anywhere near Fulham. That would tell me if it really could be her, but like a lot of famous people, she may have opted to have her name omitted from the public database. Up popped the listing: Jill Wendy Dando, 29 Gowan Avenue, SW6 6RF. *Bloody hell.*

I hurtled down the two flights of carpeted stairs at our Westminster office and joined a cameraman already primed and waiting in a crew car with the engine running. I called my source, demanding an update. 'Fuck me, Brunty,' he said, 'gimme a break, the cops haven't even got there yet.'

Was this a typical day in the life of a crime reporter? Hardly, but hopefully it demonstrates the erratic nature of the job from boredom to shock and – yes, I admit – excitement in three seconds. Such stories are great motivators and not just for journalists but for detectives, too.

Cops and hacks will rarely acknowledge it to anyone outside our world, but we relish the chance to rise to the challenge of crimes that grab huge public attention. We want to be at the centre of something that everyone is talking about. We are fellow travellers on a mission to explore momentous and shocking events, though I work under few of the pressures a detective feels. My brief is to report terrible things. I can't stop what's happened, but I can tell a story that should help the search for witnesses and clues.

At thirty-seven, Jill Dando was at the height of her fame as the host of national BBC TV news and the popular travel programme

*Holiday*. Ironically, she also presented *Crimewatch UK*, in which police appealed for the public's help in solving crimes. She was unflappable, beautiful and engaging with a warm, girl-next-door appeal. She was like a television version of Princess Diana, who had died in a car crash two years earlier. Jill was the most unlikely murder victim and her sudden, violent death was almost as much of a shock as that of the mother of our future King.

The cameraman drove as fast as he dared five miles along the Thames Embankment, through the back roads of Chelsea, past the Earls Court Exhibition Centre to the crime scene at Gowan Avenue, a long residential street of pretty, two-storey Victorian terraced houses. We couldn't get anywhere near No. 29. There was a police cordon across both ends of the road, but from where we were held back, we could see a great deal of activity around the house. In Scotland Yard's press office a helpful voice confirmed, with a bit of careful questioning and strictly unofficially, that the victim really was Jill Dando. I reported on air that the presenter had been attacked and hurt.

Just before I got the call about Jill Dando, a small posse of detectives charged out of their base at Kensington Police Station, west London, and squeezed into two anonymous saloon cars parked in the 'Police Only' bay. It was 12.05 p.m. and the start of the most baffling case most of them had ever tackled. If they had a satnav in those days, it would have told them it was a journey of just over two miles and would take them thirteen minutes, but with blue lights and sirens some were there in half that time. One of their colleagues, a fingerprint officer, heard the emergency call on his car radio and was already on his way. The detectives were known as Team Two of the Metropolitan Police's Central Area Major Investigation Pool.

Within days, even the commissioner was calling them 'The Dando Squad'.

When they got to 29 Gowan Avenue, the victim was still where she had fallen or been pushed, on the doorstep of her terraced house. 'It was obvious she had been shot, not stabbed. The bullet had gone into the side of her head. Her face was quite intact, but there was a lot of blood,' said a detective. And it was obviously Jill Dando.

So began one of the most extraordinary police investigations and one that is still unsolved today. In the 1990s Jill Dando was probably the most famous presenter on British TV. Her murder was a sensational news story. She had been shot as she returned from a morning shopping trip. I made another call to Scotland Yard and – an odd thing to say – my luck was in. I asked a different press officer for an update, and he explained he was just reading a computer screen that was showing internal police messages. 'Oh my God,' he said in genuine shock before he could stop himself, 'she's died.' I reported that, too. I was told later that her brother Nigel, also a journalist, watched the tragedy unfold on TV with fellow journalists at the *Bristol Evening Post* newspaper where he worked.

If that's true, I'm sorry. I can't imagine how devastating it must have been to learn of the sudden, violent death of your sister like that in front of colleagues who themselves, for all their sympathy, must have been contemplating the enormity of it as a news story. Some days later I learned the BBC, Jill Dando's employers, made a formal complaint that we had broadcast the tragic details too early, before we could be certain that all her family had been made aware of her death.

It would be different now. In the more sensitive times encouraged by the Leveson Report into press ethics, the media gives much more consideration to people's privacy. I don't remember details of the conversation 1 had with my news editor before I went on air. He would have asked only that I was sure of my sources and their information before reporting what I knew. It would have been a big thing to have got wrong, but then reporters are only as good as their sources.

Today we would probably wait for official confirmation from the police or the victim's family before we reported that she had died. That change of approach has taken away some of the competitiveness of the job. We are more risk averse. Getting something wrong undermines our credibility. For many years the proud and often justified boast in our advertising was 'Sky News – First for Breaking News'. The joke among our rivals was that as a 24-hour news channel we could quickly put right any errors, and the whispered rejoinder to our advert was: 'Sky News – Never Wrong For Long.'

There was later criticism from within the Dando Squad about the quality of the early house-to-house inquiries, carried out largely by uniformed officers. 'Frankly, they weren't done thoroughly and the officers doing them weren't debriefed properly,' said a detective.

Everyone who was spoken to should have had their details entered on a personal description form, to eliminate them as a suspect. But there were some glaring omissions. In some cases a simple thing like a date of birth wasn't put down and without that you can't check someone's previous convictions.

The mistakes meant that nine months into the investigation officers had to revisit many homes and ask the same questions again. That's not unusual in major unsolved investigations, but if it's the reason the Dando killer is still free then it's highly embarrassing. And it's not just that. On a second visit officers will miss any relatives or friends who stayed overnight, owners and tenants who have since moved out, maybe house-hunters who had been there at the crucial time and never came back. On a smaller case the detectives themselves would do the door knocking, but from the moment Jill Dando was identified as the victim senior Scotland Yard officers ordered a huge investigation with up to sixty-five officers and civilian support staff.

There were lots of theories: a contract killer, a former lover, a would-be lover, a TV rival, a nutter, the Russian mafia, a Serbian terrorist angry that she had fronted a televised appeal for Kosovan war victims, a villain she had helped expose on *Crimewatch UK*, or a troubled former patient of her doctor fiancé. The couple were due to marry a few months later. From the start, the two main theories were that Jill had been killed by a lone criminal or criminal gang, or that she was the victim of an obsessive who may have stalked her without her knowledge.

Another detective told me that contract killings often bore a certain hallmark, known as an OBE, which stands for 'one behind the ear'. Jill Dando died from a clean, close-up targeted bullet, fired from a handgun pressed to the side of her head. Such a shot, the detective explained, was virtually guaranteed to enter the brain and cause instant death. Neighbours found her dead, slumped against her front door with her handbag open beside her.

The officer in charge of the case was Detective Chief Inspector Hamish Campbell, one of Scotland Yard's most experienced investigators, whose skills had been honed pursuing Irish Republican Army terrorists. His real professional passion, though, was for murder. He and his various teams had solved some fascinating cases, with no apparent link between victim and killer: the stabbing and stamping to death of an elderly man by three deaf mutes, a headless woman in an abandoned garage, a mistaken-identity road-rage shooting.

From the start, Campbell believed the Dando case was solvable and that he would find the killer quickly. Some of his personal diary entries he has since shared with me illustrate how his thinking soon changed. After only a fortnight he wrote: 'Who killed her? Really no good clues yet. The murder in such an assassination style is perplexing. There is a lack of motive which troubles me and could indicate the lone stalker or obsessive, or something so deep in her life that it will take ages to emerge.'

A week later he wrote:

Three weeks now since her death and no arrest, nor one to emerge immediately. My initial thoughts remain much the same. Loner, obsessive or the organised gang or individual. I feel it is criminal, as opposed to Serbian or political. There is something about it which is so clinical, yet the weapon and ammunition tell me crime and not professional.

Police had identified the murder weapon as a 9mm semi-automatic pistol, a gun available on the black market for £100 and popular with street gangs in Europe.

Another two months on and Campbell's diary captured his frustration:

Can we solve it? I still maintain we can. In clear moments, when I have the opportunity to think quietly and clearly, it becomes blind-ingly simple and obvious, but the daily onslaught and attrition make it difficult to see the plan of attack. I feel a day away, perhaps with everyone, would be a good idea in trying to see the way forward.

Nine months after the murder, Campbell was feeling quite troubled at his lack of success. He wrote:

Why absolutely nothing? How can nothing come out of so much publicity, so much money? I'm not sure that a contract, however good, would have been possible to be kept so tight. I fear the loner, the ill man. Dando was not being stalked, not in the ordinary sense of the word, yet the quiet psychopath could have been at work.

Within three weeks of the murder a reward of £150,000 was on offer from the *Daily Mail* and the Crimestoppers charity.

There was no evidence that Ian Tucker was the man the Dando Squad was looking for, but he had featured on *Crimewatch UK* as a suspect in another case, and eventually his name rose to the top of the list of people the detectives thought worth interviewing, albeit informally. The police spoke to lots of people, about 100 of whom were considered potential suspects. There were many others on a database that changed all the time as intelligence was gathered. Of most interest were those with records of violence, past odd behav-iour and access to firearms. Ian Tucker accepted that he fitted loose-ly into this category and was surprised that it took police so long to get around to questioning him.

He was washing the personalised number plates of his BMW, on the front drive of his home in the Kent countryside, when two detectives from the Dando Squad slowed to a halt in their rather more modest Ford Mondeo. Tucker, thirty-four, pulled himself up to his full, gym-honed 6ft 2in. The diamond-stud earring, the gold Rolex and the scar above his left eye completed the intimidating image.

'It wasn't a surprise, I reckoned they would come eventually,' Tucker told me as he sprawled across a sofa, his eighteen-month-old daughter perched tenderly on one knee. 'They said my name had come up, somebody had put me in the frame for the Jill Dando thing. Could they have a word? They were proper lovely fellas; they weren't getting heavy or anything. It wasn't the first time I had been questioned about a murder,' he freely admitted as he bounced the little girl up and down.

Tucker had expected a visit because a year earlier he had been featured twice on *Crimewatch UK*, after the alleged attempted kidnap and robbery of a wealthy Arab businessman in west London. It was, he insisted, a £200,000 debt collection that got out of hand and, while two other men were arrested, Tucker disappeared and went on the run for nine months. On both episodes of the programme, presented by Jill Dando, appeals were made for information about Tucker's whereabouts. His photograph and description were broadcast. While he was away the two suspects arrested at the scene were both tried and acquitted, though not before Tucker – who denies he had a weapon – was named openly in court as the gang's gunman.

Eventually, through his solicitor, Tucker was told he wouldn't be charged, but he arrived home to find his cafe business and his reputation in ruins. He demanded, but didn't get, a public apology from *Crimewatch UK* for branding him an armed robber and kidnapper. Weeks later, the programme's presenter was shot dead. The Dando Squad detectives, now sitting in Tucker's lounge, had reflected on all of that, put two and two together and made three: means, motive and opportunity.

> I said to them: 'Listen, I had the hump at the time of the programme, but I don't even know the bird.' They said they were just here to ask me where I was at the time. The fact was, they had me down as a main player and I had been jumping up and down about *Crimewatch UK*, like you can't imagine, over the fact it had wrecked my business.

Fortunately for him, Tucker had an alibi. On the day of the shooting he was in Doncaster, South Yorkshire, repossessing a vehicle for a friend who had the receipts to prove it. That didn't stop the detectives questioning Tucker and his pal for the best part of two hours before they asked to see the documents.

> They wanted to check it all out, they wanted to know what phones I had used, all that shit. There was paperwork that confirmed everything, but they weren't just gonna take my word because, at the end of the day, I'm a villain and they've never believed me before. They were asking me about the weapon, the 9mm automatic, sort of picking my brains and seeing what I had to say about it. But I wouldn't entertain using anything like that, even if it was brand new, because there isn't anyone who has ever had one who's not had it jam up.

As his partner relieved him of their daughter, who was beginning to demand more attention, Tucker continued:

> To do something like that with the weapon that was used was totally unprofessional, or it was taking a chance. Nothing's fool proof, but

if you use a revolver, it will fire a hundred times out of a hundred, nothing will get jammed and it doesn't leave anything behind. The 9mm fires, reloads and spits out a cartridge – and that's evidence. The session with the detectives was just a chat really. It was all very friendly. They sat there and drank their tea and when they were leaving I told them I had put an ecstasy tablet in each cup.

A year after the murder, the pendulum had swung the theory slightly away from the criminal killer to the stalker, though nothing was being ruled out. Among crime reporters, the police team had become known as the Desperate Dan(do) Squad, after the comic cartoon character. New experts were being asked for their opinions. The old-school detectives involved must have found it irksome to be consulting psychologists and what they considered the new-fangled phenomenon of the criminal profiler; a controversial non-police figure who aimed to deduce the likely characteristics of the killer from an unscientific study of the crime scene.

A basic form of profiling was first used to try to identify Jack the Ripper, the killer who slaughtered at least five young women in London's East End in the late 1880s, but its more regular application was pioneered by the US Federal Bureau of Investigation's Behavioural Science Unit in the 1970s, as a tool to catch serial killers. To some police officers the profiler offers up nothing more than 'the bleeding obvious', a feeling captured some years ago in a TV police drama where a young detective at the scene of a murder rushes up to his boss and informs him: 'The profiler is held up in traffic and sends his apologies,' to which the chief inspector replies with a broad grin: 'Well, we'll just have to try and cope without him, won't we?'

But the unsolved Dando investigation was steering its frustrated detectives into uncharted waters. Some were readier than others to take the plunge. When I interviewed DCI Campbell for *GQ* magazine, he admitted that the idea of a celebrity stalker was a new concept for him, but with the help of specialists at the UK's National Crime Faculty, he was becoming an expert himself. He told me: 'It's the first time I've had to deal with stalking. I've read up on it. You have to understand aspects of it, the psychology of it.'

One of his appeals for information concentrated solely on the search for a man who, in the months before the presenter's murder, tried to obtain details of her household accounts, telling the utility companies he was her brother and wanted to switch the accounts to his name. The first attempts were made the day after her engagement to gynaecologist Alan Farthing was made public.

That could have been the rare, but not unknown, stalking behaviour of a disturbed fantasist trying to get close to her, but experts in the field had never seen such a pattern of behaviour actually leading to murder. And most victims of erotomania – a recognised mental illness in which someone develops an imaginary relationship with the object of their obsession – are men.

Among the amiable Campbell's reading material was the academic study *The Psychology of Stalking* edited by forensic psychologist J. Reid Meloy. He quotes research that shows most stalkers aren't violent, but if they are, they rarely use a weapon and very few victims die. That didn't sound like the killer Campbell was hunting, but nonetheless he was impressed enough with Meloy's theories that he sent two of his team to California to talk to him. In a two-hour chat in his book-lined office, Meloy came up straight away with an intriguing thought. He told the British police it was likely that Jill's killer had stalked other celebrities, including Princess Diana. Especially Diana.

I was keen to know more and asked Sky's US correspondent Keith Graves, who was in Los Angeles, to interview Meloy in his San Diego office. Delighted with yet more British attention and in his rather homey Californian delivery, the psychologist explained:

> I became aware through photographs of Jill Dando that her physical habitus was very similar to Princess Diana, that she was tall, she was blonde, I think the hairline was about the same. I also learned that her public presentation invited affectional feelings by the audience, the same as Princess Diana, that here's a woman who's very open, sociable, extroverted, communicates affection to other people.
>
> When people do that, they tend to invite that same kind of reaction. And sadly, those are also the kinds of women in public life that are stalked. Typically, women who are very cold, very withdrawn, angry, are not pursued by stalkers. Stalkers will pursue, because of their fantasies, women they feel they may be destined to have a relationship with. Or if they're psychotic, delusional, they may believe they actually do have a relationship with that particular woman.

One of the things that broadcasters are told early on in their careers is to imagine that they are speaking to an individual, perhaps someone they know, rather than a mixed audience of strangers. If Jill Dando had followed that advice, it may have contributed to her fate. Meloy said:

> The interesting thing that happens here, particularly with female presenters, different from film actresses, is that the newscaster is looking into the camera. And the newscaster's market value is often-times tied to the degree the viewer believes, sitting in his home, that

he has a personal affectional relationship with that newscaster and that newscaster cares about him.

It's a very one-on-one relationship. You never see a movie star look into the camera. There's not the personalised relationship we see in female news anchors that can boost ratings tremendously, if the viewer believes, you know, this is a nice gal, you know, she's affectionate, she is trying to communicate with me. We know that most people who stalk celebrity figures have a major mental disorder and are severely mentally disturbed and are at times psychotic. In other words, they've created their own private, idiosyncratic, internal reality.

Now, that psychosis can breed rejection. For instance, the stalker begins to believe that if Jill wears a red sweater when she's on the news on Wednesday, she's sending me a special message. If she wears a blue sweater on Friday, she's communicating that she loves me. If she wears a brown blouse on Monday, it means that she is rejecting me. But see, this is all delusional fantasy and Jill Dando knows nothing about it. Yet in his mind, just on the basis of those beliefs, he can now feel that she has rejected him.

Meloy compared Dando with other celebrity stalking investigations in which he was consulted, including the case of Dante Soiu, a pizza delivery worker from Ohio who stalked Hollywood star Gwyneth Paltrow. For eighteen months, Soiu sent her many letters and emails with explicit sexual content. The actress said Soiu's behaviour gave her nightmares and deeply affected her life. In one letter he warned her: 'Do not marry Ben Affleck. He's a slob.'

Meloy said Soiu was suffering from a delusional disorder and believed his feelings for Paltrow were reciprocated, and he got angry when he read about her romantic involvement with fellow actor Affleck.

> This is all fantasy, but now he's very jealous of the actual boyfriend.
> It feels because of his delusional relationship with her that she's now
> rejecting him because she's with this other guy. So these sources of
> anger, if not fury, can lead the stalker to then devalue the person and
> decide 'if I can't have her, nobody will'.

Twice Soiu, fifty-one, turned up at the Santa Monica home of Paltrow's parents to 'rescue' her because he believed Affleck and her security staff had mistreated her. On his second visit, he was arrested and charged with stalking but was later found not guilty by reason of insanity and committed to hospital.

A year after Jill Dando's murder, police arrested and charged Barry George, a man of low IQ who suffered from epilepsy and a personality disorder, was obsessed with guns and celebrities and had a previous conviction for attempted rape. He lived a few streets away from the TV presenter and was known locally for pestering women. Seventeen years earlier he had been caught, armed with a knife and rope, hiding in bushes outside Kensington Palace in an attempt to see Princess Diana.

George, forty-one, was convicted of the Dando murder after the jury heard a microscopic speck of gunpowder residue had been found in his coat pocket. The only other forensic evidence to link him to the shooting was a single polyester fibre on Jill's coat said to come from a pair of trousers found at George's home. He spent seven years in jail, before winning an appeal and a retrial in which the new judge ruled the gunpowder evidence inadmissible because it could have been picked up from a number of innocent sources unconnected to the shooting.

In a second Old Bailey trial, George was acquitted after his lawyer William Clegg told jurors:

> The only reason the prosecution say that this is the work of the local loner, the local nutter, the man with these serious psychological problems, is because that is the man they arrested ... Who was the man who outwitted Campbell of the Yard? Our Barry – what do you think? Lightbulb's flickering maybe but remember, it is only a forty-watt bulb when it is completely lit.

Most crimes reported to police remain unsolved, but homicides – murder and manslaughter – usually end in someone being charged. They are sometimes complicated and may take longer to solve, but homicide investigations are always given big resources, usually include public appeals for information and the victims are more often than not killed by someone they know. So-called stranger murders are rare, especially of women.

Today it's more than twenty-three years since DCI Campbell arrested Barry George, his one and only suspect, and the prospects of a new breakthrough are remote. Months before George's arrest I asked Campbell if it bothered him that his career could be defined by the Dando murder and whether he caught her killer. 'I can live with that small footnote in history,' he acknowledged with a smile. Then he waved a hand towards his junior detectives along the corridor. 'I remind my team that they share the responsibility as well.' Campbell retired as a detective chief superintendent in 2012 and since then has been employed investigating homicides committed by police officers in Jamaica, a country that vies regularly with El Salvador, Brazil, South Africa and others for the unenviable title of Homicide Capital of the World. Since Campbell arrived there have been more than 1,000 homicides committed by police.

> In one way of course the case did define me. The reporting was intense, and I seemed to become strongly aligned to the inquiry, which was understandable but equally not the correct approach. It would not happen like that now. But I was prepared to speak with the media and engage. The case did explode on to the media and generated so much attention, misinformation and speculation, which deflected me. I used to say, if it was the same murder, without being Jill Dando, it would have been long solved. I can understand the constant theorising, but in fact I never really considered the Serbian, Russian or gangland scenarios. Maybe that was wrong, but none of my senior colleagues did either, nor did the intelligence.
>
> It didn't define my career as much as one would imagine. There was another thirteen years of my CID career which followed; not all of it went as I would wish, but I remained within homicide. I also became involved in lecturing and training of detectives in major investigations. I learned a lot from the case which I wanted to pass back. Homicide investigation in all its aspects, and the need for the investigative body to get it right, remains my passion.

Campbell was also happy to tell me that having seen Barry George initially convicted, his later acquittal was his only not-guilty verdict in a murder case.

# CHAPTER 7

# THE STORY TIPSTER

*So his case, such as it was, sounded dismal. However, sometimes, where there is a very strong body of evidence, all is not lost*

– BARRISTER MARK TOMASSI

The contact who tipped me off about Jill Dando's murder was a man called John Ross. He was an ex-cop and became a good friend of mine. His opening words were always: 'I've got a good one for you.' No one ever said they had a bad one for me. All crime stories are bad news for someone.

For once I am happy to reveal a source, largely because, after a couple of drinks, John would admit his own key role in the latest big crime story to anyone who would listen. He is also no longer with us and, although confidentiality would normally accompany a source to the grave, I suspect John would be happy to have 'major source' as the epitaph on his gravestone. I've still got his number in my phone, as much a reminder of his journalistic ability as it is of our long friendship.

His main market for exclusive stories was the tabloid press, especially the red tops *The Sun* and the *Daily Mirror* and their Sunday paper stablemates. He was well paid for his tips and information, sometimes several thousand pounds for a story splashed over the front page. He provided plenty of those, but he also knew that some stories, such as the Jill Dando murder, would quickly become breaking news, and it was more profitable for him to tell all his journalist contacts at once before we heard it officially from the police or another source who would get paid instead of him.

I was introduced to John during my Fleet Street days in The Wine Press, a modern bar that unusually became a gathering place for journalists from all newspapers, unlike most of the older, traditional pubs that tended to be the favourite and fiercely guarded watering holes of staff from particular papers. Most lunchtimes John Ross toured the pubs, knowing instinctively which of his stories would suit which newspaper. He would usually end up in The Wine Press to meet a mix of *Mirror* staff, including me, who had walked from our desks at nearby Holborn Circus and journalists from *The Sun* and *News of the World*, who had arrived in taxis from their new offices in Wapping near Tower Bridge.

When I joined Sky News my studio base was thirteen miles away from central London drinking haunts, in Osterley, west London. As a broadcaster likely to be called to do a live report at any moment, I had to give up lunchtime drinking and socialising. From then on, I tended to get John's 'seconds', the less exciting tips, because I couldn't match the big payments he got from the papers. To TV news executives, the idea of reporters finding their own stories and expecting to pay their sources for them was a new and slightly uncomfortable concept. That sort of thing certainly didn't happen at the BBC.

Thankfully that changed when it dawned on my new bosses that a 24-hour news channel should be competing with newspapers for the same stories. John played a big part in that process and helped boost my career.

John, J. R. or Roscoe, as we variously knew him, was a former Flying Squad detective sergeant with the Metropolitan Police and had left after being cleared in a corruption trial involving the alleged fitting up of an armed robber. A shotgun had been found where no shotgun had existed before, allegedly. Despite his acquittal at the Old Bailey, John was sacked after an internal disciplinary hearing but reinvented himself as a brilliant supplier of news stories. It was no secret that most of his tips came from his former colleagues, serving police officers. He introduced me to some of his police pals in pubs, clubs, even his home and would often tell me what stories he was working on for other journalists. He trusted all – well, most – of his reporter contacts, but just like the majority of hacks, he found it difficult to keep anything secret. When he described himself as a journalist, few of us would argue with him. His transition from policeman to pressman seemed effortless, but J. R. possessed bucketloads of the 'nous' essential in winkling out information. He made people feel comfortable about telling him stories and that they could trust him. He was a natural.

So, he swapped his police officer's warrant card for a press card issued by the *News of the World*. I don't think the National Union of Journalists would have given him one and he certainly didn't get one from Scotland Yard, whose press officers were thrown into disarray whenever we called to question them on the latest John Ross tip. Senior Yard staff regularly complained about his methods, but they and we couldn't fault the quality of his scoops.

John didn't just rely on police leaks, though, because like all good journalists he had an enquiring mind, a keen sense of history and an uncanny knack for spotting a story. He rang me once to say he had just driven past Biggin Hill airfield near his home in Kent. He had seen a 'For Sale' sign on the former officers' mess building at the most famous of all Battle of Britain RAF bases. It was from Biggin Hill that many Spitfire and Hurricane pilots helped defeat the German Luftwaffe during the Second World War. Few younger journalists would have seen the news value in that.

John had a big interest in horses and at weekends could be found in his tweeds and Barbour coat, a world away from Fleet Street bars, at point-to-point race meetings or equestrian events where he had a share in a promising show jumper. Every summer without fail he would spend a week at the Royal International Horse Show at Hickstead, where he could combine his twin passions by picking up horsey people gossip and selling it to newspaper diary editors.

The secret of his success was simple: he talked to people, whether it was someone standing next to him in a bar, a stranger in the queue at the post office or the minicab driver taking him home from Fleet Street. He treated everyone he met as a potential source of stories. When a driver turned up one night in an expensive limousine to ferry him back to Kent, he gave him his card and asked him to ring if he ever picked up celebrities, especially if they were with someone who wasn't their partner. A few weeks later the driver called to say he had just had TV presenter Paula Yates – then married to Bob Geldof – and rock star Michael Hutchence in the back of the car. They were acting like they were more than just good friends. Cue another *News of the World* exclusive.

John was a gregarious, friendly guy and it paid off, literally. He wasn't a football fan, but he was first with the news that England star John Terry had been fired from the national team captaincy – over an alleged affair with a team-mate's ex-girlfriend – after a short and much-anticipated meeting with head coach Fabio Capello. I reported the sacking within minutes of it happening while our rivals' reporters spent most of the day outside Capello's office at Wembley Stadium telling their viewers they didn't know what was going on. It was many hours later when an official Football Association statement finally confirmed our scoop. How did J. R. do that? I know exactly where he got the story, but I can't say because the source still needs protecting.

John didn't care where he found his stories and neither did I. If I ever queried the accuracy of a tip-off that he considered 'a belter', he would tell me it was '110 per cent' and sometimes reveal exactly where the information had come from. If I ever thought he was paying a police source, perhaps I should have considered more seriously my own role in aiding and abetting that dubious process, but I didn't. How could I ignore him when he rang one Saturday lunchtime to tell me the Queen Mother had just died and I was one of only a handful of reporters in the world who now knew that? The relationship between John, his contacts and me was severely tested when he was arrested with a detective pal in a pub underneath Charing Cross Station in central London in July 2004. It set off an extraordinary chain of events.

His arrest was part of a Scotland Yard corruption inquiry sparked by a story in *The Sun* that told of a police investigation into racist threats made against the comedian and actor Lenny Henry. Apparently, Henry had complained about the leak and refused to cooperate with detectives. Their colleagues in the Directorate of

Professional Standards, known as the rubber-heel squad (because you don't hear them coming), had put a suspect detective under surveillance and followed him to the Ha! Ha! Bar. What followed was no laughing matter.

John and his contact Detective Constable David Dougall were arrested after the officer handed John an envelope of copied documents about two terrorist operations. John was accused of paying the officer £200 for them. The pair were taken from the bar to Sutton Police Station in south London and eventually charged with corruption. The arrest turned out to be a mixed blessing for John because, like everyone taken into custody, he was assessed by a doctor to make sure he was fit enough to be questioned. The medic was happy for the interrogation to go ahead but was concerned about the prisoner's ruddy complexion and decided it wasn't merely his embarrassment at being arrested. He advised John, at the age of fifty-eight, to see a heart specialist as soon as possible. Several weeks later, urgent open-heart surgery probably saved John's life, or at least prolonged it. It also meant his trial had to be postponed and, on medical grounds alone, he welcomed the breather.

John's good fortune didn't end there. Recuperating in hospital, he chatted to a fellow patient who let slip that his daughter worked on the BBC's hugely popular soap opera *EastEnders*. With a bit of encouragement from John, the patient passed on gossip about one of the main actors. Painfully, John eased himself out of bed, shuffled in his gown and slippers out into the corridor and phoned an exclusive and well-paid story to *The Sun*. More than a year later he was passed fit to stand trial and although he was fully recovered, he cut a forlorn and lonely figure behind the glass of the dock at Inner London Crown Court. He pleaded not guilty to the charge of 'aiding and abetting wilful misconduct in public office', but he expected to go to prison if convicted. His co-defendant DC Dougall had already pleaded guilty to a corruption charge and was awaiting sentence, although John's jury wasn't told that because it could prejudice its eventual verdict after hearing the case against him.

The trial hinged on the question of whether the money that changed hands was a bribe for information. But the case was also a public examination of the relationship between journalists and police officers. I agreed to give evidence for John's defence, not simply as a character witness but as someone who had regular contact with police officers. I was asked about that relationship and, among other things, explained how the recently retired Scotland Yard commissioner, Sir John Stevens, had invited crime reporters to call up his senior investigating officers and question them about their cases.

The prosecutor Sarah Whitehouse, now a King's Counsel and leading barrister, appeared to me to be badly briefed. She suggested that reporters carried around a copy of the Yard's media code of conduct, or some such document, at all times, which we whipped out at the start of any meeting with a police officer and announced: 'Hold on, before we go any further let me just check we are abiding by the guidelines.' I explained that I had read the code but didn't keep it in my pocket wherever I went, much to the amusement of some jurors. The prosecutor also asked if I knew a detective contact of John's who had been sacked for passing on confidential information to him. I said I did, but pointed out the officer had been suspended, not sacked, and had been reinstated. I was beginning to sound like a clever dick.

In his own evidence, John told jurors DC Dougall was a contact to whom he often lent money, which the officer always paid back. The £200 he'd given Dougall, he said, was unrelated to the documents handed over in the bar during the meeting that led to their arrest. John described the documents as low-grade intelligence that, although marked as restricted, could be viewed on a police internal intranet site by the whole of the Metropolitan Police staff of around 40,000. He said they were of little news value. The jury agreed with John and acquitted him. It was a remarkable and important victory. John told the journalists' trade paper, *Press Gazette*:

I was on trial for Fleet Street. This is a great day for the free press … If I had gone down, I would have gone to prison without a doubt. After this, perhaps cops will start talking to us again. That's why this is a big victory for the free press.

I left court with a mix of delight and relief for my friend John but rather puzzled by the jury's not-guilty verdict. Surely, John had been caught red-handed? I had thought the next time I saw him would be over a cup of weak tea and a Mars Bar across a table in the visitors' room of Wandsworth Prison. I didn't know why he was acquitted because I couldn't ask any of the jurors. It's a crime to approach a juror during or after a trial. By law each of the twelve people making up a jury must remain anonymous, and their deliberations kept secret.

His barrister Mark Tomassi, who appeared to have plucked John from the jaws of certain misery, explained to me years later what he thought had happened. He said:

In law there was really no defence, and the meeting and surveillance witnesses were impossible to forensically controvert. So his case, such as it was, sounded dismal. However, sometimes, where there is a very strong body of evidence, all is not lost. The police officer sold confidential information to a third party; this was actually witnessed and proved. My client bought it, thus was part of the 'unlawful exchange of alleged confidential information', so a slam dunk for the police and CPS. Well, not quite.

I do not claim that anything I did was actually or palpably the reason why the jury decided the case in the way they did. However, the trial, the defence stance, undoubtedly provided a platform from which a reasonable jury could make a reasonable assessment. It was in this instance in his favour ... it could have been otherwise. I see jury trial as a well-structured debate, and the twin platforms of legal assessment and factual determination in the one trial is a great cocktail. The judge must follow the law and the jury must follow the judge in those directions. I and many others also see it as a way the citizen, and any citizen, can hold the state to account ... a sort of hybrid justice where the litmus test is the common sense of a jury and its sense of right and wrong and even consequences. I suspect our friend received this kind of result.

So those who apparently break the law can expect to be arrested, charged and prosecuted, but remember, the final backstop of what is in the public interest lies not so much with the CPS, but with judge and jury. If the jury do not think that the prosecution ought to have been brought, even though in law it was correct to do so, then does anybody really mind when they acquit against the weight of the evidence? We don't need to blame [the] CPS for bringing the charge in our case, indeed it's rather difficult to see how they couldn't in the absence of some very pressing reason. The judgement *not* to prosecute is as much a problem as to prosecute; each can be criticised and a judgement to prosecute on clear evidence of involvement seems, at least to me, to have been on this basis actually correct. I see absolutely no problem with twelve people drawn at random deciding on public interest grounds to acquit where they consider there is no reason for someone to be convicted. A trial is almost perfectly equipped to work out the right result. This is I believe the reason for the acquittal.

'Nice people (like our man as it were) don't get convicted' is another way of putting it, at least not by jurors. There is, I believe, a traditional sense of fair play and 'so what' in the pragmatic way that the jury likely approached the legal task that they ineluctably faced in our case. As you know, a jury is bound by an oath to return verdicts in accordance with the evidence. I do not see it as necessarily a breach of that oath to look at the evidence in its full context; indeed I see it as a safeguard and always regarded from my first days the fundamental right of a jury to acquit, *whatever* the evidence, to be a fundamental liberty and a necessary part of a well-functioning democracy.

John didn't pause for long to consider how his good fortune had been achieved. In the lively basement of Berries Wine Bar, near Blackfriars Station, we celebrated his miraculous escape. The word Houdini was heard more than once. When he climbed the stairs unsteadily at the end of the night and turned to wave goodbye, his friends and supporters applauded and cheered. John enjoyed that so much he came back in and did it again.

Meanwhile, John's co-defendant DC Dougall, aged forty-nine, was given a nine-month suspended prison sentence after he admitted misconduct in a public office. His lawyer Pippa McAtasney described the case as a personal disaster for him, telling the judge: 'He cannot believe he has been as foolish as he has.' Judge Simon Davis said the officer had betrayed the trust of the public and the Metropolitan Police. DC Dougall, who worked at Chelsea Police Station, had resigned from the force eleven months earlier after twenty-three years' service. He must have wondered what would have happened if he had pleaded not guilty and fought the charge like his co-accused.

Within days John was back in action with another potential scoop, which sent me haring off to Putney Police Station. I arrived just too late to witness the release from overnight custody of *Sun* editor Rebekah Wade, who had been arrested for alleged assault on her actor husband Ross Kemp, *EastEnders* star, at their west London home. Police said Kemp suffered a cut lip but refused medical treatment and his wife was not charged. Everyone used the story.

Nobody I knew at Scotland Yard seemed bothered that I had given evidence for John Ross – and effectively against its own detectives – and both our careers carried on as before, though the relationship between police and the media, especially the Murdoch press, was coming under increasingly close scrutiny.

Two years earlier, the botched investigation into the murder of private eye Daniel Morgan, found with an axe in his head in the car park of a south London pub in 1987, had led to questions being asked about the *News of the World*'s behaviour. Its reporters were thought to be interfering with a renewed investigation into the case, in a bid to protect suspects who supplied the paper with other stories. After confronting the *NoW* editor, a certain Rebekah Wade a year before she took over *The Sun*, the police decided to take no action against a paper with which senior Scotland Yard staff had close connections.

At the time the whole question of press self-regulation was already under debate, so it didn't help Fleet Street's case when Ms Wade went on to tell a committee of MPs: 'We have paid the police for information in the past.' Her paper's parent company, News International, had to issue a hasty statement in an attempt to clarify her remarks: 'It is not company practice to pay police for information.' Labour MP Chris Bryant said he believed it was illegal for police to be paid for information and added: 'If newspapers are suborning police officers, encouraging them to think that there is money to be made from selling information, that can only be bad news for the criminal justice system.'

Not long after John Ross's acquittal came the start of the phone-hacking scandal involving *News of the World* journalists, and the first of two police investigations into the allegations they had intercepted and listened to voicemail messages left on the private mobile phones of celebrities, politicians and other people in the news. To other journalists, the Sunday tabloid was known for its salacious stories as the *Screws of the World*, *News of the Screws* or simply *The Screws* – you get the idea – but because of its regular exclusives on all manner of subjects it was essential reading to most people working in the news media, and I often followed up its scoops. When the practice of phone hacking was revealed, it was a bit like the discovery that top athletes used drugs to beat the competition: so *that's* how it was done! For the journalists who did it, phone hacking was like taking performance-enhancing drugs. And many became addicted.

The police probe led eventually to the Leveson Inquiry into media ethics and big changes in the way police and reporters interact today. Over several years, the phone-hacking saga prompted allegations that Scotland Yard was originally reluctant to investigate the journalists involved and failed to fully explore the evidence it accumulated. In a later, very public, row, Assistant Commissioner John Yates insisted the guidance he got from the Crown Prosecution Service was that phone hacking was a crime only if a journalist had listened in to a voicemail before the recipient had accessed it. The Director of Public Prosecutions, Keir Starmer QC – who went on to become the leader of the Labour Party – said that had never been CPS advice. Once the first prosecution was launched, the Yard had accepted News International's insistence that any criminality was the work of one rogue reporter, the *News of the World*'s royal editor Clive Goodman, and private investigator Glenn Mulcaire, both of whom were imprisoned.

In 2007, Goodman admitted hacking the phones of royal aides, a crime revealed when Prince William became suspicious of a newspaper report about his knee injury, while Mulcaire confessed to hacking the phones of high-profile figures including model Elle Macpherson, publicist Max Clifford and footballers' union boss Clive Taylor. The paper's editor Andy Coulson, who went on to be the director of communications for Prime Minister David Cameron, resigned after accepting responsibility for his staff's behaviour but denied any knowledge of it. During that first hacking investigation, the police amassed evidence against suspects other than Goodman and Mulcaire and details of thousands of hacked phones belonging to celebrities, sports stars, crime victims and former Deputy Prime Minister John Prescott, but all of that was kept quiet. In 2009, Yates was asked to consider reopening the hacking investigation and decided, within hours, that it was not necessary.

Four years on, in 2011, the original evidence was re-examined and used in a second wave of hacking prosecutions. Nine people were convicted and four journalists, including Coulson, were jailed. Rebekah Wade, who by then had married racehorse trainer Charlie Brooks and become Rebekah Brooks, was acquitted along with several others, including her husband, who had been charged with conspiracy to pervert the course of justice by hiding a laptop and other material on the day of her arrest. *The Guardian*'s Nick Davies, who had done much to expose phone hacking, later summed up the scale and impact of the second probe:

> The investigation launched that day has morphed into 12 operations, and 210 people have been arrested or interviewed under caution about phone or email hacking, payments to public officials, accessing data on allegedly stolen phones and perverting the course of justice. From that first day, this was not simply an inquiry into allegations of crime but an attempt to rescue Scotland Yard from crisis, to prove it was capable of taking on the power of Rupert Murdoch's company where earlier attempts had failed.

The revelation that journalists had hacked the phone of missing schoolgirl Milly Dowler before her murdered body was discovered prompted Murdoch to close down the *News of the World* after 168 years of publishing.

Around this time, I and several colleagues were called in by the head of Sky News John Ryley and asked if we had ever hacked a mobile phone. I hadn't. I was informed that the company had hired a legal firm to trawl our email history to make sure that none of us had engaged in hacking or committed any other potential crime. I never heard any more about it.

On 5 April 2012, I read this in *The Guardian* newspaper:

Sky News has admitted that one of its senior executives authorised a
journalist to conduct email hacking on two separate occasions that it
said were 'in the public interest' – even though intercepting emails is
a prima facie breach of the Computer Misuse Act, to which there is
no such defence written in law.

Gerard Tubb, the broadcaster's northern England correspondent,
accessed emails belonging to John Darwin, the 'canoe man' accused
of faking his own death, when his wife, Anne, was due to stand trial
for deception in July 2008. The reporter built up a database of emails
that he believed would help defeat Anne Darwin's defence; her husband had pleaded guilty to seven charges of deception before her
trial.

The paper carried a statement from my boss Ryley, in which he said
that as part of an investigation into criminal activity the hacking
was in the public interest and justified breaking the law. It had been
a 'finely balanced judgement'.

Two years later the Crown Prosecution Service announced that
my colleague Tubb would not face any charge. The CPS deputy head
of special crime Malcolm McHaffie said in a statement:

Having considered the factors set out in the guidelines on cases af-
fecting the media, it is our view that the evidence indicates that the
public interest served by the conduct in question outweighs the potential overall criminality, should an offence be proved. In reaching
this decision, we took into account that the emails were accessed
with a view to showing that a criminal offence had been committed

and that a number of the same emails were subsequently lawfully obtained.

The architect of the *News of the World* phone hacking was its news editor Greg Miskiw. He left the paper in 2005, before the scandal broke, and avoided prosecution in the first police investigation. I worked with Greg at the *Sunday Mirror* and nearly followed him to the *NoW*. I'm glad I didn't, because I could have got caught up in the controversy. In 2014 he admitted his role and was jailed for six months.

The newsroom that Greg ran worked under enormous pressure to get scoops. I don't know if he was solely responsible for that, or a victim of it. After his release from prison his daughter Sophie wrote, in *The Spectator*, a riveting analysis of her father's journalistic life at the *NoW* and its effect on his family:

> The paper was a presence in my daily life even if my dad wasn't. It was a Sunday paper, so his hours (or at least the hours he worked) were the crack of dawn on Tuesday morning till late Saturday night. After a day hunting 'exclusives, not excuses' he would resume his regular stance in the nearest Wapping pub, chain smoking Marlboro Reds and knocking back a stream of double Famous Grouses. By the time he roused himself mid-Sunday morning, he would be so agitated, adrenaline still pumping, the day would be spent trying to avoid setting him off. His job dictated nearly every part of our lives. I knew the phone number for the news desk before I started school and thought 'contacts' was another word for 'friends', because my dad had dozens although no-one ever came round for dinner.

Greg died in 2021, aged seventy-one, after a long period of poor health, including heart and lung disease so typical of a life in the fastest of Fleet Street fast lanes. Today, media bosses are concerned about their staff's work and life balance. If anyone ever worried about Greg's, it wasn't him.

The relationship between top figures at Scotland Yard and News International senior staff continued to haunt both organisations. In July 2011, the Met commissioner, Sir Paul Stephenson, chose to resign after it was revealed the force had hired a PR company run by former *News of the World* deputy editor Neil Wallis. It turned out that Wallis had been hired while the *NoW* was being investigated over yet more criminality. Wallis went on to stand trial himself, accused of overseeing the phone-hacking operation, but was acquitted.

Assistant Commissioner John Yates swiftly followed his boss out of the door after admitting he had played a part in the appointment of Wallis, who was a personal friend of his. Eight months on, the Yard's communications chief Dick Fedorcio, who had approved Wallis's PR contract, resigned.

Those three senior Scotland Yard figures were all people I knew well. I had eaten and drunk with them at official gatherings and socialised with them and their wives on other occasions. All three helped me with stories. At the time it was very much a natural part of the life of a crime reporter, an aspect of a relationship built on a common need to share stories about crime with the public; for one reason or another, I've been in touch with all of them since their resignations. I felt sorry for them in the way they left their jobs. None of them faced any criminal allegations, but it wasn't difficult to understand that, despite their denials of wrongdoing, the clear public perception was that they were too close to senior editors at the *News of the World.*

In the same month as the commissioner's resignation, Home Secretary Theresa May asked the former Parliamentary Commissioner for Standards, Elizabeth Filkin, to examine the ethics of Scotland Yard's media relations. Her findings weren't quite what we had expected. She accused journalists of 'late-night carousing' with officers. I had to look up the word 'carousing' in a dictionary. It sounded like something I would really enjoy. According to her, I was already doing it. She warned detectives to beware of 'flirtatious' reporters and being plied with alcohol 'designed to get you to drop your defences'. Did she mean their trousers? Or their knickers? It was rather laughable stuff, but Filkin did recommend more, rather than less, communication between police and the media and said the Met needed to be impartial, not have favourites, in its dealings with journalists.

Never before had we, the free press, been under such intense and prolonged scrutiny. I watched the police pursuit of my newspaper colleagues. I covered the court cases and witnessed our profession's reputation being severely damaged. And it got much worse. In November 2011, while the second phone-hacking investigation was underway, police officers arrived at the Windsor home of *Sun* reporter Jamie Pyatt. It was a few days after a boozy family barbecue, at the end of which he and his son had chased away burglars from a nearby community centre. Detectives had interviewed them about it. Pyatt told the journalists' trade paper *Press Gazette*:

> I was sitting in my office and saw a couple of police officers walking up my drive so I assumed they had returned to ask a few more

questions or congratulate us on our reckless, if rather tipsy, bravery on behalf of the community. But more and more coppers kept
coming up the drive until there were about a dozen and nobody was
holding a congratulatory cake. It was then that I was told they were
from Operation Elveden and I was under arrest.

It was a new Scotland Yard investigation into News International
journalists and payments they allegedly made to police and other
public sector workers in return for information. The new inquiry
was prompted when, for reasons journalists find difficult to understand, the company supplied detectives with thousands of confidential staff emails, many of which revealed the names of story sources.
For a journalist, revealing the identity of a confidential source of
information is the worst professional sin. The company's extraordinary cooperation with the investigators may have been designed
to avoid potential corporate bribery charges, but in a later meeting
with *Sun* journalists Rupert Murdoch actually admitted handing
over the emails had been a mistake.

When Operation Elveden ended after five years it had cost nearly
£15 million, with ninety suspects arrested and thirty-four people,
including nine police officers, convicted. Most of the twenty-nine
journalists who were charged, including Jamie Pyatt, were acquitted
by juries after arguing that the stories they wrote from their paid
sources were in the public interest. Three journalists were found
guilty but then had their convictions quashed by the Appeal Court.
It ruled that the trial judge had misdirected jurors by failing to tell
them the threshold for conviction was high – it needed overwhelming evidence – on charges brought under a little-used thirteenth-
century law of misconduct in public office. The journalists were

charged with aiding and abetting a public official's misconduct. In one case the Lord Chief Justice, Lord Thomas, said that to convict a defendant, jurors had to be convinced not just that the behaviour was wrong but that it had done real harm to the public interest. He said: 'This is without doubt a difficult area of the criminal law. An ancient common law offence is being used in circumstances where it has rarely before been applied.'

In a noisy bar somewhere, clutching a fresh glass of his favourite champagne, my friend and top contact John Ross celebrated the journalists' acquittals as enthusiastically as he had his own nearly a decade earlier. While the circumstances of John's courtroom battle were rather different, he felt he had paved the way for these later victories. And he was doubly grateful for their success because some of them were his customers, the people who paid him for his tip-offs. John didn't seem to worry about much in his own journalistic life, probably because he seldom got involved deeply in the stories he initiated. He simply got the broad details, the essence of what made them headliners, and sold them on to me and my colleagues. Sources like him never had to immerse themselves in the tragedies that are a regular part of a crime reporter's life.

# CHAPTER 8

# THE SCHOOLGIRL MURDER

*I'm not thinking about Roy Whiting.*
*I'm thinking of my daughter, Sarah*
– Bereaved mother Sara Payne

Sarah Payne was eight years old when she vanished as she played hide-and-seek with her two brothers and sister in a cornfield near the Sussex coast on a summer's day in 2000. The idyllic setting, their innocent game, Sarah's captivating school photograph and her eloquent and media-friendly mother all ensured the story got more media coverage than some other child abductions. So, too, did the timing, because it happened at the start of the school holidays when traditionally there isn't much news around, largely because Parliament and many law courts are shut.

Journalists call it 'the silly season', because they have to fill up their newspapers with frivolous or silly stories that wouldn't normally get reported: stories about piano-playing parrots and skateboarding ducks, that sort of thing. We've all done them. Somewhere in the Sky archive is the video tape of my aforementioned goldfish walk.

There was nothing silly about Sarah's disappearance. It was difficult for reporters to avoid the cliché 'every parent's nightmare'. Detectives arrested her abductor Roy Whiting, a known local paedophile, within twenty-four hours of Sarah's disappearance. He was eventually convicted of her murder, though Sarah's fate wasn't known until a fortnight after she disappeared and it took another six months for police to find enough evidence to charge Whiting.

Sarah's abduction resonated with me for several reasons, not least because it played out from beginning to end within a few miles of my home in West Sussex. The search for Sarah and the hope that she was still alive gripped our viewers and dominated news bulletins. In that time, I spent every day driving to the incident room at Littlehampton Police Station across a gorgeous South Downs bathed in early-morning sunlight and then home again in the warm glow of a midsummer evening. Most lunchtimes I bought a sandwich and strolled on the seafront before compiling my report. It was such a welcome change from the hot and sweaty daily train ride into my London office. Each day I contrasted my good fortune with the inevitability of Sarah's fate and the grief of her family. I was certain there would be no happy reunion.

I always think about the terrible bad luck Sarah suffered that day. She hit her head and ran crying from her siblings, back towards her grandparents' home a few minutes' walk away. She crossed the field and popped through a hedge out into a narrow country lane where predatory child-abuser Whiting was sitting in his Fiat Ducato van. He may have spotted the children playing in the field, but he can't possibly have known that Sarah would suddenly emerge alone. He had only a brief moment to snatch her and put her in his vehicle before her siblings followed her into the lane, but it was enough.

Her brother Lee, who was thirteen at the time, was a few seconds behind Sarah and although he didn't witness her abduction, he saw a white van speeding away with its driver waving and grinning at him. Lee's remarkably detailed description of the driver helped convince the trial jury it was Whiting. Sarah's brother told the court:

> He was quite scruffy, looking like he hadn't shaved for ages. He had little white stubbles on his face and little bits of grey in his hair. He was greasy and stuff. He had yellowish teeth when he grinned and his eyes were really white and stood out from his face.

Years later Lee said he still felt guilty that he hadn't been able to prevent his sister's abduction. If only he'd run after her faster, he might have caught up with her. He didn't even realise she was in the back of Whiting's van along with his rapist kit of ropes, a knife, baby oil and plastic cable wrist ties.

I often warned my own kids that there is sometimes such a thin line between life and death and nothing I've ever reported has so vividly and horribly illustrated that point. My daughter was a couple of years younger than Sarah at the time. Sarah's body was discovered early one morning by a young farmhand removing toxic ragwort plants from a field of hungry cows eighteen miles away. She was in a shallow, hastily dug grave a few yards from the A29 and a couple of miles from my favourite village pub, where the farmhand was a regular drinker. Two miles from the site in the opposite direction is the country estate of Pink Floyd guitarist David Gilmour.

Sarah's murder is one of those terribly sad cases that prompt people to ask me how I cope, how do I deal with the horrific details, how on earth am I able to switch off? The truth is, I don't find it difficult. I rarely see anything more than the public sees reproduced in the media. It's not as though I'm there when the bodies are discovered, though I have been in other circumstances before I became a crime reporter. Several years earlier I covered the civil wars in the Balkans and witnessed the aftermath of atrocities and the combat injuries of dozens of dead and wounded men, women and children. The first dead body I saw was at Mutla Ridge on the desert road north out of Kuwait City, from where Iraqi troops had fled at the end of the First Gulf War. The defeated Iraqis, laden down with plundered loot, were heading home on Highway 80 towards Basra when coalition bombers caught them in a bottleneck and pounded them with cluster bombs.

When I got there, troops had already cleared the area of most of the bodies, but the twisted wrecks of hundreds of armoured vehicles, trucks and cars trapped in the inferno were still scattered where their panicked drivers had tried to escape across the sand and rocks. The body of one Iraqi soldier was left, darkening in the hot sun, propped up with his rifle on top of a ridge as though guarding the scene of devastation. I couldn't decide if it was some victorious trooper's idea of a joke or a mark of respect to the fallen enemy. I don't know if I had been brutalised by what I'd seen and inured to it or if I was, for some unexplained reason, insensitive to it all and simply capable of doing my job and switching off afterwards with no lasting effect. But it was many more years before anyone at Sky News asked me if I needed any 'help' in dealing with my experiences. The short answer was 'no'.

By that time I had become a crime reporter and was unlikely

to witness anything akin to my experiences in war zones. It's not like the movies where the hack turns up with the body still warm and lying on the floor, a dagger protruding from its back. I've only once seen a murder victim at the scene of the crime, when bungling IRA gunmen shot dead two Australian tourists they mistook for off-duty British soldiers at Roermond in the Netherlands. Dutch police threw blankets over the bodies as they lay where they fell on the town's market square, but they carelessly left one pair of feet exposed, and they stayed that way until the corpses were collected hours later.

I always felt that the national news business, particularly the war and crime briefs, attracted resilient and experienced reporters who could take the grim stuff in their stride. That doesn't mean we aren't moved by what we see and hear, but for me it has always stopped short of fear, distress and the need for counselling. As a crime reporter I cover bad news, a relentless round of people doing terrible things to others. I can still recall the wailing of young acid-attack victim Awais Akram as he fled the witness box of an Old Bailey courtroom, too traumatised to continue describing his ordeal. He'd paid a terrible price for an intimate relationship with a married woman, Sadia Khatoon, who he had met on Facebook.

In revenge for the 'dishonour' brought on the woman's family, Awais was lured from his flat by her and her relatives, beaten up, stabbed and had concentrated sulphuric acid poured on his head, causing burns to almost half his body. His attackers had tried to pour the acid into his mouth. He was lucky to survive, if lucky is the right word. In court a year later he stood in front of the jury with a heavily scarred face, almost no hair, a closed-up right eye and only one ear, which was shrivelled. To emphasise the horror inflicted on him, jurors were shown a photo of Awais taken a month before the attack. It showed a handsome young man, a head of thick black hair, smartly dressed, with a garland of flowers around his neck. The prosecutor David Markham quoted a witness to the attack: 'With his clothes in tatters and literally falling off him from the acid, and blood coming from his nose and eyes and covering his bare chest, the witness said he looked like a cross between a zombie from a horror movie and the Incredible Hulk.'

After the woman's brother was convicted of his attempted murder, Awais agreed to a TV interview but wore a wig and spoke to me with a spotlight behind him and a shadow concealing the worst of his facial injuries. He said the pain of the acid burns at the time had been so bad he wished he had died, but he was now looking forward to the future, though he wasn't sure how much the doctors could do to repair his face. People stared at him in the street.

He met me at Scotland Yard where his wife sat in on our interview. They hadn't long been married when he began his relationship with Ms Khatoon, and I asked him what he thought of her continuing support after he had cheated on her. He shuffled in his seat and giggled uncomfortably, turned and smiled at his wife and said he didn't have an answer to the question. He said he was glad to be alive, but I wondered what sort of life that would be, especially since he still feared another attack.

Increasingly, we run 'health warnings' ahead of stories with shocking details or graphic images, though it has become harder to justify anything that might upset viewers. Part of that may be the shift in concern about an individual's privacy, but we live in more sensitive times where people are more easily offended and prepared to let it be known. Writing a letter of complaint was a tiresome task, but it's much easier now to voice upset or disapproval with the tap of a keyboard in the online comments box. An audience may still want to know the details of a gory crime but be spared the images. Sometimes, though, it seems we can be too protective of others' feelings. During the edit of one murder story I was told I could not show a coffin being removed from the victim's home, yet we show countless dead bodies in war zones. Perhaps the context, and the expectation of familiar images, makes it easier to take in.

And it's not just the viewers that media chiefs have to worry about. Sky News and others have had to accept that staff, too, might be affected by their work. Sky has added a psychologist to the occupational health experts available for those who need them.

Sky's concern for its employees increased during the trial of American cop Derek Chauvin, who was eventually convicted of the murder of black man George Floyd, a killing that was met with violent protests and seemed to herald hope of genuine change in the way US police treat African American suspects. Mr Floyd died because Chauvin's method of restraining him, after his roadside arrest for passing a shopkeeper a fake twenty-dollar bill, was to kneel on his neck for more than nine minutes.

The jury's verdicts were a few days away when a senior news executive circulated this email:

As the trial of Derek Chauvin draws to a close, it's likely the prosecution will show again the video of George Floyd's arrest and Chauvin kneeling on his neck. I appreciate for many this video is very disturbing and we've given much consideration as to it being broadcast. Given it's the central plank of the prosecution evidence we've decided to carry it with substantial warnings if it forms part of the court proceedings. We have our own dedicated support line to access support for those who'd like help with coping with the emotions this trial raises. Do call if you'd like professional mental health support – or do approach the Sky News Mental Health First Aiders who are happy to listen.

The email then listed the names of a dozen of my colleagues who had been trained to help others with mental health concerns.

At the time of Sarah Payne's abduction and murder there was no such organised counselling being offered so readily to me and my colleagues, though I'm sure there was help available to individuals who needed it through the company's medical scheme. It's just that I didn't go looking for it. In those days, it was something that wasn't discussed so openly. I don't doubt the nature of the protagonists in Sarah's case helped ease any discomfort I felt. The detectives in charge, Alan Ladley and his deputy Martyn 'Tosh' Underhill, were under incredible pressure to find Sarah but still readily engaged with the reporters who dogged their every step. From the first in- terview I did with them they gave me their mobile phone num- bers and encouraged me to call, a gesture of trust that was unusual then and more so today. I kept in touch with them for many years afterwards.

Sarah's mum Sara was warm, strong-willed and prepared to talk to reporters at most times, though I imagine privately she may not so easily have masked her fears and sense of doom. I've never known a parent of a missing child to grasp so firmly the need for publicity and manage to combine it with such consideration for those of us providing it. When I had to conduct a live interview with her and her family members in the grandparents' home, she made it easy for me with her calm and thoughtful responses to my nervous questions. Clumsily on air, I thanked her for being so thoughtful in the midst of her grief.

As we were leaving, I felt I ought to make some other gesture and hastily, on my way out, I gave Sarah's dad Michael a compact disc I had been playing constantly during my daily drive. It was a collection of classical choral works, which I had found sad, moving and in some way comforting. The CD included two well-known pieces: Allegri's *Miserere* and Thomas Tallis's *Spem in alium*. Michael seemed a bit puzzled, but he graciously accepted the CD. I've no idea if it had the same effect on the family as it did on me, whether they thought it a bizarre thing for a reporter to do or even if they ever listened to it. I hope they did. I also hope I didn't offer it just to make myself feel better.

After the discovery of Sarah's body, the story continued to get big coverage, and I spent another two weeks with many other reporters doing daily reports on the investigation from the field opposite the one in which her body was recovered. We all wondered what it would take, a month after it began, to knock the story off the top of our news bulletins. We left suddenly when the iconic supersonic passenger jet Concorde crashed just outside Paris. One by one, the journalists camped in the muddy field opposite Sarah's burial site took urgent calls from their news editors, packed up and drove to catch the cross-Channel ferry from Newhaven to Dieppe.

I saw Sara Payne fifteen months later and moments after Roy Whiting's conviction for her daughter's murder. It was another incongruous setting: the grand regency crown court building at Lewes, where justice has been handed down from high oak benches since 1812. Sara stood on the court steps beneath the Doric columns, picked out in the December darkness by our camera lights, and read a moving statement. Then she invited questions from the reporters clustered just below her. 'What are your thoughts about Roy Whiting?' asked one. Of course, she had the perfect answer: 'I'm not thinking about Roy Whiting,' she replied. 'I'm thinking of my daughter, Sarah.'

It was no surprise to anyone that she went on to campaign for victims and helped establish Sarah's Law, which gave parents some access to information about convicted paedophiles living in their neighbourhood.

Sara became a well-known campaigner and was awarded an MBE, but occasionally she has had to fight unwarranted claims that she had profited personally from her daughter's death.

I've not spoken to her since that day and it's one of the regrettable parts of a crime reporter's job that we build relationships with victims, often persuade them to open their hearts to us, sometimes even discuss quite personal matters, and then vanish from their lives. I can understand why we are accused of cynicism. We simply move on to the next big story.

# CHAPTER 9

# THE GETAWAY DRIVER

*I said to him: 'Look, I'm not so sure.' But he said: 'Remember your wife and kids.' I took that as a threat and agreed to do it*
— Getaway driver Kevin Meredith

**D**id you know that a diamond is at least 900 million years old? I didn't, not until a gang launched one of the most daring raids in the history of diamond heists. Some stones might be three billion years old, which really does sound like a diamond is for ever. It's the sort of specialist knowledge a reporter picks up for the duration of a story, then mostly forgets. It's part of the erratic nature of the job. An expert for a day. The heist got massive media coverage, first when the Flying Squad ambushed the robbers as they fled and later when the gang stood trial at the Old Bailey. The raid was an audacious attempt to steal the £200 million Millennium Star diamond. The huge gem was on display at the new Thames riverside exhibition centre, the Millennium Dome at Greenwich, built to celebrate the start of a new millennium. The Dome is today better known as London's O2 concert venue.

The Millennium Star was the centrepiece of a stunning display of twelve diamonds. A pear-shaped stone, it was cut from a 777-carat rough, internally flawless diamond, making it extremely rare and considered priceless. It was discovered in Zaire, central Africa, ten years earlier and remains one of the largest rough diamonds ever found. It was cut by master craftsmen in Antwerp, Belgium and New York before being polished in South Africa.

To understand the stone's allure, I spoke to diamond expert Nir Livnat who could barely contain his excitement:

> What's special about it is the quality of the stone, what we call ice material, so pure and clear that even when you look at it through a microscope of forty magnitude it looks like there is nothing there, which is quite amazing. Any way you look at it, the diamond has no dead spot, it's flawless.

It was put on display alongside the other eleven diamonds at the Dome in a purpose-built, bomb-proof vault designed to withstand the force of a sixty-tonne ram raid and monitored by CCTV with three separate alarm systems. There was a passive infra-red sensor triggered by movement, a contact alarm on the vault doors and the specially built display cases, plus a vibration alert tripped by anyone trying to smash the bulletproof glass. Tim Thorn, the security chief of the diamonds' owners De Beers, told jurors at the gang's trial that the extensive protection was designed to shield the diamonds for between thirty minutes and an hour from 'any known instrument criminals use'.

You would assume all that was enough to dissuade even the most ambitious or crazy of robbers from even thinking of stealing the diamonds. Yet Bill Cockram, the gang leader's lieutenant and a veteran armed robber, reckoned it was worth a try after visiting the exhibition and concocting a plan to smash into the Dome with a JCB digger, grab all twelve of the jewels and escape across the river in a speedboat. He said:

> I thought it was pie in the sky, but after going round there I couldn't believe the security was so light. I just tapped the glass to see how thick it was and how easy it would be to get in. I knew of a way to get into these cabinets. I'm a builder by trade so I know about glass and that stuff.

The unarmed gang penetrated the glass in twenty-seven seconds using a builder's nail gun and a sledgehammer. Not that it did them any good, because the Flying Squad, Scotland Yard's elite unit that combats the biggest robberies, had discovered the plot three months earlier. It meant that surveillance cameras followed them to the Dome and there were 120 armed officers and others waiting to pounce on them. On top of that, the real gems had been swapped with crystal copies the day before.

It was in the aftermath of the Dome raid, while I was working on a documentary to run on Sky News at the end of the trial, that I had a rare opportunity to get a real insight into the minds of two men prepared to risk everything for an audacious heist. And no, I don't know why they're always called audacious, either. Both played a part in daring crimes that captured media headlines around the world. One was Kevin Meredith, aged thirty-four, the Dome raiders' speedboat getaway driver. The other was Bruce Reynolds, mastermind of the Great Train Robbery thirty-seven years earlier, in which his gang got away with a record £2.6 million cash.

Like his father before him, Meredith was a charter vessel skipper, taking anglers out to sea for a day's fishing in the English Channel, but he was in debt and struggling to pay for repairs. He spoke hesitatingly, but candidly, aboard his own boat the *Random Harvest* in Brighton Marina. It was a rainy February day near the end of the gang's trial. He had been granted bail and was fifty miles away from London, where the judge was summing up the evidence for the jury at the Old Bailey.

It's not unusual at that stage of a trial, when the jury has heard all the evidence, for police and prosecutors to brief reporters on the background to a case, though we have to sign an embargo form and promise not to publish anything until the verdicts have been delivered. To do so, anyway, would break the Contempt of Court law and land reporters and their bosses in the dock. But to get a defendant to talk while they await their own verdict is almost as rare as a flawless diamond. It involves a good deal of trust that the journalist isn't going to cause trouble by reporting their words too early or inadvertently letting the jurors know that the defendant has recorded an interview that they might hold against them and that may be reflected in their decision. That was the agreement we had with Meredith.

Meredith described how he got caught up unwittingly in the Dome heist after borrowing money from gang member Bill Cockram, and failing to pay it back. He denied he was part of the gang or that he had been promised a huge pay-out. As Meredith told it, the gang trapped him into taking part in a venture he would never normally have considered:

> I met Bill when he came on the boat as a fisherman. He came out a couple of times and the second time we had a very good conversation, just normal chit-chat, and I explained to him my situation because the vessel wasn't running properly. I had a lot of problems with the engine.

A year earlier the *Random Harvest* flooded, because of a broken brass fitting, four miles out to sea with six anglers on board and had to be escorted into the marina by a lifeboat. The coastguard rescue helicopter had been alerted but stood down when Meredith managed to stop the water pouring in. A Marine Accident Investigation Branch report had urged Meredith to improve his boat's safety. It concluded that a contributory factor to it needing to be rescued while out in the English Channel was that he hadn't lifted it from the water for an annual maintenance inspection.

Meredith said:

> I was in a bit of dire straits with money really, and Bill offered to lend me thirteen or fourteen hundred pounds. That's how I got to know him, but I didn't see him again for over a year. Then my father got a call from him one Saturday afternoon and I went to meet him in the Katarina pub in the marina. And it went from there, that's how I got into this situation. We had a general conversation and then he asked about the money, had I got it? And I said no, it's been over a year, and I just haven't got it, so he asked me to do him a favour: to

drive a speedboat, just for fifteen minutes. I said to him: 'Look, I'm not so sure.' But he said: 'Remember your wife and kids.' I took that as a threat and agreed to do it. There was no way I would ever put my family in danger. I saw him as a bit of a wide boy, he looks hard, being from the East End and everything. The position was, I had to say yes. He was the sort of guy who knew people you didn't say no to.

I had known Bruce Reynolds for a long time and had often interviewed him about his infamous robbery. His take on the underworld was always instructive. After some persuasion, he agreed to come into the Sky News studios and turned up dressed immaculately as always: a well-cut suit and beautifully polished footwear. In an edit suite he analysed footage of the heist with more than a little envy; the recruitment of gang members, the planning, the excitement of the raid and the huge prize on offer, it had all thrilled him, clearly. Except the bit where the gang got caught. Reynolds said there were clear parallels between the Dome heist and the Great Train Robbery. Both gangs were aiming to pull off a raid that had never been done before and win themselves respect among their peers. No villain considers the flip side of failure and lasting public notoriety until later. If they get caught.

Reynolds, who got a 25-year prison sentence, said:

The greater the prize, the greater the glory. They wanted to reach the top of their profession. It's like the explorers, everybody looking for their El Dorado. I was amazed at the audacity [that word *again*] and I could understand that, doing what people haven't done before. In one fell swoop you cut off your life of crime and retire, satisfied you made the most of your chosen career.

He doubted that, in the minutes before the raid, the Dome gang would have felt any different from his own team as they waited to sabotage the railway signals and ambush the overnight Glasgow to London Royal Mail train at Bridego Bridge, Buckinghamshire, in August 1963.

Reynolds asked me to stop the footage for a moment. He looked directly at me, through the large, round, metal-framed spectacles he wore, and said:

If you're a thinking man, lots of things go through your mind. As with all dangerous occupations you think, what am I doing here? I've got a wife and a child at home. You hope your security is good, and if you think there's been a leak you call a board meeting to decide whether or not to abort. But once you're all in agreement, and the die is cast, it becomes like the dressing room of a rugby match with 'let's go boys' or 'let's get it done'. There is always acute nausea beforehand; the enormity of what you're about to do reaches down deep inside you. You have moments of terrified anticipation until the action begins, and then your head is very clear, and you have your focus.

But what about the speedboat getaway driver Meredith's claim that he had been recruited under threat because of the debt he owed? Did it seem likely he was telling the truth and was so intimidated by the gang that he had to take part? I asked the Great Train Robber. 'I imagine he was in an absolute state of panic,' said Reynolds.

The thing about getaway drivers is you don't have to be a good driver, but you do have to have plenty of nerve. He wasn't a regular member of the team, but he would have known there was something not quite legal going on by the temperament and character of the people that had employed him.

Meredith went to London two days before the raid and Cockram introduced him to the gang's leader, 38-year-old Raymond Betson, a market-trader-turned-thief who had already made a fortune from alcohol and cigarette smuggling. 'To be honest, I suppose I was very successful,' was how Betson, with a complete lack of irony, later described his dishonest career to the jury. Meredith said it was Betson who took him to the River Thames and showed him where to put the speedboat into the water: at Bow Creek, a winding inlet across the river from the Dome. That night, Meredith stayed with Cockram at his home and watched television, while his host spent the evening taking a series of phone calls.

> He was very relaxed, but I still didn't know what was happening. I didn't think I was in a position to ask. I didn't sleep at all that night. I knew it was partly to do with the Dome, but I didn't know about no diamonds. My job was to pick up two people, I didn't know what for, and I just wanted to do that and get them across the river and go home.

At 6.30 the next morning, Meredith was picked up by gang member Terry Millman, another villain with a string of convictions, and taken in a van to Newcastle Draw Dock on the Isle of Dogs to collect the speedboat, which had a top speed of 55 mph. Millman, who died of cancer awaiting trial, had bought the boat for £3,700 and signed the receipt with the alias T. Diamond. Together they drove the sleek, red and white eighteen-footer to Bow Creek and put it in the water. Millman went off to join the others, leaving Meredith to await instructions about exactly when to head 500 metres across the river to the north Greenwich pier beside the Dome. The plan was for him to pick up the fleeing gang with the loot and whisk them back across the river. A getaway van would be waiting, which they would drive to a pub rendezvous in nearby Rotherhithe. Meredith told the Flying Squad and me he didn't know any of that.

I went into Bow creek, turned the boat around and pulled up against a little ladder, and then I got a phone call, or a call on the radio, asking me if I was there. I said yes and didn't hear anything for about twenty minutes. Then I was told I would get a call saying 'five minutes', and when I heard that I should make my way across to the pier. I got the call over the radio and started moving away and just when I got to the entrance of Bow Creek, which leads to the Thames, that's when I heard the words: 'Attack, attack, attack,' and then I just froze, you know. I just didn't know what to do; I didn't know who was speaking, I was scared, and I just headed straight for the pier. From that moment, it was just pure panic.

Once I had actually moored up to the pier, I was just checking the engine and the next thing I knew I saw a white RIB [a rigid inflatable boat] shooting down the river, and when I turned back, there was another black RIB that came alongside with a load of armed police shouting 'armed police, armed police, show your hands'. I was just in absolute shock.

The story of his arrest was dramatic, but at least it was done without the force employed by the armed officers who, minutes earlier, had ambushed the rest of the gang as they tossed smoke bombs and began smashing into the diamond display cases inside the Dome. At that stage the police didn't know for certain that the robbers weren't carrying guns. They may have assumed they had weapons as the gang were wearing body armour. In his police mugshot taken soon afterwards, Cockram was sporting a very obvious black eye, but he still appeared to manage a half-smile. Or was it a smirk? Meredith said it was only when he was taken to Peckham Police Station, and questioned, that he realised what he had got involved in. 'At that point it was relief, you know, because I was out of the situation with Cockram,' he added. The TV interview was almost over. I was surprised how much he had revealed. He looked relieved, unburdened perhaps.

Relief was certainly not what came over Great Train Robber Bruce Reynolds when he suddenly found himself having his collar felt by a police officer. He'd spent five years on the run in London, Canada, France, Mexico and Devon, after pulling off what became known as the Crime of the Century. 'I've never been arrested quite as violently as this little team was,' he said, watching the video showing the moment the Flying Squad swooped on the Dome robbers,

> but it's your worst nightmare, the end of all your dreams, what you planned for your family, plus you're looking ahead to all those years in prison. You can't get any lower than that. It's a total nightmare and you have a sense of abject failure, and then you start thinking [about] how you can reduce the charges against you to soften the blow. Can I turn [the] Queen's evidence, are the police corruptible, will they take money or information? You try to make the best of it.

On the eve of the verdicts, Kevin Meredith cut a very different figure to the seasoned old villain Bruce Reynolds. The fishing-boat-skipper-turned-getaway-driver didn't strike me as someone who had considered bribing the police or nobbling the jury. Like the others in the Dome gang, he had been charged with two things: conspiracy to rob the Dome and conspiracy to steal the diamonds. The four main defendants, who had tried to steal what they thought were priceless diamonds, admitted the lesser theft charge but denied the more serious robbery allegation after arguing that they were unarmed and had threatened no one. They were carrying ammonia gas, but Cockram said that was purely to pour on any blood they might shed in the smash-and-grab, to contaminate it and confuse forensic investigators in their search for evidence, had the gang got away.

Meredith had denied both charges, on the basis he had been recruited at the last minute and had played no part in the planning. The judge must have viewed him as a peripheral player because he eventually freed him on bail before the trial began. That hardly reduced the tension Meredith was feeling as he travelled from Brighton to the Old Bailey for the final days, hoping for his acquittal. 'With the judge's summing up [and the jury about to start its deliberations] I have good days and bad days,' he said.

> Some days you go in feeling really good, thinking you know it might just happen, and the next day it's totally out of the window. It's for the jury to decide, they've heard all the evidence and hopefully they'll come up with the right verdict. It's going to be really hard, you know.

Meredith had spent more than nine months in prison before being freed on bail. He chose not to be in court for the judge's summing up because he wanted to spend precious time with his wife and family.

He probably knew he was going to prison. 'I'm trying to prepare myself. It's got to the stage where it's getting harder and harder every day, but we're a strong family and we'll get through it.' After a three-month trial the jury took their time, needing more than a week to deliver verdicts that even then not all of them agreed on. The main gang members were convicted of robbery. Betson and Cockram were jailed for eighteen years. Robert Adams and a fourth robber, Aldo Ciarrocchi, who used scanners to monitor police communications and also tossed the smoke grenades, got fifteen years each.

Meredith was cleared of robbery but convicted of the conspiracy to steal the diamonds and got five years imprisonment. It later emerged that, the day before the trial began, he had taken five officers from Belmarsh Prison on a fishing trip on his father's boat. The officers were sacked after an internal investigation. On the day of the verdicts, I was waiting outside the Old Bailey to break the news. My producer inside told me Meredith was the only one of the raiders who appeared to show any emotion. And there was sobbing in the public gallery as Judge Michael Coombe said of Meredith's claim that he had been threatened into taking part because of the money he owed Cockram: 'In all my years at the Bar and bench I have never heard a defence of duress with less merit or substance.'

Meredith may have enjoyed Judge Coombe's discomfort, two years later, when the judge admitted, during an appeal by Betson and Cockram, that he had fallen asleep at various stages during the gang's trial, but he denied snoring. Betson's lawyer argued that by nodding off during his defence, the judge had given the jury the impression he took such a dim view of his client's case that he could not be bothered to stay awake and had prejudiced jurors against him. The Appeal Court judges refused the appeal, but they gently reprimanded their judicial colleague after TV researcher Tamsen Courtenay, who had sat through the trial, told them Judge Coombe appeared to be asleep half-a-dozen times, his head once lolling 'so far forward as to be almost in contact with the table'.

Betson did eventually get three years taken off his eighteen-year sentence, but he returned to crime soon after his release and demonstrated that he hadn't learned his lesson or improved his criminal craft. He targeted a cash depot in Kent, but he smashed down the wrong wall, searched an empty warehouse, grounded the getaway car in a bumpy field and then dumped in a hedge a balaclava with his DNA on it. He went to prison again for another thirteen years.

After spending three hours with me in the Sky edit suite, Bruce Reynolds's own verdict was that the Dome robbers would have got great kudos among their fellow jailbirds when they began their sentences because of the publicity their heist had generated. Everyone would know who they were and afford them much respect for their ambition and daring at least, but the reality would soon kick in. Speaking from his own experience, he said:

> Because of your reputation, you have to maintain a front and you walk along the landing with your head held high. But then the cell door slams shut, you collapse onto your bed and the tears start welling up. You think of your little boy and how you miss him, and you wonder what's going to happen to him, because it's inevitable that marriages are going to break down under that sort of strain. I asked Ian Barrie, who was nicked with Ronnie Kray for the murder of George Cornell, and went down for life with a minimum twenty years, how do you do such a long sentence? And he said: 'It's easy, you just do it five years at a time.'

Reynolds was one of those criminals it would be easy to glamour-ise. For a start, he was tall and handsome, had developed an early reputation as a Raffles-type burglar, drove a Jaguar car and then led the Great Train Robbers, who escaped with a fortune. They were regarded largely by the public as latter-day Robin Hoods who had got one over on the Establishment.

In his book, *The Autobiography of a Thief*, he wrote poetically of the uncertain moments spent waiting for the mail train to arrive:

> The August moon was as white as a five-pound note. From the top pocket of my camouflage smock I took out a leather cigar case and selected a prepared Montecristo No. 2. Moistening the tapered end, I struck a match, carefully ensuring the flame burned the leaf evenly before I drew in the smoke. I exhaled into the night air. I knew I wouldn't have time to finish it, but a Montecristo No. 2 is a fine com-panion to have whilst awaiting your destiny. I knew this would be my greatest moment, a night to remember. Whatever happened in the next few minutes, my life would never be the same again.

I was asked to read that passage at his funeral. It was held at the 900-year-old Church of St Bartholomew the Great in Smithfield, barely a smoke grenade's throw from the Old Bailey. Other speakers were the actors David Thewlis and Ray Stevenson, punk poet John Cooper Clarke and writer Jake Arnott. It was a rather glamorous gathering, but the reality of most of Reynolds's adult life was quite different. He had two decades in prison and his twilight years were spent living on benefits in a housing charity flat. As his musician and artist son Nick, a friend of mine, whose band Alabama 3 played at the funeral, told mourners: 'He chose a lunatic path and paid the price.'

Reynolds himself wrote that the infamy of the Great Train Robbery became a curse that followed him around and stopped people from offering him work, legal or illegal. Comparing his fate with that of the sailor in Samuel Taylor Coleridge's *The Rime of the Ancient Mariner*, he said: 'The notoriety was like an albatross around my neck.' To survive, he once told me, he had to 'separate the myth from the man'.

Less than a year later, five miles upstream from the Dome, the River Thames was the scene of a less dramatic, but unprecedented and altogether more gruesome, crime that took detectives around the world and is still unsolved today.

# CHAPTER 10

# THE SACRIFICE

*We didn't expect to find human body parts openly on sale here,*
*but we were told they might be available if we were*
*to ask the right questions to certain sellers*

– FORMER DETECTIVE CHIEF INSPECTOR WILL O'REILLY

Just before 4 p.m. on Friday 21 September 2001, Aidan Minter, a video games brand manager, was climbing the steps up to the road that crosses Tower Bridge in London, when he spotted what he thought was a tailor's dummy floating in the River Thames below. When he looked closer, to his horror, he realised it was the headless torso of a child. The body was recovered by river police, as the incoming tide took it gently upstream, three bridges along, near the Globe Theatre.

The Thames throws up around fifty bodies a year – drunks, suicides and murder victims – but not many of them have their head and limbs chopped off. The officer who took charge of the case, Detective Inspector Will O'Reilly, had an unidentified murder victim

with no face, dental records or fingerprints, no witnesses, no suspects and no motive. There was no murder scene to comb for clues.
To their frustration, detectives discovered there was no register of
boats that used the Thames, either. What was left of the little boy
did not match any of the seventy missing children reports they had.
What they did know was the body had been in the water for up to
ten days, and any forensic evidence of the killer had been washed
away. The police couldn't even be sure of the child's precise age.

Detectives could get little media coverage for a public appeal for
help. It was ten days after the 9/11 United States terror attacks and
the deaths of 2,977 innocent victims were dominating news bulletins. A colleague had reported briefly on the torso discovery, but
my news editors were not interested in it beyond that. The sad truth
was that few people, especially at that time, really cared about the
fate of one small unidentified boy. Even a £50,000 reward couldn't
persuade someone to give police information. When the murder
squad later asked the US Federal Bureau of Investigation for advice
they were told: 'Don't bother, it's unsolvable.'

But, despite the odds, or perhaps because of them, the Scotland
Yard team did bother and set off on a remarkable investigation that
sent detectives thousands of miles and stretched the boundaries of
forensic science. I'm not sure I grasped the significance at the time,
but this was the Metropolitan Police's chance to demonstrate it was
prepared to learn from the Macpherson Report a couple of years
earlier, which had branded the force 'institutionally racist'. Judge
William Macpherson reached that damning conclusion after his
public inquiry into the way the Met had failed to properly investigate
the murder, by a white gang, of black teenager Stephen Lawrence in
south-east London in 1993. Macpherson's definition of institutional

racism was this: 'The collective failure of an organisation to provide an appropriate and professional service to people because of
their colour, culture or ethnic origin. It can be seen or detected in
processes, attitudes and behaviour which amount to discrimination
through unwitting prejudice, ignorance, thoughtlessness and racial
stereotyping.'

Macpherson made seventy recommendations for the force
to change its racist ways, but broadly he put its officers and staff
under huge scrutiny over their racial awareness. There would be
a giant spotlight aimed at unsolved homicides. The murder squad
had every reason to shelve the investigation early on because of the
obvious difficulties it faced. Indeed, that was the recommendation
of the senior officer who initially oversaw it, but some enlightened
figures saw this as a golden opportunity to try harder.

One of the first things the police did was to personalise and restore a little dignity to a tiny body that no one wanted to claim. 'In
the absence of his own, we will become the boy's family,' declared
DI O'Reilly's incoming new boss, Commander Andy Baker. They
called the victim Adam, the name chosen 'to represent all of mankind'. When reporters did finally catch up on the story, we were
encouraged to call it the 'Adam investigation', rather than the more
brutal 'Thames torso case'. It reflected the compassion and drive of
the team Baker put together to catch whoever had murdered him.

When Baker outlined his investigation plans to Yard chiefs and
to the Metropolitan Police Authority, the group of local politicians
and independent monitors who held the force to account, they all
agreed with him. Baker said:

I really believed there were opportunities to find who Adam was, who had killed him and why, and slowly we began to make progress. We had a fly-on-the wall TV documentary team with us and then invited some trusted news journalists, all with the backing of the press office and senior management, including the commissioner, Sir John Stevens. They saw the commitment we had, but I guess there was also that concern that this was a young black child and if we just shelved it, were we being judgemental? There were colleagues who asked me why we were bothering when my predecessor said we should drop it, but then after we got some publicity, people would come up to me in the pub and say they hoped we find the poor boy's killers.

A pathologist spent six hours on Adam's post-mortem examination. After ruling out the possibility that the boy had been mutilated by a boat's propeller, he told police he had seen similar knife wounds before, but only in the ritual killing of an animal. Adam had died from a neck wound, his body drained of blood and then his limbs cut off. Toxicology tests showed that he had been fed cough mixture not long before his death, but if someone had been caring for him, why hadn't they reported him missing? It was an astonishing case and, but for the 9/11 attacks, would normally have kept me busy for weeks. What the story was to demonstrate, much later, was how important science was becoming to criminal investigation.

The theory of human sacrifice looked promising when a search of the river discovered, two miles upstream, seven candles wrapped in a white sheet. An African name, Adekoye Jo Fola Adeoye, had been carved on the side of the candles and written three times on the sheet. Was that Adam's real name? Thousands of pounds and much dogged detective work later, police uncovered the truth when they traced the name to a former British resident living in New York. Mr Adeoye had been on business at the World Trade Centre when the hijacked planes hit the twin towers on 11 September, and he had survived. He was as puzzled as the detectives, until they discovered that his sister in London had been worried about him and wanted to bring him good luck with a traditional ceremony beside the flowing waters of the Thames. It was one of many dead ends that frustrated the murder squad.

Forensic scientist Ray Fysh launched the first of several initiatives that had never been tried in criminal investigations. Ray is a genial, roly-poly character whose south London vernacular belies a sharp scientific mind, thirst for knowledge and pioneering spirit. He suggested using the one certain thing of Adam they had: his DNA, his unique chemical profile they got from what little blood was left in him. They could try to identify Adam by putting that profile into what was, back then, the fledgling DNA database. It was possible that one of Adam's parents was one of the many thousands of people whose DNA had been recorded if they were charged with a criminal offence. If so, Ray thought he might be able to detect a link with Adam, via a familial DNA search. 'We needed to identify Adam. There were no guarantees this would work but we were desperate and we had to start somewhere,' said Fysh, who after his retirement spent ten years as a university lecturer talking more about the Adam case than any others.

With the exception of identical twins, a DNA profile is a genetic code unique to an individual – a sort of chemical fingerprint – and the most accurate way of identifying someone. But we all share certain traits with our parents and other relatives and that will be reflected in similarities in our DNA. Today if you want to trace members of your family, you can do it with a programmed computer DNA search: the more similarities the closer the relative. You couldn't do that in 2001 because computer programming was in its infancy, so Fysh had to do it manually. Britain's first ever familial DNA search was carried out in the front room of the forensic scientist's timbered Kent cottage over many days and nights, with a variety of coloured pens, reams of paper, lots of coffee and a good deal of faith.

At the time, the DNA database contained the genetic profiles of more than 750,000 people. Fysh restricted his search to those of an Afro-Caribbean heritage within the wider London area and came up with 39,000 names. When he examined those closely, he boiled down his list to thirty-five males and eleven females who might possibly be Adam's parents. When police checked the forty-six individuals, they ruled them all out as relatives of Adam. Another dead end, but Fysh had set an important precedent.

He explained:

Forensic science had traditionally been used to corroborate other evidence, but for the first time we were being proactive and becoming investigators ourselves. Forensic science always piggybacks off other scientific techniques, like DNA, which wasn't developed for criminal investigation but was adapted for it. The one thing that Adam did for me, the detectives Will and Andy were always asking questions. What about this, what about that? That's what you need, somebody to ask the questions, to push you to go and find out the answers.

While Fysh looked for answers in the world of science, the detectives headed further afield to boost their knowledge of ritual killing. They knew as much about the subject as they did about aliens. First stop was South Africa, where they went to explore the grim phenomenon of muti murders. Muti is the Zulu word for medicine, and a muti murder is one in which victims are killed so their body parts can be used to cure illness, bring power or restore virility. I knew Commander Baker from previous cases and so was one of the small group of journalists invited to go with him and O'Reilly on an adventure that was to take us all out of our comfort zone.

Baker was in charge of all murder investigations in London and one of four commanders on Scotland Yard's Serious Crime Directorate. I couldn't imagine any other senior cop asking journalists to tag along and witness what could have been an expensive and unrewarding trip. He was direct and honest in his media relations and, as I have already said, an extremely compassionate individual, determined to do all he could to find whoever had mutilated and murdered a small child. It didn't take much to persuade my bosses it was an important story for us to cover.

On the 7,000-mile flight to Johannesburg, Baker summoned me through the curtain from my economy cabin to explain, among other things, why public funds were being spent on business-class seats for him and his colleague, Will O'Reilly. The pair of them had a lot of research to do, he explained, and would hit the ground running after the twelve-hour overnight flight. 'We have a steep learning curve ahead of us and only a week to get what we want,' he said. At least he had the good grace to offer me a glass of decent red wine, though the British Airways stewardess refused to serve me and sent me back to my cheap seat.

The British detectives planned to immerse themselves in African traditions to try to understand what might lie behind their victim's grisly death. Britain had around 800 murders a year while South Africa, despite its smaller population, had around 25,000. Muti murders were common.

None of us were sure what they would find as Baker and O'Reilly, by then promoted to detective chief inspector, prepared to explore the world of ritual killings. On the day we landed in Johannesburg, there were two reports of particular interest in the influential *Star* newspaper. One described how a group of children retrieving a football from a stream in Lenasia, a suburb of Soweto, had discovered a girl's leg. The other recounted how four defendants and four witnesses in a witchcraft trial at Durban High Court had all died suddenly of various illnesses. The judge had admitted that 'something strange' was going on after he and the prosecutor also fell ill. There was a third, much smaller story that we almost missed, headlined: 'Scotland Yard Turns To South African Ritual Murder Experts'. Below it was the memorable sub-heading: 'British Police Flummoxed'.

As the temperature outside climbed to ninety degrees, we spent our first morning in the air-conditioned headquarters of the South African Police Service's serious and violent crime section in central Pretoria. There we learned that muti cures commonly involve the use of herbs, plants and animal body parts, but for some believers, that is not enough. The most serious illnesses can be cured only by what is considered the strongest muti medicine, made from human body parts. Muti killings have been committed for centuries as part of traditional African beliefs, most widely in South Africa, but the practice was outlawed with the arrival of Western criminal justice systems.

On the polished oak table in front of us were some of the most horrific images imaginable. There was a young boy with half the skin on his face peeled away and a couple of ribs missing where his killers cut out his heart; a woman with her genitalia removed, another with her nipples sliced off. I could describe all the crime scene photographs we saw but, even now, it's hard to think that humans could do that to other humans. In muti murders it was important that the victims' screams were heard before they died because the spirits of their ancestors needed to feel their pain, explained our host, Colonel Kobus Jonker, a wiry, bearded Afrikaner who was the former head of the occult crime department. It was the only one of its kind in the world and it was clear to us why South Africa needed such a unit.

Jonker handed me a diagram of a naked woman headed 'Body Parts Used For Muti'. Arrows led to a brief description of what each body part was used for, some of which I could have guessed at. An eye, for instance, will bring you farsightedness, a brain provides knowledge, breasts and genitals, male and female, will give virility while stomach skin will cure intestinal ailments. A penis, oddly, can also bring you luck on the horses.

Muti can be made from almost any body part, which is usually burned, ground into a powder or paste and then smeared on the affected area, or mixed with milk and ingested. Jonker told us of the recent discovery of several dismembered bodies. The severed heads were found in a river twenty kilometres away.

The necks were gone: they went for the atlas bone. That's very important because our black culture believes that all your nervous systems and blood systems go through this bone. It's the connection point between the skull and the body. In South Africa people will pay 3,500 rand [then about £200] for an atlas bone.

Adam's atlas bone was missing. I asked Jonker if muti medicine worked. He didn't smile, implying that I wasn't taking the subject seriously enough. 'I doubt it works,' he said. 'I can't see how a girl's private parts can make a woman pregnant, or how using a person's brain can make you cleverer.' Nor could I.

We spent the next morning at what was known as the muti market, held above Faraday Station in south-central Johannesburg, where the scent of dead animals mixed with the smells of corn cooking on an oil barrel brazier. The young muti seller I approached might have been surprised to find a white man poring over his wares. I entered into the spirit of the marketplace, and he drove a hard bargain with me over the price of a tiny, shrivelled mongoose paw. We settled for thirty-five rand. My local fixer Japhta helped me negotiate in Zulu and thought I'd got a bargain. 'He said it will clean out all your pipes. If you cannot father children, it will do you good. You must grind it, mix it with milk in a cup and drink it.'

I had a lot to choose from because among the wonders scattered on the pavement in front of the seller were vulture heads, snake skins, lizard legs, antelope horns and a collection of bones so big they can only have come from an elephant. There was a dead rat dangling from a pole and neat piles of herbs, roots and bits of tree bark. Crammed together on a long table were dozens of filthy whisky and port bottles whose murky contents could only be guessed at. I joined the detectives as they wandered around, peering intently at what was on offer and chatting to the traders. 'We didn't expect to find human body parts openly on sale here,' said O'Reilly, 'but we were told they might be available if we were to ask the right questions to certain sellers. We've seen a number of boxes and baskets that were covered up.'

As the Scotland Yard duo built up their knowledge of all things muti, they met a man whose job was to identify muti killings, how to distinguish them from the work of sadists and psychopaths. Gérard Labuschagne was the commander of the Investigative Psychology Unit, an engaging specialist with a great sense of humour despite the grim nature of his chosen field. He explained how the effects of wild animal activity and high temperatures on the bodies of victims added to the difficulties of his investigations. So, too, did the traditional beliefs of some police, politicians, civil servants and wealthy businessmen who were sometimes reluctant to acknowledge muti killings. Labuschagne suggested it was more likely Adam was the victim of a ritual, rather than a muti murder. In muti it was unusual for a victim's limbs to be cut off and their genitals and internal organs to remain intact, which was the case with Adam's remains. Death from a throat cut and blood loss was also more indicative of a ritual, sacrificial killing, he explained to the detectives as I listened in.

The investigator offered his visitors from London a note of caution.

One must not stare blind to the fact that Adam came from Africa in origin. That does not necessarily mean the murderer or ritual was African in origin. Remember that killers seek easy victims, especially when it comes to children. The fact that no one has come forward is a conundrum. Adam may have been imported for the murder. It may even be that he and his parents were smuggled into the UK and this was a revenge murder because they couldn't pay the fee, or something to that effect.

The detectives took notes as he spoke, absorbing the words of the expert.

Twenty-five kilometres outside Johannesburg, in an area known appropriately as Brits, we turned off the highway and down a dusty track into the veldt, past some of the best-appointed properties in Gauteng province. The white bungalow home of Credo Mutwa stood in a couple of lush acres below a steep hill. A sign hanging from a tree beside the iron gate read: 'Admission by appointment only.' Two of Scotland Yard's top detectives had come to consult a witch-doctor, though we were not allowed to call him that. He was a sangoma, or healer, and one of the best-known in the country. There was bound to be some leg-pulling back in London. From the look of his place business was good, though unlike some sangomas I'd read about, Mutwa did not have his own helicopter.

He was a big guy, quite old but a striking figure as he huddled in a corner of his spacious living room wearing a blue and purple robe with heavy brass trinkets dangling from his neck. He blinked at his guests from behind large horn-rimmed glasses. He got up and bowed as the detectives approached cautiously and were introduced by Dr Labuschagne. They sat at a round table in a corner lined with bookshelves. Mutwa studied the grim photos of Adam's torso with lots of tutting and head shaking, before speaking in good but sometimes broken English and a slow, deliberate manner: 'I think this is a human sacrifice to some water deity, carried out by a gang of people who were strengthening themselves for doing some very ugly crimes.' He studied the faces of the detectives, perhaps looking for their reaction.

These people, when they do a thing like this, it's because they are filled with fear of what they are going to do; let's say a gang of big criminals planning to rob a place or terrorists about to intimidate someone. In those parts of Africa where there were wars we often saw things of this horrible nature.

The sangoma told the detectives they should turn their search for clues to west Africa, Nigeria in particular, or the Caribbean. He said:

It may be something called obeh, the horriblest form of human sacrifice, usually an innocent child not yet full of puberty. The criminals would either drink the blood, using the top of the victim's skull, or wash themselves with a mixture of the blood and water. The finger joints are used either as charms, or they are ground into a ritual paste and carried by the criminals to give themselves strength.

Mutwa had another chilling insight into Adam's murder.

I can say, with much firmness, that among the people who did this ugly thing was somebody who knew the boy. I notice, too, that the child is wearing red *brookies* [shorts]. In Africa, for thousands of years, red has been a colour of resurrection. This tells me clearly that among these monsters was someone who was related to that boy.

The Scotland Yard men spent time alone with Mutwa, emerging into the sunshine an hour later, astonished at how much insight the sangoma had given them.

As the week went on, it was becoming clear the detectives were on the right continent but in the wrong country, and they were around 3,000 miles from the place that would more likely hold the key to Adam's fate. They were already making loose plans to visit west Africa, but they still had an ace to play before they left. To the huge surprise of their colleagues in London, the Scotland Yard duo had persuaded Nelson Mandela to make an appeal for help in identifying Adam and finding his killers. Mandela was more than South Africa's first black President and the whole continent's most revered icon; he was an international superstar on a constant quest for peace. When he spoke, everyone around the world listened.

Bathed in bright sunshine, Baker and O'Reilly stood rather nervously in suits and ties, the top buttons of their shirts firmly fastened, on the immaculate lawn of a lovely villa in the suburb of Houghton. There was a buzz as the gates swung open and a police car escorted a gleaming Mercedes into the compound. For those of us who had never seen Mandela, this was quite a moment. Rather stiffly, the elderly passenger emerged and pulled himself up slowly to his full height. In a distinctive grey paisley shirt, with matching white collar and cuffs, Mandela briefly acknowledged us waiting media and turned along the path towards the rear of his former home, which was now the headquarters of his charitable foundation. Only then, at the sight of the great man himself, were the Scotland Yard detectives convinced he was actually going to help them. Throughout the trip they had worried, they later admitted, that something would scupper Mandela's involvement.

A few minutes later they were summoned to climb the steps to the house for a private audience with Mandela and the chance to brief him on their mission before he faced our cameras. It soon became clear they had done a good job – or he'd been won over by the presentation of a London bobby's helmet – because his public appeal was much longer and more heartfelt than they had expected. Baker told me later he had brought with him a copy of Mandela's autobiography for him to sign and I kicked myself I hadn't thought to do the same.

Sitting beside the officers on a table set up on the lawn, in front of our camera and those of my BBC and ITV rivals, plus various South African journalists, Mandela spoke with a passion that suggested he wasn't simply reading a statement prepared for him by the Scotland Yard press officer who had just arrived from London. He made it clear it was his show and he was in charge. He said:

Scotland Yard has appealed to us to add our voice to theirs, imploring people from around the world to come forward with any information that can help identify the young, murdered victim and to track the perpetrators of this horrific crime, and I conceded to make this appeal without any hesitation.

Establishing the true identity of the boy is crucial to a successful conclusion of the investigation being conducted by police. Hence, we appeal for all people in the UK and across the world to come forward with even the least bit of information that can help solve this murder and, as it seems likely that the boy might have come from South Africa and has been the victim of some ritualistic murder, I wish to direct my appeal even more specifically to the people of Africa.

If anywhere, even the remotest village in our continent, there is a family missing a son of that age who might have disappeared around that time, 21 September last year, please contact the police in London either directly or through their local police. The South African Police Service and the South African pathologist have already made a sterling contribution towards trying to solve this terrible murder. The Metropolitan Police Service has dedicated itself to solve this murder.

But even Mandela had to acknowledge that his words might not be enough. He said: 'One of the problems I see is this – that this may be a child that comes from the remotest area of our country, where people have not had the advantage of even the most humble level of education and our appeal may not be able to reach them.' Despite that parting shot, Baker and O'Reilly could not have hoped for more. Mandela even name-checked them, undoubtedly a highlight of their careers. He stayed beside the detectives to answer our questions, even flirting mildly with a young female journalist at the front and cajoling her into asking a question. I shared her sense of awe of the saintly figure in front of us. I didn't get the attention she did, but he did answer my own rather garbled question about his involvement.

The detectives got home to discover that Ray Fysh had been pushing the DNA boundaries once more, engaging the help of geneticist Andy Urquhart at the Forensic Science Service. DNA was commonly used to determine a person's identity, but there were other parts of DNA that could, potentially, be used to reveal more about an individual. Like Fysh, Urquhart had a particularly enquiring mind and agreed to expand some research he'd already been doing on exploring DNA to determine someone's skin colour. He began studying Adam's DNA to see if it could give clues to his ancestry. He focused on two strands of DNA. Put simply they were: mitochondrial DNA, which is inherited from a person's maternal bloodline, and the Y chromosome, which is inherited from the paternal line.

With an enthusiasm that matched Fysh's pioneering spirit, Urquhart used the two strands of Adam's DNA to narrow down his African heritage to west Africa. It was most likely the boy hailed from Nigeria.

Eventually such work led to the building of an international database of DNA profiles. In the short term it corroborated what Credo Mutwa had suggested: that the key to solving Adam's murder lay in west Africa, probably Nigeria. There was still a long way to go.

As publicity about the case grew, slowly it began to show results. A sharp-eyed detective in Glasgow called O'Reilly's office to report a bizarre exchange during a court appearance by a Nigerian asylum seeker called Joyce Osagiede. She was a troubled woman with psychiatric problems, who was trying to retrieve her two young daughters from the care of social services. She spoke confusingly of black magic and child sacrifices, including the killing of her own newborn son. At her flat social workers found what they believed were ritualistic objects. The Adam team got a search warrant for Osagiede's home and found children's clothing from the same German supplier as the orange shorts the dead boy had been wearing. Osagiede had lived in Germany before arriving illegally in the UK. What detectives couldn't establish was any firm link between Adam and Joyce and they had no reason to detain her. When her asylum application was later rejected, O'Reilly and another officer, Detective Sergeant Nick Chalmers, accompanied her on a deportation flight to Nigeria. Frustratingly, she refused to say any more and the officers flew home without getting off the plane, but they hadn't finished with Osagiede and her connections.

The Glasgow search had turned up Joyce's links with an address in south London and a tenant called Kingsley Ojo, a Nigerian from Benin City where Joyce was from originally. The Adam team began to suspect that Ojo was involved in Adam's death, but they couldn't prove anything. A separate investigation established Ojo had entered Britain illegally in 1999, then used a false name to get a passport and, with a variety of aliases, help smuggle fellow Nigerians into the country. He was later jailed for people trafficking and deported. Police thought Ojo may have brought Joyce and Adam into Britain, but it couldn't be proved.

Although officers believed they had established Adam's ancestry, they were advised his links with Nigeria could be ancient. It didn't mean he had ever been to Nigeria. To help identify him and boost their chances of finding his family and killers, they needed to discover where he had spent his few short years and especially the crucial time just before his murder. Pollen from birch and alder trees, typical of London in the autumn, was found in his large intestine, which confirmed he had been alive in the capital. That also assured detectives his murder had actually been committed in London, that his body hadn't been brought into the country and then discarded. But they needed to know more.

Again, it was Ray Fysh who came up with an idea, based on the principle 'we are what we eat.' He went to see Ken Pye, professor of environmental geology at Royal Holloway University in Surrey and an old acquaintance, and together they explored the possibilities of a different scientific analysis of Adam's remains beyond his DNA. Fysh explained his thinking to me:

Geologists determine the age of rocks by analysing their chemistry and measuring the ratio between two isotopes of the chemical element strontium. Soil derives from the erosion of rocks. We eat plants that have grown in the soil and animals that have fed on those plants. The water we drink has gone through that soil as well. From everything we ingest our bodies absorb a vast array of elements, including strontium. What our bodies don't excrete is put into long-term storage in our bones, teeth, nails and hair. Here's the interesting thing: the original strontium isotope ratio in rocks stays the same as it travels through the soil, plants, animals and into our bodies. So that ratio in Adam's bones would tell us the type of rock structure where he was born and bred. Was it Nigeria, the Caribbean or south London?

'When we applied this to Adam's bones,' said Fysh,

we got a very high strontium ratio, which meant he was born and bred in an area where his food came from a very old rock structure. It told us he wasn't born and bred in Peckham because it doesn't have a rock base that old. The isotope ratio pointed to the rock structure of a large swathe of west Africa, from Guinea to Cameroon. That matched the familial ancestral DNA results that pointed to the same region and the likelihood that Nigeria was Adam's birthplace. It was still a big area.

To narrow it down Fysh, DCI O'Reilly and Andy Urquhart were sent on a mission to Nigeria to collect soil samples, animal and human bones. After three weeks travelling around the country, they returned with 150 samples. Over the next two months, analysis of these was compared with Adam's bone chemistry, which narrowed down his home as a region of southern Nigeria from Ibadan to Benin City. Detectives were getting closer.

Nearly eighteen months after Adam's torso was discovered, I went on another unusual trip with the Adam investigation team. This time it was to the sweltering villages scattered around Ibadan. Here, accompanied by interpreters and armed police guards, the camera crew and I watched the detectives meeting puzzled village elders to explain their mission in the hope they could help solve the case. In khaki trousers and a short-sleeved shirt, DCI O'Reilly addressed a crowd gathered outside a wooden hut: 'Does anyone in the village have children missing?' DNA mouth swabs were taken in the search for Adam's relatives, reward posters were stapled to palm trees and wind-up radios were handed out so villagers could listen to local radio reports of their visitors' investigation.

In the beautiful, sacred forest of Osogbo, with monkeys leaping across the treetops, we saw shrines with multi-headed wood figure carvings where worshippers come to offer gifts to the Yoruba gods. Among them was a statue of Oshun, the river goddess in whose name detectives now believed Adam may have been sacrificed. As we wandered through another village, Commander Baker acknowledged that witnesses might be reluctant to talk. He said: 'Ritual killing is a taboo subject, and we have to be mature about it. We must maintain that we are not here to judge a culture, we're investigating a murder.' When I interviewed Nigeria's police chief, Inspector General Tafa A. Balogun, he said of his British colleagues: 'I'm highly optimistic that they will achieve 100 per cent success.' And they very nearly did.

Another visit to Joyce Osagiede in Nigeria prompted her to tell detectives that she had looked after a young boy when she was living in Hamburg. She later admitted handing him over to a man she knew as Bawa, who took him to London. A decade on, she named the boy and police managed to find a photograph of him, but they also found the boy in the picture, by then a young man, alive and well. Osagiede admitted buying orange shorts like those Adam had been wearing and claimed she had left them in one of her temporary homes, but both premises had been searched and those shorts weren't found.

Osagiede's estranged husband, Samuel Onojhighovie, had been a suspected human trafficker on the run from Germany and early on in the investigation was arrested in hiding in Dublin. There were now so many lines in their inquiry that convinced detectives that Adam had been trafficked into the UK from Germany, specifically to be sacrificed in a ritual murder. The Adam team wanted to put Osagiede on trial for trafficking the boy, but the Crown Prosecution Service declined to charge her. The case against her was compelling but circumstantial. For all the groundbreaking forensic work done in the investigation it produced no evidence against her, and in her interviews, she had been too confused. She has since died.

It would be easy to view the Adam investigation as a failure. For all the effort and cost, he wasn't identified, and nobody was charged over his killing. The unsolved murder of a child always rankles with police officers. Still without his real relatives, Adam was buried in a blue coffin in an unmarked grave five years after his body was found. His only mourners were the detectives and Ray Fysh. Today, however, Andy Baker looks back on the investigation not with dissatisfaction but with pride of what was achieved and its legacy. He said:

> We identified the gang involved in trafficking Adam, I'm sure of that. They went to jail. Joyce was certainly involved as a loose facilitator and got herself and her daughters into the UK illegally by handing over Adam to the gang. We passed on our knowledge of African trafficking to other European countries. Italy, Spain, Holland and Ireland all asked for our help in their own investigations. We learned a lot about the dark world of rituals and all that was useful to others.

As for the pioneering science, searching for relatives through familial DNA links became standard practice, as did ancestral DNA identification. The rather more complicated chemical analysis of isotope ratios was used in a variety of criminal investigations. In another case, three men were jailed for a gangland shooting after Fysh and colleagues at the Forensic Science Service matched bullets found at a suspect's home to those from the murder scene. The spent bullets were too damaged for comparison by firearms experts, but using techniques developed during the Adam investigation, the scientists were able to establish the link by analysing their chemical composition.

Dr Stuart Black, associate professor at the University of Reading, was one of several academics who worked with Fysh on complicated cases after the Adam investigation. He said: 'Ray inspired us, he was thinking outside the box and that's what it took to push those new methodologies. Early on in my career, he was always saying, would you be interested in trying to analyse this or could you do something with that?'

For the detectives and me, cases that involve torture, mutilation and death are rare, but on the path to finding out the motive for Adam's murder we learned that muti killings in South Africa were running at about one a month. Like no other, the Adam case supplied enough gory detail to satisfy anyone with a craving for true crime horror.

The Met's determination to pursue the investigation, against the odds, led to groundbreaking forensic work, which is another area of crime that fascinates many people. Just look at the proliferation of Crime Scene Investigation TV series and their video game spin-offs. The Adam murder squad might not have appreciated it at the time, but the public's awareness of increasing forensic possibilities may have been willing them on to crack the case.

It's only through writing this book, and pestering Ray Fysh to explain to my unscientific brain what exactly he and his academic colleagues did, that I have begun to understand the success they had. Four years after the Adam case, some of the pioneering science used in trying to solve his murder was applied during the investigation of a crime that heralded the start of a deadly new threat to Britain: Islamic terrorism.

# CHAPTER 11

# THE TERRORISTS

*I remember taking various shots, trying to neutralise
him by shooting him in the head*

– Specialist Firearms Officer PC WS5

'We're next,' came the chilling warning from the UK's most senior policeman, Sir John Stevens. The Scotland Yard commissioner was addressing members of the Metropolitan Police Authority, whose job it was to oversee both his and his officers' actions in their mission to keep our capital city safe.

It was two days after the 9/11 Islamic extremist terror attacks on the United States and Sir John, as usual, wasn't pulling his punches. He was certain Britain would be the next target of those inspired by the terror group Al-Qaeda. I was sitting at the back of the room and, unfortunately, didn't actually hear what he said. There had been plenty of other interesting stuff, and for once I rushed out of the meeting to prepare a report and missed the usual huddle with my colleagues to discuss, as we normally did, what we all thought was the main headline. I can't remember exactly what my news editor said later when our rivals ran the story and we didn't, but I'm sure it was something pretty unpleasant.

Of course, Sir John was right, although it was another four years before a gang of British citizens, motivated by the same hatred of the West, blew up themselves and their victims on three underground trains and a red double-decker bus during a Thursday morning rush hour in central London. The 7/7 suicide bomb attacks on 7 July 2005 killed fifty-two innocent men, women and children. Hundreds more were injured. I headed straight to Scotland Yard and, for the next three weeks, barely left my spot on the pavement outside the Metropolitan Police headquarters. In the wake of the bombings the government hurried in new counter-terror laws, which, among other things, would punish the supporters, helpers and promoters of terror. Britain was under attack from within and Prime Minister Tony Blair declared: 'The rules of the game have changed.'

He wasn't the only one who had to rethink some fundamental ideas about terrorists. We were familiar with Provisional Irish Republican Army bombings and shootings in the UK, but they were carried out by people desperate afterwards to cover their tracks and vanish. Here now were criminals who didn't need a getaway driver. Far from trying not to get caught, they set out on their mission carrying their own identification. Indeed, they wanted to be saluted for their actions and hailed as martyrs. Before midnight on the day of the blasts, police had retrieved from the debris a membership card in the name of ringleader Mohammad Sidique Khan. They later found two of his bank cards. The former teaching assistant wanted the world to know he was proud of his personal death toll: six innocent commuters killed and another 163 injured, including construction manager Daniel Biddle, who lost both legs, an eye and his spleen. Along with the shrapnel surgeons had to remove from his body were his door keys.

It was a week before the police officially published the bombers' names and said they believed they had intended to die, but detectives had worked that out much earlier. It was the question we journalists kept asking more than anything in the daily media briefings we were getting from Scotland Yard. Of course, we speculated that these were suicide attacks, but still had to wait for official confirmation. One of the difficulties for the police was how to deal with the bombers' families. Were they grieving relatives or co-conspirators?

The other question that went unanswered for days was just how many had died. As someone who had covered wars, bombs and plane crashes I knew only too well the difficulties in identifying bodies that had been torn apart, but the families whose loved ones were still missing could not understand, three days after the attack, why no victims had been named. Detective Superintendent Jim Dickie, the senior identification manager, got exasperated when he tried to explain how and why forensic examination of the crime scene was holding up the removal of the dead to the morgue. When he started talking on live television about torsos and limbs it became a bit too much for his superiors. I don't remember seeing or hearing much of him after that, though the identification process did pick up speed.

Because the bombers had, in crime detection terms, been careless, much of the forensic work for Ray Fysh and his team was straightforward, but under the cosh of the Anti-Terrorist Branch and impatient government ministers, they had to work much quicker. It didn't take long to work out that the bombs' main ingredient was the chemical hydrogen peroxide, used in a much more diluted form in cleaning products and hair bleaching and readily found in high-street pharmacies. At the inquest into the bombers' deaths four years later, there was still astonishment at the ease with which they had bought what had been their key ingredient. Coroner Lady Justice Hallett pointed out: 'So you get cross-examined by the chemist if you want to buy too many aspirin, but you can buy as much hydrogen peroxide on the market.'

It wasn't quite that simple, though. The bombers needed to increase the hydrogen peroxide concentration in the products they bought, so they boiled it up on a kitchen stove to evaporate off the water to turn it into a high-concentration deadly substance. Within a few days, police had found the bomb factory, a small two-bedroom flat in an anonymous block in Leeds. Inside were pots and pans used to boil the hydrogen peroxide, a bath full of chemicals and plastic tubs of an explosive yellow-brown sludge. So far, so good, but the world was watching the investigation into this unprecedented terror attack on the British mainland and the detectives wanted and needed to know everything. For starters, how long had the bombers been preparing the ingredients? This is where Fysh and the scientists were able to apply, for the first time, some of the techniques he had pioneered in the Adam investigation four years earlier. He worked out the answer by chemical analysis: not of the bones of a small child, but of the hair of the ringleader, Khan, which, remarkably, was retrievable.

Scientists describe hydrogen peroxide as an aggressive chemical. When the bombers boiled it up in their flat, they used pans that contained lead. The hydrogen peroxide attacked the pans, releasing lead into the air, which was then breathed in by the bombers. By measuring the lead levels along a strand of Khan's hair, working backwards from the day of the bombings, analysts could actually work out how long he had been cooking hydrogen peroxide. It was several weeks. Fysh explained:

> The increase in lead levels in the hair provided a time scale for the concentrating of the hydrogen peroxide from 18 per cent to approximately 60–70 per cent. Together with this, the lead isotope ratio in the hair at the maximum concentration matched the lead isotope ratio of the pans.

What's more, by going back even further, the analysts could also tell that Khan had travelled to Pakistan. Khan's hair revealed that he had been eating, drinking and inhaling in a geological region with lead isotope ratios that matched Pakistan's. This corroborated other evidence that Khan had spent time there at an Al-Qaeda training camp.

When the bombs went off, I was on a train in south London, travelling into my office at Westminster. The first hint of trouble was my train stopping unexpectedly – nothing new to Southern Rail passengers – and the guard walking through the carriages telling us all there were problems on the underground. A power surge, or something like that. Minutes later he informed us the whole network was not working. I'd never known the entire tube system to be out of action. And what, I thought, was the ultimate power surge? An explosion. I called my news desk and was told they knew no more than me. I rang the Scotland Yard press department and detected an air of controlled panic.

In more calls over the next fifteen minutes it became clear there had been explosions and people were injured. 'Are there people dead?' I asked a senior press officer. 'I think so,' he volunteered with some hesitation, 'but please don't report that yet.' Things moved very quickly and soon I was reporting live on air, directly from where I sat on my stranded train, that it was a suspected terror attack, much to the dismay of my fellow passengers. When we were eventually diverted to Cannon Street, I was the only one on board leaping off and eager to head into central London.

It was four years since Sir John Stevens had warned of such an attack, but he had just been replaced as Metropolitan Police commissioner by Sir Ian Blair. It was certainly the toughest of starts for Blair, but the new chief endeared himself to me when the BBC asked him what the first thing he did when he was told of the attacks was. He replied: 'I did what everyone else did; I turned on Sky News.' To their credit the BBC producers used his comment, but they must have agonised over doing so.

For each of the next twenty-one days, I stood for up to sixteen hours a day outside Scotland Yard, beside the iconic triangular sign known as 'the revolving cheese', reporting every twist and turn in the police investigation. We had regular, live daily briefings at the QEII conference centre, but often developments or appeals were so urgent that senior press officers, even the Met's director of public affairs, Dick Fedorcio, would come down from their office and give us hot news on the pavement. More than once I paused briefly during my own live report to listen in, jot down or simply memorise the headline and then turn back to the camera and tell viewers what I had just learned. They were heady, exciting times, and it didn't matter if our coverage looked a bit rough around the edges because our audience was getting a real sense of breaking news.

Some evenings a few crime reporters were called in for extra, more informal briefings with the head of special operations, Assistant Commissioner Andy Hayman, one of the most senior Met officers. He would appear with Fedorcio's deputy, Chris Webb, at his side and take us into his confidence, giving us a sense of where the investigation was going. For some reason these briefings were held in a pub around the corner from the Yard. Not that any of us were complaining. I stuck to water and for good reason, because one night I slipped out three times to deliver a live update on new developments. Those of us from the Crime Reporters Association invited along felt privileged to be given such an insight into what was a constantly moving investigation. With what now seems like appalling bad taste I dubbed us the Provisional CRA.

I had known Andy Hayman for a few years by then. He had been a commander at the Yard and chief constable of Norfolk before returning to the Met in his latest job. He was always a friendly, good media operator who clearly enjoyed the company of journalists he trusted and treated us with respect. From the start of 7/7 he adopted a new and welcome policy of telling us more than we might have expected, though at times insisting some things were not to be reported until some later date.

It's usual, in an ongoing criminal investigation, for police to keep key details out of the public domain, so as to use them in any future trial. Although it was eventually established that the London bombers had all died in their attack, for a long time, anti-terror investigators believed others had been involved in the planning and could end up being prosecuted. Hayman seemed to take the view that the public shouldn't have to wait for a trial – that might be several years away – to learn more about the dangers they faced, there and then, from 'home-grown' terrorists and, even more frighteningly, any others who might follow in their wake.

It was after 9/11, amid fears that a similar attack could happen in London, that Chris Webb had created a new media strategy for use should that awful prediction come true. It was based loosely on a protocol Scotland Yard and journalists already had on kidnaps, where we agreed to a news blackout in return for being told what was going on. Webb, who went on to become a successful crisis management consultant, said:

I always felt, and I still hold this view very strongly, that the media is a stakeholder and a partner, and we should do what we do with other partners and engage and have a relationship with you and keep you informed of things that are going on. Now, we do that within certain parameters, understandably.

We knew full well that your editors would be making demands on you to find something different or whatever. We had a lot of covert operations going on at the time in different parts of the country. The last thing we wanted was for you to find out a snippet of information and, on the back of that, go and make your own enquiries in the local area, which would then completely blow out of the water that covert op. The other thing was, it was a two-way process because we knew that you might be finding out information in the enquiries that you were making that would actually help and support our investigation. Bear in mind, in 2005, there was no social media. We were wholly relying on the press, getting the right tone and the message to the public. You can only do that if you're prepared to engage with them.

It was astonishing how quickly London got back to normal after the horror of the 7/7 bombings. Within days, tube trains were running almost as usual. Commuters were packed once more into overcrowded carriages, with armed undercover police not always as hidden as they thought they were. Was it a defiant spirit or a belief that it couldn't happen again? And then it did, well, almost. On 21 July, two weeks later, four more bombers launched copycat attacks on the capital's transport system, but their explosives failed to detonate. They managed to escape and the city became the centre of a huge manhunt, with police fearful the gang had more bombs and were planning to set those off.

The next day, police and army surveillance teams were monitoring a suspect they believed was one of the failed bombers, Hussain Osman. They followed the man as he left his south London flat, caught a bus and walked the final part of his journey into Stockwell tube station, just south of the River Thames. There, his fate was sealed because his pursuers had been ordered to kill him if he entered the underground network. The police rules of engagement dictated he must not be given a chance to detonate any explosives he could be carrying. After their suspect descended the escalator and took a seat in a train carriage, the police surrounded him and shot him at least six times in the head at close range. The news travelled fast, particularly among the officers involved in the manhunt who must have felt relief and pride that the threat from at least one of the bombers had been removed.

I was standing outside Scotland Yard, fortunately off air, when Fleet Street crime reporter Peter Rose called me. He was working as a freelancer and had great contacts. He told me police had shot dead one of the suicide bombers at Stockwell. I hesitated about going straight on air because I felt I needed some sort of official confirmation. I made some frantic calls but got nowhere. Then a former Flying Squad inspector I knew walked past and said, quietly and without stopping: 'Have you heard? We've shot one of the suicide bombers.' I barely had time to mutter my thanks as he walked into the building.

That was enough to go with the story. I called my news desk, out of earshot of the other reporters nearby, and very quickly was on air saying that it was understood police had shot a suspected bomber. As I was speaking to the presenter, I could sense the competition turning their heads and leaning in to catch what I was saying. Before I'd stopped talking, I could hear their own phones ringing. Moments like that justify a journalist's time spent nurturing contacts. I was feeling pleased with myself, but I didn't stop to think about how my journalistic pride was over a young man who had just had his brains blown out. And an innocent man, as we soon found out.

The man police killed was a Brazilian electrician called Jean Charles de Menezes, aged twenty-seven. He was the victim of mistaken identity, poor communications and the heightened fear of another terrorist attack. There can have been few worse days in Metropolitan Police history: an ongoing investigation into co-ordinated suicide bombings, more terrorists on the loose and public outrage over a terrible, tragic error. It was my job to hold the force's top brass to account, but it was difficult not to feel some sympathy for them. The commissioner, Sir Ian Blair, told reporters de Menezes was challenged by his officers and refused to obey their instructions. That wasn't true. In a statement, his press department said that de Menezes's behaviour and clothing at the tube station had added to police suspicions. That wasn't true either. Eventually, Sir Ian admitted the shooting was a big mistake.

His force was later fined £175,000 over the fiasco under Health and Safety laws. At an inquest into the death of de Menezes three years later, the jurors were prevented by the coroner from returning a verdict of unlawful killing, but they rejected Scotland Yard's argument that the killing was lawful in the circumstances of the ongoing terror alert. Instead, the jury chose an open verdict. Police flew a senior officer to Brazil to apologise to the dead man's family, who settled on a compensation payment of £100,000. The victim's cousin, Patricia da Silva, said in a Sky News podcast in 2021: 'This happened sixteen years ago but the outrage is still the same. I don't know if one day we will have justice, but in my view, to be honest, I don't think so.'

The four failed bombers were eventually found and arrested within a week, including Hussain Osman, who had fled to Rome, where he became a test case for the new European Arrest Warrant system of fast-track extradition back to the UK. When police discovered two of the bombers holed up in a west London flat, our cameras were not far behind them, thanks to a resident's tip-off. We filmed the scene live: the security being set up around the flats and armed officers nearby putting on their body armour, as though preparing for a raid. I had several calls from Scotland Yard insisting we stopped filming. If the bombers had access to Sky News and saw the police preparations, they could be tempted to blow up themselves and the residents. Obviously, we complied and resumed filming only when the two bombers emerged at police gunpoint, naked but for their underpants to show they were not carrying explosives.

Two years later, the relationship between police and the media turned sour over yet another, in some ways even more chilling, terror investigation. Several reporters, including me and my colleague, Tim Marshall, Sky's foreign affairs editor at the time, had got wind of a massive police operation, planned for the next day, to arrest 'a major terror gang'. I didn't know a lot more, other than it would be in Birmingham, though I had no idea where. We sent a crew to lurk around the city centre in the hope they might spot a convoy of West Midlands Police vehicles heading out for dawn raids. I stayed in London, ready to break the news at Scotland Yard once the arrests had been made. A newspaper colleague had the same tip-off as me but even fewer details, and he sent a photographer on a wild-goose chase to Manchester.

When news of the arrests was released officially by police, there was very little information given out. I spent several hours badgering contacts to try to establish what the story was. Reporting is often like that. Rarely does anyone tell me everything I want to know all at once. It's a bit like putting together a jigsaw adding pieces as you get them and hoping you beat your rivals in assembling the full picture. As the day wore on, my description of the terror plot to Sky viewers changed from 'major' to 'unusual'. More endless calls meant I was able to add 'chilling' and 'kidnap' to the puzzle. Once I had managed to add the awful elements of 'beheading – soldier – and Muslim' to my live report, a frustrated senior police officer finally rather grudgingly admitted: 'Well, now you've got the lot.' It was a plot to abduct and behead a Muslim British soldier.

Our reporting of the details caused a stink and angered the anti-terror police national coordinator Peter Clarke, a deputy assistant commissioner at Scotland Yard. In a speech to the influential Policy Exchange think tank he said:

On the morning of the arrests, almost before the detainees had arrived at the police stations to which they were being taken for questioning, it was clear key details of the investigation and the evidence had been leaked. This damaged the interview strategy of the investigators and undoubtedly raised community tensions. I have no idea where the leaks came from, but whoever was responsible should be thoroughly ashamed of themselves.

Well, for a start, nothing of the police operation had actually been reported before official confirmation that it had already happened. News of the raids was given to me and other journalists in a press release by West Midlands Police at around eight o'clock in the morning and before all the arrests had been made. Clarke seemed to have been unaware of that, or forgotten it. Or maybe it was that West Midlands early press release he was driving at when he said, elsewhere in his speech:

What is clear is that there are a number, a small number I am sure, of misguided individuals who betray confidences. Perhaps they look to curry favour with certain journalists, or to squeeze out some short-term presentational advantage – I do not know what motivates them. The people who do this either do not know or do not care what damage they do. If they do know, then they are beneath contempt. If they do not know, then let me tell them. They compromise investigations. They reveal sources of life-saving intelligence. In the worst cases they put lives at risk. I wonder if they simply do not care.

I pointed out at the time that it was Clarke who appeared to have signalled an important change in the police policy of never revealing details of ongoing operations, when *he* announced, *during* an earlier terror raid, what his officers had found. In another investigation, it was Clarke again who detailed the number of computers police had seized, suggesting that they would need a long time to properly examine them. I figured he did that as part of a police campaign for a change in the law to give them more time to interrogate terror suspects before they had to charge or release them.

Following the rumpus over who said what and when to the press during the Birmingham terror operation, the Liberal Democrat home affairs spokesman, Nick Clegg, urged the chief constable to investigate whether there had been a breach of the Official Secrets Act, which Clegg insisted 'prohibits the release of information that "impedes the … apprehension or prosecution of suspected offenders"'. There was a police investigation, but it was a more mundane leak inquiry with three main suspects: a senior Metropolitan Police officer, an employee in the Prime Minister's office and an official at the Home Office. Two detectives came to Sky to interview me and Tim Marshall. We told them only that we could not reveal our sources. They must have thought we had something to hide. Which we had, of course. We heard nothing more and as far as I know they didn't find the source of the leak.

What was clear was that terror was now firmly on the agenda of crime reporters and, as time went on, it slowly overwhelmed everything else. Others and I had to share the terror beat with our home affairs colleagues. The continuing threat from groups or individuals inspired by jihadist groups meant we were all constantly waiting for another attack, more arrests of suspects caught red-handed, the next court appearance or the start of the latest trial. From 2006 the government started to publish its current terror threat level assessment, a scale of five categories from Low (an attack is highly unlikely) though Moderate, Substantial and Severe to Critical (an attack is highly likely in the near future). The level has never fallen below Substantial, which means an attack remains likely.

According to Home Office figures, around a sixth of terror suspects arrested in the year to March 2022, were under eighteen. The British government launched various initiatives under the banner of a programme called Prevent, aimed at stopping the radicalisation of the young and vulnerable and supporting them afterwards. One of its aims was to encourage schools, community leaders and even parents to report concerns about individuals. It got a lot of referrals initially, but it was later criticised for failing to stop terror plots.

The two years of on-off lockdown during the coronavirus pandemic brought fears of increased radicalisation as people spent more time online. It coincided with a period of negative publicity over poor police performance and falling behavioural standards, which inevitably damaged public confidence in the police.

Ali Harbi Ali, a young British national and Muslim of Somali heritage, was a textbook example of someone who was radicalised by online propaganda and reported to the Prevent programme yet wasn't considered a serious threat. In 2021 he stabbed Tory MP Sir David Amess to death during a constituency surgery in Essex because of the politician's support for British air strikes on ISIS positions in Syria. Ali also represented the counter-terror authorities' biggest concern: the home-grown jihadi acting alone.

The first person I ever heard say 'communities defeat terrorism' was Commander John Grieve, when he was head of the old Anti-Terrorist Squad at Scotland Yard. He had retired before 7/7, but as an academic he went on to help establish the John Grieve Centre for Policing and Community Safety. He recognised the importance of neighbourhood policing, of small teams of officers rooted in and dedicated to specific residential areas where they got to know the locals. He must have been distraught to see that model of policing being dismantled under public spending cuts from 2009, and then hailed again, in 2022, as the key to restoring public trust.

It wasn't just Islamist fundamentalism that counter-terror police had to worry about. The growth of right-wing extremism, often fuelled in online forums with thousands of members, has sometimes erupted into terror. In 2016 the Labour MP Jo Cox, a vocal opponent of the Brexit campaign for the UK to leave the European Union, was shot and stabbed to death by a 52-year-old constituent. Thomas Mair was a loner who had long harboured a hatred of liberals and the Left. During the murder outside a West Yorkshire village library he was heard shouting: 'Britain first, keep Britain independent, Britain will always come first.' The judge told him: 'There is no doubt that this murder was done for the purpose of advancing a political, racial and ideological cause, namely that of violent white supremacism and exclusive nationalism most associated with Nazism and its modern forms.'

Scotland Yard Assistant Commissioner Matt Jukes, who became head of Counter Terrorism Policing in 2021, warned that children as young as thirteen were unknowingly being drawn into extreme right-wing terrorism. Many were seduced by propaganda drawn from 'first person shooter' video games in which players inhabit the main character. 'This is a group which is substantially younger than what we have seen in the past,' he said, '[young] people who are spending a great deal of time online, day and night, living their lives in that space, building friendships and relationships in that digital world.'

In March 2022, Jukes briefed journalists that half the 186 terror arrests in 2021 were related to Islamist extremism, while 41 per cent were connected with right-wing ideology. Twenty of the arrests were of children under eighteen, and all but one were suspected of right-wing extremism.

Often, it's difficult for me to keep up with everything that's going on. Counter-terror police say they are regularly investigating hundreds of terror plots, and the security service MI5 has 3,000 individual 'subjects of interest' under live investigation at any one time. Several police officers I knew told me they were among hundreds being recruited to boost the ranks of counter-terror command. It usually meant they were even more guarded in what they told me.

Some good things have come out of counter-terror activity and made my job easier. When new terror suspects were charged, the Crown Prosecution Service began giving out a case summary that included a lot of detail on the alleged plot. We had to agree not to publish most of the information before the trial, but it was enormously helpful to reporters juggling several often-complicated cases, some of which overlapped. Helpful, that is, until one newspaper printed much of the detail of a case before the suspect had even appeared in court. It was a flagrant breach of the deal between reporters and prosecutors. The CPS withdrew the case summaries in great anger. Journalist Duncan Gardham, who specialises in stories about security, often has to badger courts to hand over documents to which the media is entitled. He said:

In theory we're still entitled to the full summary. If you push and throw your toys out of the pram you might get it, but how much information is given varies enormously from case to case. The reason it's like that now is because one paper decided to act outside the journalists' agreement.

Reporters also, now, have contact with the spooks, the officers of MI5. Since 9/11 the organisation has been swamped with intelligence, mostly about Islamic extremist plots, and after 7/7 its budget and staffing levels were increased massively. It opened up regional offices and forged relationships with local police forces in a new joint offensive against what Tony Blair called 'the war on terror'. The relationships had not always been good. The spooks had usually been to posher schools than the police and looked down on them as rather pedestrian investigators. A police contact believed MI5 officers had little regard for the preservation of evidence because they seldom had to produce it in court. The spooks called the police 'plod'. Police officers referred to the MI5 riverside headquarters Thames House as Toad Hall. Old rivalries had to be overcome. What helped the police, several sources readily acknowledged, was the high-level surveillance equipment MI5 brought to their joint investigations.

Once, the security service's existence was barely acknowledged officially, but after 9/11 it was thrust into the limelight, eventually developing its own website and advertising jobs in national newspapers. Now, its director general gives public speeches and, on a non-attributable basis, some individual officers speak about the current terror threat. They will never discuss any detail of ongoing operations, referring all such questions to the police. We've got used to a different sort of language, especially when things go wrong.

What I might once have thought of as an 'intelligence failure' is, in fact, an 'intelligence gap'. The new openness also gave us access to other once-secret areas. I was invited to Fort Halstead, the government's explosives research laboratory, where forensic analysis was done on the 7/7 bombs. According to my car's satellite navigation system, the place didn't exist.

We were full of expectation when Sir Stephen Lander, the first boss of the new Serious and Organised Crime Agency, invited reporters in for a chat. SOCA was set up a year after 7/7 to tackle the country's top criminals, the drug and weapons traffickers. I went in with John Twomey, the *Daily Express* crime correspondent. The office was in an old anonymous building tucked down a narrow Westminster side street. It was a disappointing meeting because Sir Stephen, a former head of MI5, hadn't got the message about the new policy of openness. When we asked about his media strategy, he said he wasn't going to have one. Once a spook, always a spook, I thought. He didn't seem to grasp that the public had a right to know how he was going to be spending his first £427 million budget of taxpayer's money.

He told us SOCA would be working with regional police and he was quite happy to let those forces take the credit for any successful investigations. He and his staff would be content to stay in the shadows with no public profile at all. I couldn't imagine that was going to go down well with the new SOCA recruits who I knew would be gagging for recognition.

Fortunately for us, it wasn't long before a period of government financial austerity had every public body scrambling for continued funding and desperate to show how it deserved it. SOCA was replaced eventually by the National Crime Agency, which was more than happy to be known as Britain's equivalent of America's Federal Bureau of Investigation and help journalists sing its praises.

Those who work in counter-terror are, understandably, guarded in what they say. Sometimes the information offered, if any is offered at all, is so vague I struggle afterwards to decide if I've really learned anything new. Anyone listening in to our conversations might think we are talking in riddles. I wonder how police officers get on with the various intelligence agencies, now they have to work together more regularly. At least they're on the same side.

Detective Inspector Brian Tarpey had to deal with Russian intelligence officials when he went to Moscow in 2006. It was in the wake of the radioactive metal poisoning in London of former KGB agent Alexander Litvinenko. Scotland Yard had identified two Russians as witnesses and potential suspects, Andrei Lugovoi and Dmitry Kovtun. They were later named as Litvinenko's killers during a UK public inquiry into the murder, but long before that happened the Russians said: 'Sure, please come and speak to us.' In Moscow, Tarpey and a colleague met and interviewed Lugovoi, who denied any involvement, and then asked to see Kovtun. They were told they would have to speak to Kovtun in hospital, where he was seriously ill. Tarpey said:

> A colleague was taken into a room and met a man lying on a bed, completely wrapped head to foot in bandages just like an Egyptian mummy. All you could see were his eyes. The Russians said that far from being the killer, he himself was a victim who was poisoned by Litvinenko. To this day, I still don't know if we interviewed the man we thought he was.

In 2017, there were four terror attacks in London: at Westminster Bridge, London Bridge and Finsbury Park and a failed bomb blast on a tube train at Parsons Green. Fourteen innocent people, including unarmed PC Keith Palmer who was guarding the Houses of Parliament, were murdered and nearly 137 injured. Twenty-two people, mostly teenagers, were killed by a suicide bomber at Manchester Arena at the end of a concert by pop singer Ariana Grande. Over 1,000 more were injured. It was the deadliest UK terror attack since 7/7. A damning report, at the end of a long public inquiry into the bombing, was highly critical of the venue's security, the emergency services' response and MI5's 'significant missed opportunity' to take action that might have prevented the attack.

Mark Rowley, who was then head of Counter Terrorism Policing and still to be knighted, told me that after the London Bridge attack a fortnight later, in which eight people were murdered by three terrorists who drove into pedestrians then ran amok with knives before being shot dead by his armed officers, he went out onto the balcony of his eighth-floor Scotland Yard office at 4 a.m. He stood there alone for a long while to clear his head and marshal his thoughts for the days ahead. He didn't do it to sober up, because he'd given up alcohol when he took on the high-profile role three years earlier.

The awful wave of attacks prompted internal reviews of the monitoring of potential jihadis by police and MI5, according to *The Guardian*. Two of the attacks were carried out by former 'subjects of interest' and one of many changes implemented was a more focused monitoring of suspects previously thought to pose only a small risk, a source told the newspaper. Victims' families complained bitterly that known extremists had not been under some kind of surveillance, an issue that crops up in the aftermath of every terror attack with the question to counter-terror chiefs always asked during press conferences or briefings: 'Was the suspect known to you?' Too often, the answer has been 'yes', with the frustrated explanation that 'we cannot possibly follow everyone who might pose a threat'.

When Home Secretary Amber Rudd admitted that the Manchester Arena bomber Salman Abedi was 'known, up to a point' I asked a police source with specialist experience what it takes to put a suspect under full 24-hour surveillance.

His answer was that you need sixty people to monitor one suspect around the clock. Here's the breakdown: two teams of fifteen officers working a twelve-hour shift each. They would have to have time for travel, brief and debrief, evidence logging and meals. Some might lose their sharpness, because of sleep deprivation, fatigue and boredom, and they might get spotted.

So, there would have to be a third team of fifteen on stand-by, ready to replace those who drop out. Long-term surveillance presents other problems. Officers get ill, or must sit promotion exams, or go to training and safety update sessions. Family issues crop up. Some simply need a day off. Very quickly the operation requires a fourth team. To watch closely all of MI5's 'subjects of interest' with a team of sixty would involve 180,000 surveillance officers, a number far higher than the combined staff of UK police forces and the security service.

In 2019, convicted terrorist Usman Khan was at a prison rehabilitation meeting in a building at the north end of London Bridge when he went to the toilet, retrieved two knives he'd hidden there and stabbed to death two of the event organisers, Saskia Jones and Jack Merritt. A year earlier he had been freed from an eight-year prison sentence for a foiled terror plot. He was released without a parole board assessment of any lingering public danger he posed. He had convinced officials he was rehabilitated.

Khan was chased outside by others and attacked on the pavement thirty yards or so onto the bridge. Moments later armed police arrived, cleared away his attackers and shot him dead. Most of that, including the fatal shots, was captured on video from a passenger in a passing taxi and from a bus and posted on social media. Within minutes news outlets were running the footage without showing the moment of Khan's death, but you didn't have to search far on the internet to see the whole grim episode. We had come a long way since the pre-social media days of 7/7 when police press officers such as Chris Webb could engage the media to control the flow of information and perhaps reduce public alarm. Watching the unedited footage of police deliberately shooting dead a man in broad daylight on a London street, not long after it happened, must have scared the living daylights out of most viewers. Today, the redacted versions shown by mainstream broadcasters have been reposted on YouTube and watched by millions, despite or perhaps because of the warnings of distressing images. Some show Khan still moving after the first shots and it's quite unsettling, even though recorded from a distance. What's more chilling, maybe, are the conversations going on behind the smartphone cameras; mundane, excited rather than shocked. We've got used to terror on our streets, just as we have of real violence on social media.

The various videos barely captured any of the chaos and confusion of the moment. All of it was recounted by the police firearms officers who gave evidence at an inquest I covered two years later. At times it sounded surreal. The first officers scrambled to the scene were told initially that a woman had been stabbed and thought only their first-aid skills were needed. As they got closer, they learned they might have to use their weapons but still didn't know the suspect was a terrorist. Three officers from a specialist armed-response vehicle ran towards a group of men attacking Khan on the pavement and tried to assess the risk.

The officers were all granted anonymity during the inquest. PC YX99 was a firearms officer with less than two years' experience carrying a weapon. He often hesitated as he gave his evidence, recalling how he thought Khan was unarmed and reached through the crowd to grab him. Khan looked at him and said: 'I've got a bomb.' The officer told the inquest jury: 'At that moment I was slightly stunned. I thought, you selfish cunt, you want to die and you want me to kill you. You start to think of all different outcomes and what you're going to do.'

Suddenly, the officer started worrying that Khan might be mentally ill and that he risked shooting an innocent man. Still, he checked him for hidden explosives and found a belt, copper wire, containers and what looked like white plasticine. 'I thought the bomb was 100 per cent real and that he would detonate it and we were all going to die,' he said. 'The last thing I remember thinking is, it's going to hurt, and also thinking, try and shoot him, get people off and shoot him. You are relying on muscle memory and training to make the best of a situation you can.'

The officer pulled off the men tackling Khan and fired twice. He thought he had killed Khan, but the terrorist continued to move as he lay on the pavement, raising his arms and, after eight minutes, even tried to sit up.

The officer said:

I was in shock, in a bit of a panicked state to be honest. I was relieved to be alive still and my ears were ringing because I didn't have Peltors [ear defenders] on. I had fired a couple of shots and was fully expecting him to be dead so when he moved, I was stunned. I was partly doubting myself just because of the way other people reacted when I said 'he's got a bomb' – they weren't reacting as quickly as I was because you don't want to be anywhere near it. I was beginning to doubt myself, thinking I had definitely seen something around his waist. I was wondering, is it a real device?

PC WS5, a former member of the armed forces, was just behind PC YX99 and said that after the first two shots he moved away when he saw what he thought was a real suicide belt. He said he realised he was in 'no man's land', too close to the device, so he moved fifty metres away where there was a wall to use as cover. 'At the time I was on the radio just trying to get control to send more units, to shut off the foot passage under the bridge,' he said. 'I remember distinctly there was a lady pushing a pram without a care in the world, and there were also city-river cruises going on.'

Khan kept moving and the officer told the inquest:

I believed he was a threat and needed to be neutralised as soon as possible. I couldn't get a clear shot or a clear view of him so I moved a bit closer to the footpath, maybe fifteen metres from him. I remember taking various shots, trying to neutralise him by shooting him in the head.

He was aiming for the mandibular nerve, which he described as the 'on-off switch' for the brain, adding: 'Without that you can't have any mobility to move or detonate or do anything at all, so I was aiming for that.' Looking through his rifle sight he could see one shot go across Khan's forehead. 'He put his hand up and wiped it across his forehead in disbelief, so I then went for the body mass. I believe some of them hit.' PC WS5 fired ten shots.

In all, six officers fired twenty shots between them. Eventually it was established that the suicide belt was a fake, but jurors were told all officers were trained to treat all devices as potential explosives. The inquest was told that eight out of twenty bullets missed their target. None of the critical head shots, designed to kill Khan instantly, hit him. When officers on one side of London Bridge heard shots being fired from a different direction, they didn't know at first whether they had heard colleagues' guns or were being fired on themselves by potential accomplices of Khan. The vivid recollections of the highly trained firearms officers were a fascinating and chilling insight into the challenges of their job. It was far from the smooth, clinical operation the public might have expected. Few police operations are.

# CHAPTER 12

# THE FUGITIVES

*This is no holiday lifestyle here. We have no money*
*and struggle from day to day to make ends meet*
– FUGITIVE WAYNE SMITH

P ounding the crime beat day after day is always challenging, but it can be wearing, too. There is precious little fun or good news. If terrorism is the most grim, serious part of a crime reporter's brief, then hunting fugitives from justice can sometimes feel like light relief. Many journalists have spent a lot of enjoyable time on the trail of Lord Lucan, the earl who vanished after the notorious murder of his children's nanny, Sandra Rivett, in the family's home in Belgravia, London. Apparently, he had mistaken the nanny for his wife Veronica, Lady Lucan. Since he disappeared in 1974, there have been regular supposed sightings of Lucan across the world, but his fate is unknown and he's still a wanted man. Reporters haven't stopped looking for him.

An old *Daily Mirror* colleague, Garth Gibbs, claimed that not finding Lucan had been the highlight of his career. He acknowledged that his rivals, too, had enjoyed some success in not locating the missing peer, but insisted:

> I regard not finding Lord Lucan as my most spectacular success in journalism ... I have successfully not found him in more exotic spots than anybody else. I spent three glorious weeks not finding him in Cape Town, magical days and nights not finding him in the Black Mountains of Wales, and wonderful and successful short breaks not finding him in Macau either, or in Hong Kong or even in Green Turtle Cay in the Bahamas where you can find anyone.

No one has calculated how much journalists have claimed in expenses as they travelled the world in pursuit of Lord Lucan. His nickname 'Lucky' could be applied to those who've been sent to look for him. Of course, some don't really want to find him. The canny Scots editor and columnist Sir John Junor once observed: 'Laddie, you don't ever want to shoot the fox. Once the fox is dead there is nothing left to chase.'

I've never gone hunting for Lucan, but I've pursued plenty of other wanted suspects. As Gibbs suggested, except for Wales, fugitives tend to head for warm, sunny places and not some bleak, frozen outpost that few of us would want to visit. It's always a bonus to go on a foreign assignment with sun cream, rather than a woolly hat, in your suitcase. These days, though, news editors tend to want rather more assurance that the trip will be successful. And not 'successful' in the Gibbs sense of the word.

'This is no holiday lifestyle here. We have no money and struggle from day to day to make ends meet.' The words of Wayne Smith, a wanted man. We were sitting drinking coffee on the beautiful curve of a sandy beach fringed with pine trees, overlooking the sparkling Mediterranean Sea outside Kyrenia in Northern Cyprus. Smith was a man who'd had enough of life on the run from British justice. He wanted my help to give himself up. I know I shouldn't have done, but I felt a bit sorry for him. He was trapped in paradise.

Smith, aged thirty-eight, had been an account executive with a mobile phone company. He and a friend were racing their cars along a Birmingham street when both hit a pedestrian, 22-year-old waiter Mohammed Idrees, as he crossed the road. Smith's car dragged the victim along for more than 100 metres. When he finally stopped, he found him dead, trapped under the wheels. Smith said he fled the scene in shock because he could see, in his car's wing mirror, a group of Asian men running towards him and he feared for his life.

Smith was later arrested and charged with causing death by dangerous driving. Terrified of going to prison, and claiming to be the target of death threats, he skipped bail before his trial began, but it went ahead anyway and he was convicted in his absence. By that time he had already fled to the Turkish-controlled part of Cyprus, popular with British ex-pats and holidaymakers, where the European Arrest Warrant system was not recognised and there was no extradition treaty. Northern Cyprus was one of the few remaining European safe havens for runaways and a much nicer place to live than the others, especially Albania.

The day before we met, I'd been in Greek-controlled southern Cyprus, in the divided capital city of Nicosia, where UK authorities had launched one of their occasional public appeals for help in locating British fugitives from justice. Smith and his girlfriend Julie

Skelding were two of the names on the list of nine Most Wanted targets in Operation Zygos. She fled with him after being convicted of giving him a false alibi when she appeared alongside her boyfriend at Birmingham Crown Court. The joint appeal by the UK's Serious and Organised Crime Agency, the British charity Crimestoppers and Cyprus Police, featured fugitives thought to be hiding somewhere on the island, north or south. From those I spoke to, no one in any of those organisations really expected to track down anyone in the north, never mind get them extradited.

Smith had seen my TV report and, through an old Sky News colleague of mine who lived locally, Tom Roche, managed to get in touch and asked me to meet him. He and Skelding wanted to give themselves up. Tall and slim, Smith wore a polo top and cargo shorts and, with his tan, blended in easily with the large British ex-pat community. That, of course, is one of the attractions for fugitives in such European resorts: they feel at home and they can speak English. He said that watching the television report had been painful, especially an interview with his victim's brother who said Smith should be man enough to own up to his actions. As we sipped a second coffee beside the deserted sands, Smith defended himself:

> I was involved in a tragic accident. It was hurtful to see myself described as Most Wanted. I would never put myself in that category, with terrorists and murderers. What I did was wrong, I killed a man, but it wasn't intentional. I was charged with the wrong offence and I am going back to launch an appeal.

The couple had lived in Northern Cyprus for six years. Smith worked as an odd-job man, while Skelding did shifts in various bars used mostly by UK ex-pats. They had struggled financially and I believed them. Some fugitives I've pursued were habitual criminals, often wanted for drug trafficking but enterprising enough to continue doing exactly the same thing, sometimes using contacts they already had. Smith and Skelding weren't like that. He said:

> We have been lucky to make some unbiased friends and they have supported us. No one knew our background, but obviously they do now. I didn't come here and change my name or my appearance. When someone challenged me, I told the truth. It's become a living nightmare, because eventually your passport runs out. I never wanted to escape justice, I wanted time to consider my actions because I felt I was unfairly convicted. I want to go back and face justice. It's about closure for me and closure for the family of the man who died. Their loss is tragic and I sympathise and I'm truly and deeply sorry. No one wants to turn back the clocks more than I do, if I could.

The couple's surrender wasn't going to be easy. They would have to drive across the border, through one of the few checkpoints, into southern Cyprus and give themselves up to the police there. But both Smith's passport and Northern Cyprus visa had expired and the pair of them had unpaid fines for minor driving offences. They feared they might be arrested at the checkpoint and jailed before they could cross to the south to give themselves up. They alerted the British High Commission in Nicosia of their intention. But on the day I had agreed to accompany them, I had to go back to the UK to cover another story, the abduction of five-year-old April Jones in mid-Wales, an investigation that became the biggest police hunt in British history and tragically ended in her murder.

Eventually, the couple realised they had no option but to take a chance with the border police. Newsman Tom Roche agreed to go along and help navigate them through any complication, but in the end there was no hold-up. They were met in the south by police and a High Commission official and held in custody on an existing European Arrest Warrant (EAW). They were extradited soon afterwards. Prior to agreeing to surrender, Smith had asked me what sort of prison sentence he should expect back in Britain. I told him I reckoned he'd get three years. He got seven years and ten months. Skelding got one year and ten months. I never heard from them again.

My meeting in Northern Cyprus with another British fugitive on the same Most Wanted list didn't go quite as well. Timur Mehmet, aged thirty-nine, had been on the run there for five years after his conviction over a £25 million fraud at Northampton Crown Court. After skipping bail and fleeing, he was jailed in his absence for eight years. He was one of a gang of twenty behind a complicated scam involving the buying and re-selling of computer parts and gold bullion. It was known as a carousel fraud – basically fiddling VAT payments. When I found Mehmet at a plush new villa and knocked on the door, he denied it was him, until I showed him his photograph on the Most Wanted poster. Then he admitted:

Yes, it's me. I am trying to do a deal to return to the UK. People who think I should be serving my sentence will get their wish very soon. I was already talking to my lawyer before the Crimestoppers appeal. I am going to resolve this, but I don't see the benefit in talking to you about it. It's complicated.

When I asked him what he did in Cyprus, he said 'nothing', but we established his connection with a US-style burger restaurant called Johnny Rockets in Famagusta. He was pictured at the opening party two years earlier, but he said it was run by his family and not him. The previous year, he had been selling space in a new twelve-storey office block in Nicosia and the constructor told me Mehmet and his father owned the building. I left him standing by the gate of the villa, which he said was not his. The last I saw of him, he was holding his hand over his eyes to shield them from the bright sunshine. As far as I know, he is still in Northern Cyprus.

Police and politicians agree that the introduction of the EAW, even if it didn't work in Northern Cyprus, was a brilliant idea. It cut through the red tape that used to hold up, and sometimes block, the extradition of suspects between European Union (EU) countries. The EAW system was created in 2002, in response to the terror threat after the 9/11 attacks in the United States a year before, but was also intended to help the fight against serious cross-border crime. It replaced the different bilateral extradition treaties that existed between most EU member states. The change simplified the process and meant that, as long as the warrant's paperwork was in legal order and the alleged crime was a recognised offence in both countries, then a suspect could be returned in as little as three weeks. One of the first successful EAW extraditions was of suspected London tube bomber Hussain Osman from Rome, where he fled after the failed suicide bombings on 21 July in 2005. Italy had signed its EAW agreement with the EU only three months earlier. His extradition took eight weeks. Osman was convicted and jailed at Woolwich Crown Court for forty years.

The EAW hasn't always received universal praise. In 2011 there were warnings that it was open to abuse. The Council of Europe's Commissioner for Human Rights, Thomas Hammarberg, said:

Human rights organisations have expressed concerns about the imprisonment of innocent persons, disproportionate arrests, violations of procedural rights and the impossibility in some countries for an innocent person to appeal against a decision to be surrendered. The problems appear to have worsened with the increase of the number of EAWs – there are now an average of more than one thousand per month, the overwhelming majority of which relate to minor crimes.

Ten years later, the international criminal justice charity Fair Trials said it had heard of cases where the warrants had been used to extradite suspects for stealing two video games, a Christmas tree and even a toothbrush. At the time the charity was campaigning to prevent the European Parliament extending the list of offences that could be used to issue EAWs.

The new warrant certainly changed Spain's attraction as a bolthole for British fugitives. In the 1970s and '80s there was no extradition treaty between the two countries. Many British criminals escaped to Spain and lived cheaply in the sun, untouchable so long as they behaved themselves. There they could vanish into what had become huge British communities with little need to learn a new language; they could even drink their favourite beer and eat familiar food. Perhaps even dabble in a bit of smuggling in a country that had long been the European gateway for illegal drugs from north Africa and South America. In a recent count there were 310,000 British-born people living in Spain, with 18 million annual visitors. It is easy to hide in a foreign land that has become a home-from-home where many settlers have learned not to ask too many questions of new arrivals. The Schengen Agreement between most EU countries – the UK is a notable non-signatory – also meant that after 1985 anyone could travel across internal European borders without having to show a passport and be subject to only rare, random checks. It was for good reason that the Costa del Sol in southern Spain became known as the Costa del Crime.

I went there in 1987 for fugitive robber Ronnie Knight's wedding to girlfriend Sue Haylock. It was held in great splendour at the Ocean Club near Marbella. I wasn't invited, but I wasn't the only gatecrasher. I stood outside with other reporters, photographers and undercover Flying Squad officers, all of us trying and failing to look inconspicuous. Then campaigning journalist Roger Cook and his TV crew buzzed overhead in a helicopter, capturing footage for the first episode of ITV's groundbreaking Cook Report. Together we all watched several notorious villains arrive, dressed to the nines, with broad smiles on their faces. None of them seemed much bothered by our presence. The bride turned up in a ribboned, chauffeur-driven, old-style saloon that could only be described as a gangster's car.

During the reception we watched a slightly sozzled Knight, dressed in an immaculate white suit, wobble towards us with a tray of filled champagne glasses. He plonked the brimming flutes on the grass and snarled: 'Here you are guys. Thanks for coming. Now, drink up and fuck off.' Knight eventually tired of his fugitive life and came back to the UK, where he was jailed for his part in the £6 million Security Express robbery in east London. It was the introduction of the EAW that finally closed what had been a much-used legal loophole for plenty of others like him.

A year after the new EAW got into full swing, UK police and Crimestoppers launched Operation Captura. It was the first media initiative to name and shame the UK's Most Wanted hiding somewhere on the Spanish Costas. It was the forerunner to the similar Operation Zygos in Cyprus and Operation Return in the Netherlands, two other favourite fugitive boltholes. It's difficult to overstate Captura's success. Between 2006 and 2019, Captura published the identities of ninety-five fugitives, of which eighty-seven were caught or surrendered and returned to face UK justice. The list included murderers, rapists, kidnappers, paedophiles and drug traffickers. A lot of drug traffickers. By the time they featured on the Most Wanted list, some had already been convicted of their crimes and had skipped bail, others were simply wanted on suspicion of committing offences, although the evidence against them was very strong.

Only a minority of all fugitives wanted in the UK have appeared in the Most Wanted campaigns, because there are, at any time, many more suspects on the run than most people would imagine. By the time Britain's participation in the EAW system ended with Brexit, the country's withdrawal from the EU in 2020, Spain had provided the return of more British fugitives than any other European country. For example, figures showed that between 2010 and 2014 alone, Britain got back 675 wanted criminals from within the EU, 189 of them from Spain.

I've lost count of the number of times detectives stood in front of a giant screen showing the mugshots of their latest Most Wanted fugitives and told me: 'Our message to these suspects is that you can run, but you can't hide.' Such comments were inevitably followed by a tribute to 'the wonderful cooperation' and 'sense of purpose' shared between the police forces of Britain and Spain. There was always an opportunity to show senior police chiefs from both countries smiling and shaking hands. Viewers would be forgiven for thinking that every Spanish cop had the fugitive mugshots in his or her pocket and was patrolling the streets looking for them. The reality was rather different.

Each suspect's details might well be held on the Spanish national police computer system, but they were unlikely to come to the authorities' attention and be discovered unless they committed a crime, were involved in a traffic accident or ended up in hospital. Any of those episodes inevitably meant official scrutiny of documents and identity. Lifesaving treatment could be tricky as any fugitive living under an alias would probably own up to his true name, particularly if his survival depended on drugs for an existing health issue, or a transfusion from the right blood group.

Matthew Sammon, a first-aid instructor from Croydon, south London, had been living and working for two years as an odd-job man on the Costa del Sol when his name and photograph were included in an Operation Captura appeal in 2016. He was living modestly, sleeping in an old camper van in which he kept his tools, and had built up a reputation as a reliable, hard worker employed mostly by ex-pats. He was forty-six and was able to earn a living because he hadn't told his customers the real reason for his presence there. He was on the run after admitting downloading and possessing 34,000 indecent images of children. He had also confessed to having nearly 900 videos, which police believed he filmed while working with a diving club at various swimming pools in the UK. He was given bail by a British court and promptly fled abroad.

On the Most Wanted list he was in notorious company. The rogues' gallery included Jamie Acourt, a man wanted for a drugs conspiracy but who was better known as one of the original suspects in the racist murder of black teenager Stephen Lawrence.

Acourt was eventually arrested, extradited and jailed in the UK two years later.

Sammon was captured within hours of his face appearing on Sky's coverage of the appeal. Ex-pat building developer Danny Reid rang a local news agency, which in turn called me to say Danny had employed Sammon as a labourer. What's more, he knew where Sammon was likely to be that night.

Within an hour, we were staking out a vast car park behind a shopping centre along the coast in Fuengirola. Sure enough, just as Danny predicted he would, Sammon drove his camper van in and parked in his usual spot. After chatting to another camper driver, he walked his dog briefly before returning to his van. We filmed it all discreetly from a distance. He appeared to have no idea his photograph was all over the media and his cover blown.

After assuring ourselves the man in our sights really was Matthew Sammon, and not being confident we could tail him if he drove off, I called the NCA's fugitive chief and told him what we had seen. He asked us to stay put but keep out of sight until his officers came and found us. We could then witness the arrest. How naïve I was. It was dark two hours later when, completely by chance, we spotted two Spanish men in casual clothes walking through the car park, chatting like a couple of mates out for the night. As they got nearer, one of them began talking on a mobile phone and something about their manner told me they were undercover policemen. Obviously not very good ones. They strolled past our car, completely ignoring us, and headed for Sammon's camper van. We had to scramble to get the shots we needed. We were just in time to see them haul Sammon out of his vehicle and begin questioning him, before demanding his passport. At the same time, they tried to stop us filming, claiming we had no right to do so. So much for the tip-off we'd given them.

When we got back to the beach restaurant, across from the hotel where the British cops were staying, we found the police team enjoying a noisy meal and celebrating 'their' success. Sammon was extradited back to the UK within a fortnight and ten weeks later was jailed at Southwark Crown Court for thirty months. Oddly, there was no mention during the hearing of his two-year absence, and he was certainly not punished separately for it.

I wasn't the only one a little dubious over the real depth of co-operation between the Spanish and British police. A man who called me out of the blue said he had alerted both forces to what he considered another travesty of justice. A neighbour of his, a fellow ex-pat, had settled in Mijas, even though he was wanted for benefit fraud in Liverpool. My caller said that, over two years, he had sent the cheat's Spanish details to the UK's Department for Work and Pensions, Merseyside Police, Crimestoppers and local Spanish police, but no one had done anything about it. It wasn't difficult to track down the seventy-year-old fraudster Norman Brennan. I found him out walking with his dog and drinking at an open-air bar in a park near his apartment, a daily habit he'd developed in the five years since he jumped bail and fled to Spain. When I confronted him and introduced myself, he replied, matter-of-factly: 'And?'

Before he had gone on the run, Brennan had appeared before Liverpool Crown Court where he admitted seven fraud charges. Brennan had pretended to be his brother, who also lived abroad, and claimed £120,000 in four different benefits. He disappeared before being sentenced and bought two houses beside a golf course near

Mijas. The biggest revelation was that while Work and Pensions investigators were supposed to be searching for him, other colleagues in the department were writing to him regularly in Spain, where his pension was being paid directly into his bank account. A European Arrest Warrant in Brennan's name didn't appear to have made any difference.

We ran the report during the week of the Tory party conference, where the Secretary of State for Work and Pensions, Iain Duncan Smith, was promising a government clampdown on benefit fraudsters. To his credit, the minister didn't try to bluff his way out of the scandal. When I interviewed him, he confessed he was 'outraged' at our revelations and promised action. In the 28-second clip we used, though, he couldn't help mentioning that the government was 'already spending millions and ... returning billions to the Exchequer by getting rid of fraud from the system'. Within six weeks Brennan had been arrested, extradited and jailed for three years.

The story of a conman called Mark Acklom again left neither the British nor Spanish authorities with much credit. When Acklom was on the run in Spain, the British detective hunting for him, Detective Inspector Adam Bunting of Avon and Somerset Police, told me: 'I'm getting no cooperation from the Spanish police. I've asked them to check out an address where he might be, but they hardly seem bothered at all. He is not wanted by them, so they have little interest in spending time and effort on him.' The irony in that statement was that Bunting and his colleagues had been slow to investigate Acklom and had missed opportunities to arrest him.

I spent a lot of time tracking down Acklom, who had wooed and betrayed a beautiful divorcee. Carolyn Woods was managing an upmarket boutique in Gloucestershire when he walked in one day to buy a jacket. She fell in love with the handsome, multi-lingual charmer. He told her he was a wealthy banker named Mark Conway who worked as a spy for the UK's secret intelligence service MI6 and promised to marry her. She was completely taken in by him and to this day cannot fully explain why. She told me she even watched him walk past security into the MI6 building in London 'for a meeting' and not emerge for an hour or so. Neither of us could understand how he managed that.

Acklom strung her along for a year, isolated her from family and friends and gradually fleeced her of her £850,000 life savings. Then he fled, leaving her broke and suicidal. The police showed little interest in her plight, telling her to register her loss online with the national fraud reporting centre, Action Fraud.

Officers initially treated her with no regard to her emotional distress as the victim of a romance scam, so Woods filled in the fraud form and then, through a mutual friend who happened to be a journalist, approached me, asking if I would help her find Acklom. By then she had discovered all his lies – and that he already had a wife and two young children.

I agreed to help Woods for two reasons: she had been appallingly let down by police, and I already knew about Acklom from his extraordinary past. He had launched his fraud career when he was a sixteen-year-old pupil at a public school in Eastbourne, where he claimed to be a financial whiz kid. He conned a teacher into giving him £15,000 to gamble on the stock market. He also stole his father's gold AmEx card to hire a jet and fly his teenage pals to Paris and Switzerland for lunch. He went on to persuade a building society to lend him half-a-million pounds to buy a house. I remembered his sensational trial in 1991, at the Inner London Crown Court, where a judge rejected his lawyer's claims that Acklom, by then eighteen, needed psychiatric help. The young conman was jailed for four years.

After being approached by Woods, I discovered that in the intervening twenty-five years, Acklom used a number of aliases and left a trail of broken businesses and female hearts across Europe, amazingly without attracting any media attention. Shortly before he met Woods, and using the alias Dr Zac Moss, he unsuccessfully tried to con the Prince's Trust in Bristol out of money, offering to raise £8 million for it. Fortunately for the charity, its regional chairman resisted the deal because he was convinced that he would never see the funds. Acklom may have changed his name, but clearly, he hadn't altered his ways. When I spoke to his mother, she said she believed his behavioural problems were the result of a difficult birth. He was a fascinating subject for a crime reporter. I didn't have to think too hard about Carolyn Woods's request to help track him down.

Woods knew that after he vanished, Acklom had set up a business and an office in Alicante, Spain, but was later arrested there for an old fraud offence. Freed on bail, he did a midnight flit to San Remo on the north-west coast of Italy. After a lot of digging, I turned up a brief online newspaper report that said an unnamed British fraudster his age – by then he was forty-one – had been arrested and extradited back to Spain. It sounded like our man. Officially, the Spanish police wouldn't help, but an officer I'd befriended during an earlier Most Wanted appeal confirmed it was Acklom and that he was being held in the naval port of Cartagena. He was now calling himself Marc Ros Rodriguez.

I sat in on his one-day trial in which he was convicted of conning two brothers in a property deal. He duped them into paying £200,000 as a deposit on two riverside flats in Fulham, south-west London. The trouble was, Acklom didn't own the apartments. In fluent Spanish, he tried to convince the judges it was all a mistake and appeared to blame his co-defendant Josefina Munoz, a business partner.

I wrote to Acklom at his new prison in Murcia and he invited me to visit. I met him in the sweltering jail on a Sunday morning, the two of us seated six feet apart in a divided booth, separated by a scratched Perspex window and speaking by telephone. One of the first things he did was roll up his trouser leg, not to keep cool, but to show me a scar, caused, he told me, when Irish terrorists had tortured him during one of his MI6 missions. He barely paused for breath during our forty-minute meeting. I struggled to ask him many of the questions I wanted to put to him. He denied defrauding Woods and claimed his scams were no more than business ventures that had collapsed when partners pulled out after discovering his past.

Over the next seven months, Acklom wrote me ten letters. In tone and emotion they swung between anger, defiance, denial and contrition. In his first letter, typed and printed, presumably, off a prison computer, he wrote: 'I really settled down finally to concentrate on a good, decent, honest life loving my wife and our children. The saddest thing is I am a clever guy who has been wasted by the domino effect of what happened in 1991.' He wanted my help in telling his story in a book and even suggested we become friends. In another letter, handwritten this time in blue biro, he told me he had an appeal coming up and could get bail for €30,000. He wrote: 'Is there no way Sky can lend me the bail money? They get it back once the appeal ends. I will never run away again. I only have one last chance.' He signed off with 'big hug'.

All of this I reported back to Carolyn Woods and she passed it on to Avon and Somerset Police. They had finally shown an interest in her case, though the detectives assigned to investigate appeared to her to have little knowledge of the details. They certainly didn't know where Acklom was until we told them. By the time they got a European Arrest Warrant for him, Acklom had been freed from jail. He called to tell me he had won his appeal and would stay in touch. Then he vanished again. His name was later added to the same Most Wanted list as paedophile Matthew Sammon, but the Acklom trail had gone cold.

After failing to find any new leads, I teamed up with a remarkable investigator who was tracking Acklom online. She was working on behalf of dozens of people from across Europe who had also been conned by him, either in bogus business ventures or romance scams like Carolyn Woods. The victims had joined an online anti-fraud forum, sharing their stories in the hope of discovering where he was.

Anonymous for her own security, and known only as Charlie's Angel, the investigator emailed details of Acklom victims to the National Crime Agency's public hotline but got no response. She could not understand why more wasn't being done to find the trickster. And neither could I.

The Acklom case was a bleak and vivid illustration of UK policing's poor response to fraud, a crime that now affects more people than any other crime. His appalling story helped prompt a police watchdog report into fraud, a *Times* exposé of shoddy victim support and a damning review by former Scotland Yard Deputy Commissioner

Sir Craig Mackey, who found that fraudsters were being allowed to 'operate with impunity' because police forces were not equipped to investigate them. Like Woods, victims were still being told to fill in the same online questionnaire and speak to call handlers who followed up only a fraction of cases. One detective summed up the reason behind the lack of police interest: 'It's a crime that doesn't bang, bleed or shout.'

Most fraud cases don't involve tales of spies, beautiful women and millions of pounds. They are usually much more mundane, about far smaller sums and are carried out online. The Acklom story got picked up by other media in the UK and beyond and a lot of its appeal was the light it shone on the lack of support Carolyn Woods got from the police.

In 2021 chief constables were ordered to give fraud a much greater priority.

None of that was of any help to Carolyn Woods, of course, who, in 2016, was still encouraging me and the private investigator Charlie's Angel to help her because the police weren't. When Charlie was sent a photograph of Acklom, sitting at a pavement cafe in a busy street not far from Lake Geneva, she forwarded it to me. He was with a man who looked remarkably like another well-known fraudster. The picture had been taken by a victim of Acklom's who had spotted him as he walked past. By the time I got there Acklom was long gone, but it was the launch pad for more diligent and targeted research. Charlie's Angel managed to discover what Acklom was up to in Switzerland: he was living outside Zurich with his wife and daughters, running what appeared to be a legitimate company manufacturing black box data recorders for driverless cars. He had created a dynamic website designed to lure in investors, telling them he was the European representative of electric car pioneer Elon Musk. The mega-rich US entrepreneur, Acklom claimed, had put five billion Swiss francs into the project. I interviewed a German banker who admitted investing €400,000 in the black box idea after receiving a phone call from Acklom. He didn't even meet him.

Charlie's Angel and I told the British police Acklom was in Switzerland, and eventually he was arrested. He spent nearly a year in a Geneva prison before he was extradited to the UK. He pleaded with me in one of several letters: 'Please visit me here or in UK. You are my friend. The UK can't prevent a friend visiting. Help me, Martin. I can't cope anymore.' He also claimed his life would be in danger in a British jail but refused to say why. In another letter he wrote: 'Whatever happens, the truth will never come out in a courtroom, because the government would never allow it to. There are certain things I could never publish in a book either (my collaboration with SIS etc.)'.

Acklom eventually did a deal with British prosecutors and was jailed for five years and eight months. He pleaded guilty to five of the twenty fraud charges he faced over his swindling of Carolyn Woods. He was still insisting that the money he took from her was a series of loans that she had offered him, and he always intended to pay it back. In one of his last letters to me, in his oddly unjoined-up lettering, he wrote: 'Just a point of context. CW is not a "blond bimbo" or naïve. She is a highly intelligent and very well-educated lady.' There was no mention of the coercive control he had exerted over her because a new law recognising that particular crime did not come into force until after he went on the run. Woods got on with her life, with a new job and a new relationship, yet admitted she wasn't expecting to get back any of the money Acklom stole.

When Britain had to withdraw from the European Arrest War-rant system following Brexit, police fears that they would find it difficult to get back fugitives proved largely unfounded. A new deal with the EU known as the Trade and Cooperation Agreement more or less mirrored the EAW arrangements for fast-track extradition. The first post-Brexit statistics from the National Crime Agency, covering the 2021 calendar year, showed that the UK got 156 sus-pects extradited from the EU. In the final pre-Brexit year of 2020, the number was 179. The figures were likely to be skewed anyway by the effects of the global coronavirus pandemic, when both travel and the opportunity to commit crime were severely restricted.

During the same period, the NCA and Crimestoppers had scaled back the foreign launches of their Most Wanted campaigns. It was a shame because I always believed that our audience, be it on TV, the website or our growing digital platforms, loved to play detective. While viewers didn't actually go hunting them, at least they looked out for anyone they recognised from the list of suspects. That's ex-actly what happened when Britain's most notorious gangster went on the run. Police were swamped with calls from members of the public who thought they had seen him.

# CHAPTER 13

# THE DOUBLE KILLER

*I think they will never forget, and I am nervous. Now I have*
*to live the rest of my life in fear, in danger*
— Protected witness Martin Grant

Sometimes a scoop is staring you in the face, literally, and you choose to ignore it. In this case there were two faces involved. There was mine and one I didn't instantly recognise, a photofit of a suspect in one of Britain's first road-rage murders: a vehicle cut-up followed by a roadside punch-up that ended in a fatal stabbing beside the busy M25 London orbital motorway in Kent. The victim, Stephen Cameron, a passenger in a van, died in the arms of his teenage fiancée Danielle Cable, who had been driving. The killer sped off in his Land Rover Discovery, disappearing into the Sunday morning drizzle. A huge story. Police launched a manhunt to find the young electrician's murderer. Every crime reporter was calling contacts to find out what was really going on in the investigation.

On a day off, I was in a pub with Mike Cobb, Scotland Yard's most media-friendly press officer. He had just taken me and my partner on a tour of the Metropolitan Police's astonishing collection of crime artefacts housed in its private crime museum. As we ordered our drinks, Mike picked up a copy of the *Evening Standard* and pointed to the front page. On it was the photofit, created from the description given to police by the grieving Danielle Cable. Mike said almost in jest: 'Don't you think that looks like Kenny Noye?' I replied: 'Not really, maybe a bit. Isn't he still in prison?' With that we collected our glasses of wine, headed for a table and thought little more about the mugshot.

A few weeks later, via an internal message system, all UK police were put on alert for a man called Anthony Francis, with this warning about him: 'Violent, carries knives.' *Daily Mirror* reporter Christian Gysin had good police contacts and was told by a source that Noye, one of Britain's most notorious villains, was in the frame for the road-rage murder. Anthony Francis was one of his aliases. Gysin jumped in his car and drove to Sevenoaks Police Station, where the investigation into the killing was based, to try to speak to the detective in charge. Detective Superintendent Nick Biddiss invited Gysin into his office, but he refused to confirm anything. Why then, Gysin asked, did he have an aerial photograph of Noye's mansion on the wall behind him? An embarrassed Biddiss struggled to explain.

Biddiss later called Gysin's editor Piers Morgan and said if the *Mirror* named Noye it was likely that the suspect, who was thought to be in hiding in Northern Cyprus, would vanish again and might never be caught. The paper agreed not to publish Gysin's scoop, but several weeks later the *News of the World* got the same tip and ran the story as a big exclusive. I kicked myself for being scooped, but I had only myself to blame. In hindsight I was astonished that Mike

Cobb had actually spotted the Noye likeness from the photofit. For years, despite his infamy, and as far as I was aware, there had been only one published photograph of Noye, long-haired, smiling and smartly dressed in a dinner jacket and bow tie. Talking many years after the case, Gysin had a good memory of the saga and recalled: 'When my contact said it was Noye the police were looking for, he told me to just get out that old picture of him and compare it with the photofit. I did and it was obvious it was Noye, the spitting image of him.' Unfortunately, it hadn't been obvious to me. I kicked myself again.

Noye's criminal career has weaved in and out of my own as a crime reporter. My first encounter came when I flew, with a photographer, over Noye's home in Kent in a helicopter. It was the day after his acquittal for the murder of an undercover policeman in the extensive grounds of the mock-Tudor mansion. Noye stabbed Detective Constable John Fordham, one of a team of surveillance officers hunting the gang who got away with £26 million in gold bullion from the Brink's-Mat warehouse at Heathrow Airport in 1983, to death. Noye argued he had lashed out in self-defence when he found Fordham, dressed in black and wearing a balaclava, hiding in his garden late at night. An Old Bailey jury believed Noye's version of events and found him not guilty. But the Noye story didn't end there. He was later jailed after being found guilty of handling the stolen gold. He had been out of prison for only a couple of years when he stabbed and killed 21-year-old Stephen Cameron.

After two years on the run, Noye was located and captured near Cadiz in southern Spain, many miles from the villains' traditional playground of Marbella on the so-called Costa del Crime. I went to Madrid for his extradition hearing, full of anticipation at catching my first glimpse of a criminal whose notoriety had eclipsed that of all his contemporaries. It was an extraordinary moment when he was led in handcuffs through a small door into the bullet-proof glass cage of the dock. That one old photograph of Noye in his dinner suit and dicky bow had suggested he was a tall, handsome and well-built guy, but the suspect in front of me in jeans and anorak was a small, wiry, scowling figure who looked more like a jockey than a top gangster.

Maybe years in prison and his time as a fugitive had physically diminished him, but he was still full of menace, glaring around the courtroom like a caged animal. Gysin was there for the *Mirror*, along with the rest of the British press. We were all packed together on benches on one side of the courtroom. Noye obviously knew who we were. One by one, he stared us out. No prizes for guessing who blinked first. His Spanish lawyer Manuel Murillo claimed the only evidence against him was the word of Danielle Cable. His client looked nothing like the photofit she had helped compile, said the lawyer. I agreed on that point, unlike Christian Gysin.

None of that mattered to the Spanish judges, who had to decide only that the legal papers were drawn up correctly according to the renewed extradition treaty, the absence of which had once allowed previous British fugitives to live in Spain and hold a proverbial two fingers up at their police pursuers. Noye's only hope was to convince the judges he wouldn't get a fair trial in the UK because he had already effectively been convicted by all the media reporting into the road-rage killing. Noye's urbane and affable London solicitor Henry Milner recalled in his memoir *No Lawyers in Heaven*: 'I was surprised to notice that the three judges were continually smoking. They sat in silence throughout – never asking a question, which was not a particularly good sign, and I had little doubt as to the outcome.'

Noye was extradited a year later and with his lawyers began plotting a defence for his trial at the Old Bailey. I headed to the beautiful, windswept Costa de la Luz near Cadiz to start background research on Noye's life on the run. I teamed up with ex-pat Nigel Bowden, who had started working life as a marine biologist but discovered that acting as a translator and fixer for visiting reporters was more lucrative and much more fun. By the time I got there, Nigel had already found Noye's seafront hideaway villa in Atlanterra. He told me how he watched aghast as the first newspaper reporter he took there broke in by smashing a window. I imagine alcohol played a part in that little escapade.

How Kent Police tracked down Noye is still a bit of a mystery, with various versions emerging over the years: tipped off by a sharp-eyed tourist, betrayed by a criminal informant or tapped through his personal phone by the UK spy centre GCHQ. It may have been as simple as a surveillance team following Noye's wife Brenda when she got on a plane to visit him. Up to that point newspapers had reported various 'sightings' of Noye in Portugal, Tenerife, Russia, Dubai, aboard a Mediterranean yacht and even having a meal in his local Chinese restaurant. A police contact on the investigation team told me the detectives were worried about the effect of all the publicity.

He said:

We are bound to wonder whether Noye is behind a lot of the stories, trying to create an environment in which he couldn't possibly get a fair trial. The Chinese restaurant story should have won a prize for fiction. We had to check it out of course, but it was bollocks and we wasted time. The newspaper report had him downing brandies, but everyone who knows him says he's teetotal. Even when we are 99 per cent certain a story is crap, we can't afford not to follow it up.

At that stage there was no warrant for Noye's arrest because of a lack of evidence, said my source. 'That's not to say he wouldn't be arrested, but to suggest he's sneaking in and out under the nose of dozing cops is ridiculous.'

But was it ridiculous? The theory that Noye was still living quietly in his old Kent manor was reasonable, according to a man who himself was once dubbed 'Public Enemy No. 1.' John McVicar went on the run for two years in the 1960s after escaping from Durham jail where he was serving twenty-three years for armed robbery. 'It's much more difficult to stay hidden abroad because you don't have the resources and if you are discovered you have to find somewhere else to run,' said McVicar, a reformed, thoughtful and engaging figure who later earned a living as a writer. He was staying in a flat in Blackheath, south London, while police across the UK were hunting him. 'You mustn't exaggerate the problems of staying at large in this country, they are not that great. I even managed to have a holiday in Devon,' McVicar told me after cycling to my office to meet me. 'All you need are discipline and money and maybe a woman to care for you. It's better than prison.'

In his fugitive days in the 1960s, McVicar, of course, didn't have to contend with the huge advances in communications technology and 24-hour TV news that Noye had to be wary of. Once Noye was located, Kent Police moved swiftly in case he got tipped off they were on to him. In total secrecy they flew out Danielle Cable who, from a safe distance, identified him as her fiancé's killer. He was arrested in a restaurant the next day. Noye was certainly living in style. Police grabbed him in the Michelin Guide-recommended El Campero in the fishing port of Barbate, where the local almadraba tuna was served in twenty-five different ways. Noye, whose tastes were clearly a bit more prosaic, had just finished his red mullet when four undercover Spanish cops in shorts and T-shirts pounced, wrestled him to the ground and handcuffed him. He had with him – perhaps in keeping with McVicar's advice – a female dinner companion, his Lebanese–French girlfriend Mina Al Taiba. She had presumably made herself scarce when Mrs Noye visited.

News of the arrest sent a posse of reporters to Cadiz, where we met the detective chief whose officers had caught Noye and taken him to the city's police headquarters. It was there his fingerprints were matched with those on a glass retrieved from another restaurant he had visited the day before. The detective was happy to be interviewed on camera to discuss his role in the operation and, at one stage, did something I had only ever seen happen in a movie. He very obviously placed the Noye file on his desk and left the office. I took a deep breath, leaned over and opened the file, urging my cameraman to shoot what documents he could and be quick about it. The police chief returned a few minutes later and our interview continued. The paperwork included Noye's false passport, in the name of Alan Green, with a photograph in which his only disguise was a pair of spectacles. The name was hardly an imaginative alias, though it might have been his joke at the expense of a former Director of Public Prosecutions, Allan Green.

A year later I used the passport in my report of the first day of the Old Bailey trial. Kent Police wanted to know how I had got hold of a such vital exhibit. It was something their press office had been planning to hand out to all journalists, but only at the end of the hearing. I can't recall if I told them precisely how I got it, though it was nothing more than basic journalistic enterprise. I was surprised none of my rivals had got the same help from the Spanish police chief.

The trial was sensational, with Noye denying murdering Stephen Cameron. For reasons that were never entirely made clear, the two men got out of their vehicles and confronted one another at traffic lights on the M25 slip road. Noye claimed that in the punch-up that ensued Cameron got the better of him and was threatening to do more.

I took the knife out and pointed it. I see him and then said: 'Don't come near me you nutcase.' His girlfriend was shouting: 'Get off!' He's telling me he is going to kill me. He is just in a complete wild rage. He caught me with a couple of unlucky blows and I thought if he knocks me down and gets my knife out of my hand he is going to use it on me without a shadow of a doubt. I can't fight. I was worn out. I can't remember how exactly I done it, but then I struck out. I had my head down, and we were moving about close together, and I just struck out. I can only remember striking out once, but I accept it was twice. He definitely knew I had the knife.

Noye fought the case on the grounds of self-defence. Why not? It had worked before in the very same court. The prosecutor, much as he might have wanted to, couldn't tell the jurors that Noye had once stabbed a policeman to death because it would have been prejudicial to him receiving a fair trial. But, in a high-risk move, Noye decided to tell them anyway. He and his lawyers must have worried that jurors would remember Noye's first murder trial from fifteen years earlier. It had got massive publicity at the time, and so too had his later conviction for handling the Brink's-Mat gold. Noye was a highly unusual, memorable name. Even if only one juror had a good memory, he or she was almost certain to tell the others. Noye also had to explain why he was carrying a knife. He claimed it was for his own protection because he felt a marked man after killing an officer and never knew who might want to take revenge. On top of all that, he needed to give a good reason for running away after stabbing Mr Cameron; he told the court he thought that a second time around, he would not get a fair trial.

One of the prosecution witnesses was a colourful, if rather dubious, character, Hells Angel Alan Decabral. He said he had seen two men fighting, witnessed the stabbing and watched as Noye drove away smiling. Six months after Noye's murder conviction and life sentence, Decabral was shot dead by a hitman at a retail park in Kent. He had earlier told reporters he'd had death threats before the trial, which he assumed were intended to stop him giving evidence. Decabral was himself a career criminal involved in drugs and firearms supply and alcohol smuggling. Detectives interviewed Noye in prison as a suspect in arranging the hit, and they offered protection to other prosecution witnesses, but they also thought Decabral could have been the victim of a biker drugs war. Giving evidence against Noye was beginning to appear a risky business. Stephen Cameron's fiancée Danielle Cable went into the witness protection scheme, officially named the UK Protected Persons Service, having to change her name and move many miles away from her Kent home to start a new life.

I've always thought what a huge sacrifice that must be, having to leave everything and everyone behind, for ever. It's a stark choice: stay put and worry, or completely reinvent yourself, your present and your past. And what of your future? How much would you trust police to keep you safe in either situation? Danielle Cable has spent the majority of her life under witness protection and is, apparently, now married with a daughter. Because of the secrecy around her and the scheme we can't possibly know the level of threat she was under, nor how she has coped.

Danielle was persuaded to go into hiding when the police convinced her there was a price on her head for giving evidence against Noye, but he has reportedly said he bears her no ill will and hopes she can return to a normal life. But would she want to? She has spent longer in her new identity than she did as Danielle Cable.

Some protected witnesses can't help but return to their old lives. They take the risk because they can't stand being without their family and friends or simply because they can't settle in the scheme. Other protected witnesses say they find it impossible to make new, close friends because they have to lie about everything. I imagine you have to be tough and single-minded to survive in a brand-new life. Or just very scared by the alternative.

Martin Grant is another witness who chose to live under protection because of his connection with Kenny Noye. He helped police foil a plot to clone bank customers' cash withdrawal cards.

The Hole-in-the-Wall Gang, as it inevitably became known, planned to steal millions of pounds and could have heaped disaster on the banking system. Noye was allegedly involved in the plot and later was named in court as a conspirator who had played 'a prominent role' in the scheme. Grant, a friendly but rather nervous man, agreed to talk to me and even appear on camera. He was already living his new secret life. He wasn't disguised because he said that anyone who wanted to kill him already knew exactly what he looked like. On a chilly day I sat beside Grant, a tall and balding man, on a public bench on the edge of a shopping centre and let him tell me how he grassed up Kenny Noye.

He said it was about a year before the road-rage stabbing of Stephen Cameron and Noye was, by then, a free man. At the time, Grant, a computer expert, was in jail and coming to the end of his sentence. He had served eight years for the attempted murder of his wife and child. He explained how a prison officer offered him some temporary freedom, ostensibly to help set up a computer system for the officer's friends. Grant said:

> I was finishing my sentence at an open prison in Kent and looking forward to doing a university course, when a prison officer fixed day-release work for me to install a new computer system at a nearby garage. He took me off to Meopham Van & Car Hire and introduced me to three people, including Kenny Noye. The name didn't mean anything to me at the time.

The trio badgered Grant to join their plot. They had recruited telephone engineers to help tap into bank automated teller machines (ATMs), download customer account details and put them on to blank cards. Grant's job was to put together a computer system to control the operation and, he said, it worked on test runs.

> At first I didn't want to get involved, but I was threatened by them and their friends inside prison. One asked me if I had ever lost an

eye. They showed me details of my prison record, which should have been confidential within the prison service, and where my mum and brother lived and made threats against them.

Grant agreed to help the gang, but then reported it to the police. Scotland Yard's Flying Squad persuaded him to carry on with the conspiracy but as a police informant. For three months Grant got an insight into what he described as Noye's paranoia.

The remarkable thing about Noye was his obsession with security. The others told me it was all a result of him having killed the detective years before. He thought police were following him everywhere. Of course, some of the time he was quite right. Whenever we went out, we would drive around in circles, or miles out of our way before meeting up at a safe house with the others. If he wanted to discuss what we were up to we all had to troop off to the middle of a car park somewhere. If we went out to dinner we would never sit near a window because he thought the police would stick a listening device up to the outside wall.

Noye would keep his mobile phone switched off so it couldn't be tracked. He would also never discuss business in a house with a satellite dish. He was convinced police had a way of using them to listen in. For most of the time I spent with him Noye was a perfect gentleman, much more like a businessman than the others, but it was obvious he had a violent temper, particularly when things were going wrong. He seemed to be financing the operation because whenever I needed computer equipment someone would drive me to his house, or his skip business in Dartford, and he would hand us some money.

On Grant's evidence seven gang members were arrested, just as they were about to begin milking thousands of bank accounts. They admitted the plot and most were jailed but Noye, not for the first time, managed to avoid the same fate. Roy Ramm, the former commander in charge of Scotland Yard's Organised Crime Group, said: 'There was intelligence implicating Kenny Noye, but he knew his way around the law and stayed carefully in the background.' And anyway by that time, when the case drew to a close in December 1996, Noye had already been on the run for seven months after murdering Mr Cameron.

After our interview, Martin Grant walked off into a pedestrian tunnel towards the shopping centre and I never saw or heard from him again. I don't know where in the world he is living in his enforced anonymity and have no way of contacting him. I hope he is OK, because when we met, he told me something I've heard from other protected witnesses: that he was struggling to get the authorities to provide the life they had promised him. Those who go into the system are often disappointed because they expect an improved lifestyle as compensation for their sacrifice. What they actually get is 'like for like', a necessary arrangement their handlers believe will help them adjust more easily to their new life. One thing that's unlikely to change is their fear of retribution. Grant said just before he wandered off into the shadows of an underpass and an uncertain future: 'I think they will never forget, and I am nervous. I only have to hear something at the door, and it makes me jump. Now I have to live the rest of my life in fear, in danger.'

Crime reporters tend not to worry too much about retribution from villains. A few of us have been intimidated, threatened and, occasionally, physically attacked. Others have had to take extra security measures, lay low for a while or give up their jobs, but there is no history in the UK of serious violence. In Ireland, *Sunday Independent* investigative reporter Veronica Guerin was shot dead by a hitman on a motorbike in 1996, but she often got uncomfortably close to the underworld figures she wrote about. She had various direct threats and was once shot in the leg when she answered her front door.

Author Wensley Clarkson, one of Britain's best-known true crime writers, wrote three books about Noye, including *Kenny Noye: Public Enemy Number One*, and did incur the gangster's wrath, followed by what he took to be an indirect threat. A prison officer the author knew received a copy of the book from Noye, two years into his murder sentence. Inside was the handwritten inscription: 'I'm certainly no killer, Wensley Clarkson has published loads of lies about me in his books and caused untold damage. The tables will turn one day. All the very best, Ken Noye.'

Clarkson said:

> If you receive a threat like that it isn't going to happen. If a criminal has already threatened you he is not going to carry it out later because he has already exposed himself. The time you might really be in trouble is when a villain you've upset turns up without warning. People often ask me, in that middle-class dinner party way, if I get scared in the work I do, but to be honest I'm more worried about getting a parking ticket.

There are two sides to Kenny Noye. Moments after his conviction for handling the Brink's-Mat gold his temper got the better of him. He shook and screamed at the jurors: 'I hope you all die of cancer.'

Years later, on his release from jail, City lawyer Bob McCunn met a very different Noye: thoughtful, business minded and humorous. McCunn led a small legal team hired by the insurers of the gold bullion to try to recover the robbery proceeds. He eventually completed a series of out-of-court settlements with the villains involved. Remarkably, the lawyers retrieved £26 million, the exact value of the gold when it was stolen. But by that time, that figure represented only a small part of the true value of the traceable assets, through which the profits had been laundered. More astonishing was the fact that the lawyers managed to squeeze payments out of some of those acquitted of the robbery, and even from those who hadn't even been charged with any offence.

It was largely down to the lower standard of proof required by a civil court, but also thanks to Noye, as solicitor McCunn explained:

> We were faced with taking fourteen people to court, but that would have been uneconomic and so there was enormous pressure to do deals outside court. Kenny Noye had indicated he was prepared to talk to us and he was sensible and highly regarded by the others. So we thought we would start with him, and if we could get a deal with him the rest might follow.

It worked and the rest coughed up without a courtroom fight. Noye is thought to have paid back nearly £3 million, which he could apparently easily afford, but it was risky strategy for him. Because of his willingness to strike a deal with the underwriters, other gang members may have felt they had been railroaded into making similar agreements. People in the underworld fall out over much less.

Today Noye is a free man, judged to be no threat to the public but still on licence and under threat of a return to prison if he breaches any condition of his parole. It's probably a matter of keeping that legendary temper under control. Occasionally newspaper photographers go looking for him but sensibly they tread cautiously. You never see a close-up. If he still owns his old six-bedroom Spanish hideaway villa it has proved a good investment. It was up for sale recently at €1.9 million, six times what he apparently paid for it. The estate agent's website says the property has a 'very relaxing feeling of freedom'. And that smashed window has been mended.

Seventy-six years old at the time of writing, Noye may have settled for retirement. Perhaps he still has a lot of money. Even his adversaries have paid tribute to his business brain. Less successful villains are sometimes tempted to get involved in one last job, unable to resist a final roll of the dice, the chance to secure themselves a big pension pot. For some it's the lure of getting back into action, as described vividly by Ben Kingsley's character Don Logan in the film *Sexy Beast* when he's trying to entice safe-cracker Gal Dove, played by Ray Winstone, out of retirement for one last big heist: 'It's not about the money with you and me is it, Gal? It's the charge, it's the bolt, it's the buzz, it's the sheer fuck off-ness of it all.' For whatever reason, one of Noye's long-time associates couldn't resist the challenge of one last daring raid.

# CHAPTER 14

# THE DIAMOND WHEEZER

*After all, we didn't harm anyone, did we? Just a burglary*
— PRISONER DANNY JONES

I had a tip from a former newspaper colleague in April 2015 that there had been a raid at a safe deposit centre in Hatton Garden, the street known worldwide as the centre of London's jewellery quarter. In fact, I missed my friend's call and his voice message sat in my mobile phone for an hour before I listened to it. For a crime reporter there's a rough, descending order of top stories. Diamond heists sit just below serial killers. There hadn't been a big raid like this since Valerio Viccei's raid on the Knightsbridge safe deposit centre twenty-eight years earlier. I headed straight to Hatton Garden.

A uniformed policeman stood guarding the door of 88–90 Hatton Garden, which is on the corner of a five-storey block of offices that runs 100 yards along the street. Occasionally, a forensic officer clad in white coveralls went in and out. Worried jewellers from the many neighbouring stores and workshops, back after the long Easter bank holiday weekend, began to gather as word and gloom spread in equal measure.

It turned out that most of them kept their valuables locked overnight in the safe boxes deep in the underground vault, and many weren't insured. They used the centre because they couldn't afford the insurance premiums for storing gold and gems on their own premises, either, welcoming what they believed was the vastly better security offered at No. 88–90.

Nobody on the street had any real idea of what was going on and, due to most premises being closed during the Easter break, they certainly hadn't seen anything. The police said only that they were investigating a burglary that had happened sometime over the holiday weekend. Despite having so little detail to go on, I started reporting live from the scene and soon I was joined by many other colleagues from television and newspapers. The story took on greater importance when we learned the investigation was being run by the Flying Squad.

Historically, the squad dealt with armed robberies, of which there were many in its heyday, but such crimes had largely tailed off because of better security and also because several 'pavement artists', as the police called them, were shot dead. By police. The squad developed a glamorous sheen and was immortalised in the 1970s TV drama series *The Sweeney*. Senior officers played down the idea that it was an elite group of detectives, but many aspired to join and wore with pride the squad's tie with its emblem of a swooping eagle.

The Flying Squad didn't normally investigate burglaries, but it took charge of Hatton Garden because it was clearly going to become a high-profile case, the value of the stolen loot, at the heart of a world-famous jewellery quarter, would be high and already there were whispers that those involved might be familiar to the specialist detectives. One name that cropped up early on was Brian Reader. He was a well-known villain who was jailed for handling the gold stolen in the Brink's-Mat robbery at Heathrow Airport in 1983. He had also been acquitted, alongside his friend and neighbour Kenny Noye, of the murder of undercover policeman John Fordham.

When I called Commander Peter Spindler, in overall charge of the investigation, and asked him directly if Reader was a suspect, he wouldn't confirm or deny it. He explained recently: 'The first thing I did after your call was ring John Fordham's son because I thought that Reader's name might come out and I should prepare him for that.' Reader, by then an old-age pensioner, was eventually charged and convicted over the raid, memorably arriving on the night of the heist by bus, using a friend's free travel pass.

I was forever tempted to call the raid a robbery, but it wasn't. This is because in strict legal terms a robbery has to include violence or the threat of it. Robbery covers everything from a bank raid to a street mugging, as long there is a human victim who is hurt or frightened. The Hatton Garden robbery sounded much more exciting than the Hatton Garden burglary, but that's what it was, a commercial burglary. The safe deposit centre was empty at the time, so there was no one to frighten or bash up. Robbery usually carries a much higher sentence than burglary. To avoid confusion, and to play up the spectacular nature of the burglary, we called it a heist, a word that covers a multitude of sins. The Hatton Garden Heist rolled off the tongue. It was good alliteration.

The gang hadn't even broken into the main building above the vault, because one of them somehow had keys to the front door. Once inside, to restore some professional pride, they did do a bit of proper burgling by disabling alarms, jamming a lift and removing the hard drive from a CCTV camera system. Then they used specialist equipment to bore a hole through the 50cm-thick concrete wall into the safe deposit vault. Inside were all sorts of treasures, including gold, cash and jewellery, locked in hundreds of metal boxes. The raid took a long time, because the gang's diamond-tipped Hilti drill didn't work properly on the first night and they had to hire more equipment. It all happened over two days of the Easter Bank Holiday weekend, to take advantage of the fact that the building and the surrounding offices were closed.

All but one of the gang were arrested six weeks later, after a catalogue of their own basic errors. They managed to leave one CCTV camera working. One burglar, John Collins, used his own car on the raid and when another, Danny Jones, bought a replacement bit of equipment on the second day, he gave his own name and address. They also failed to realise the police were capable of bugging their pub meetings and tracking their mobile phones after the raid, when they were under suspicion and surveillance. Commander Spindler described them as 'analogue criminals in a digital world'. The brightest one, it seemed, was a man known to the others as Basil, who had keys to the building and was the one who disabled the alarms. He had also been clever enough to disappear afterwards.

The gang appeared in the dock for the first time on 21 May 2015. They arrived in a fleet of vans, escorted by heavily armed police who shut off roads around Westminster Magistrates' Court. As they stood in the dock, flanked by prison guards, it was clear these were not young men and were unlikely to try to storm their way to freedom. *The Sun* had already dubbed them the 'Diamond Wheezers' in a play on the often-used 'diamond geezers' phrase. When the clerk asked them their names, they all managed to stand up un-aided. Seldom had the three court artists present used so much of their grey crayons in one drawing. The four who were to emerge as the ringleaders were the oldest. Brian Reader was seventy-six, John Collins was seventy-four and Terry Perkins was sixty-seven. The fourth main gang member was Danny Jones, at fifty-eight hardly a youngster. What also singled out Jones was his response to the charge. His solicitor told the district judge Tan Ikram that he would be pleading guilty. No one else gave a hint of their intentions, nor were they asked to. It was early days.

The gang were driven off to begin many months in a special unit at the high-security Belmarsh Prison in south-east London. I left court puzzled that Jones had already admitted his role. He was planning to confess to a charge of conspiracy to burgle. You can't conspire to do anything on your own. In effect, he was implicating the others. They can't have been very happy about that if they were intending to plead not guilty when it came to their own trials. I also thought that if Jones wasn't going to fight the charge, and he had said so rather blatantly in front of the media, maybe he would be willing to talk about the heist at some stage. He was certainly going to have plenty of time to think about the possibility as he languished in his prison cell. A few days later, again more in hope than expecta-tion, I wrote him a letter. I had no idea whether he would respond, or even if the jail authorities would let him receive mail, let alone a letter from a crime reporter. He was, after all, one of Britain's most high-profile prisoners and was being held in maximum security with many restrictions. To my great surprise, I didn't have to wait long for a reply.

Jones's first letter arrived, in the stamped and addressed envelope

I had also sent him, within about six weeks. It was handwritten in biro on two of the several plain sheets I had enclosed in my letter to him. In many ways, it was much more than I had expected. It was warm, informative and humorous.

This is what he wrote:

Martin thanks for your most welcome letter. Well at this moment I am in the special unit double AA cat [category]. Be truthful with you Martin as it came as a bit of a shock as it's a prison within a prison as we are not killers, paedophiles, terrorists. It was a commercial burglary. We haven't had no visits. It's took almost five weeks to get our mail as they say they're short staffed. It's really wrong as I can't see some of this so-called gang getting through this once sentenced, as a guy has cancer, he's 76, another with a heart condition aged 68, also another 75, myself 58. You probably know all this following the case at court. Myself I'm pleading guilty as I have done from day of my arrest. Martin, about telling the story to you accurately, I would but at this moment in time I think it's a bit early.

I have had other people writing to me, crime correspondents, as you can imagine. I think this has been blown out of the water, what with the media, internet, different points of view, Oceans 11. I suppose it sells newspapers as the public love all this, which I haven't any control of. As you are right, I know what went on the start to finish as I was there and I am going guilty. Martin, I myself don't want any fame from this burglary. It is what it is, a burglary, a hole in the wall. Once again the police have made it like a film. They should have turned up when the burglary was in progress and the alarm went through to central station, but they never did. I wont go on. When the time's right I will give you the truth and nothing but the truth and let the truth be known. After all, we didn't harm anyone, did we? Just a burglary, a commercial. I will finish this letter now, good luck. God bless, Danny Jones, Just a hole in the wall, nothing more.

From his words it was clear he was playing down the gravity of the crime in the face of widespread publicity. For all Jones's modesty, it was a bit more than just a hole in the wall. The initial perception was of a daring raid on a seemingly impregnable fortress, and the theft of millions of pounds' worth of gold and diamonds from wealthy owners, most of whom could probably stand the loss. Among the early suspects, in the public's mind at least, were the notorious Pink Panther gang, the infamous jewellery thieves behind a string of heists in the South of France. From the start, it was understandably front-page news and led many TV news bulletins.

When it turned out that it was a bunch of old British villains, some of them pensioners, who had managed to bypass security, scramble down a lift shaft and drill through a concrete wall, and escape with the loot, it became an even bigger story.

I thought Jones's first letter would probably be his one and only and filed it in my desk. It would be a great addition to my background report for the end of the trial of the gang members who were pleading not guilty. I got a call soon after from a friend of Jones, a man called Paul, and went to meet him. He told me a bit more about Danny and his life inside the Belmarsh special secure unit. He was speaking with Jones's permission, but he was still rather guarded. I told Jones this in my second letter to him. His reply, written on lined paper torn from a ringed pad, said:

Hello Martin, hope this finds you in good spirit. Well, I'm pleased you see Paul as I spoke to him on the phone. Martin, it's only early days at the moment and there are things I can't explain to you as you must appreciate my situation, but when the time comes right in the future and the court case is over and I know where I stand. As when I get out of the double cat AA I will send you a visit and maybe we can get things rolling as at this moment I don't know where I am. Martin, I can't understand how I've ended up in this special unit, as it's a commercial burglary not a terrorist act on mankind, as they regard money more than life in this country.

All they said in the papers, dads army. Well, let me tell you, dads army are like super sportsmen compared with this gang. Run? They can barely walk. One has cancer, he's 76, another heart condition 68, another 75 can't remember his name, 60-year-old with two new hips and knees, Crohn's Disease. I won't go on, it's a joke. If they ever make a film they would call it Rebirth of Dads Army.

The third letter was on official paper with a HM Prison Belmarsh stamp in pink on the first page. Jones had formally written his name and prison number in the spaces allocated for them. At the top was a printed instruction: 'When writing to Members of Parliament please give your previous home address in order to avoid delay in your case being taken up by the MP.' Thankfully, Danny was showing more faith in a crime reporter than a politician. This letter, I reckoned, was gold dust. He wrote:

Hello Martin, hope my letter finds you well. Martin, I have some interesting news for you and if possible let it out to the media, as I've instructed my solicitor Mark Davies six weeks ago to tell the police Flying Squad that I want to give back my share of Hatton Garden burglary. They said it's in motion. I now understand that the police said that the prison Belmarsh won't release me to the police. What a load of bull. As the police can't want it back as I'm the only person in the world to know where it is deep down. I want to do the right thing and give it back. They are trying to make me look a bad person. I'm trying my best to put things right and for some reason they don't want me to give it back. I will want them to take me under armed guard with my solicitor and yourself. I will return the goods. If I don't get the chance to go out under armed escort I hope some poor sod who's having it hard out there with his or her family finds the lot and has a nice life as you never know Martin, people do find things don't they?

I want you to let the public know my situation and that I'm trying to do the right thing and return the goods. You'd think I'm a terrorist, a killer. Fuck me, Martin, it was a hole in the wall, but as we all know money becomes more than life in this country, don't you agree? You would have thought the police would have jumped with joy, but for some reason which I don't know they are not that interested. As I do know that if the police wanted to take a prisoner from a prison they go to the Home Office and it's done as the prison have no say. As they took that sex killer out of here, Levi Bellfield a few years ago [and] he showed them where he killed those women. So there you go, Martin, a sex killer and there's me, a 58-year-old burnt-out burglar. Maybe they think I'm going to get [a] hit squad to get me out, my god how stupid.

Yes, I am frustrated Martin, wouldn't you be mate knowing I'm going to prison for a long time. All I want to do is let my two sons know I'm trying to change for the best, I know I've done wrong. I'm not crying Martin, I did it. I can't talk for other people, only for myself, and whatever I get on judgement day I will stand tall. But I want to make amends to all my loved ones and show I'm trying to change. I know it seems a bit late in my life, but I'm trying, but at this moment these police are giving me no hope. Do your best for me as there's a lot more to come in the future and that's the truth. God bless, Danny Jones.

Well, that was some confessional, and even more astonishing as it appeared Jones was begging the police to take him out of prison to show them his buried treasure. But did I believe him? I thought initially that it was a wind up, that he was having a bit of fun at my expense. It was an extraordinary story, but I would look stupid if I ran it and it wasn't true. I also thought that if I published anything he had written to me, the prison authorities would stop any more letters. As Jones had urged me, I called his solicitor Mark Davies. He was courteous enough, but he didn't want to discuss the matter. I wasn't even sure if he knew Jones had been writing to me. If he didn't, that must have come as a bit of a shock. I wrote back to Jones and received a fourth letter in reply:

I got your letter today, so out of respect I've written back. This will make you laugh: I wrote to the Archbishop of Canterbury about not getting any visits and the reply was from his correspondence sec-retary. The reply was he couldn't help me, but will pray for me in his next church service. He also said sorry you got mixed up in the Hatton Garden heist. And finished off by saying 'Just being famous must seem like a pretty poor reward, best wishes, Lambeth Palace.' A man of god. I haven't heard from the police concerning the stuff I want to give back, as I've already told you in my last letter. Apart from that the trail has gone cold. You said do I need anything, matter of fact Martin there is something I need – God. Cheers Martin, god bless, Danny Jones.

By now I was building up quite a treasure trove of prison letters for the report I would compile when the case was all over. I kept writing to Jones to encourage him to write back. When I didn't hear from him for some weeks, I thought that maybe we had come to the end of our correspondence. It had been a good run and, as far as I knew, he wasn't writing to any other reporter. Then I found a fifth letter waiting in my pigeonhole:

> Alright Martin, I don't know if you have been getting my letters, as I haven't received any of your letters, maybe the prison are holding them back, who knows? Still no visits, as I give up. It's nothing to do with the Home Office, it's the police Martin. My solicitor can't get no joy out of them. They say they are busy, I won't go on about it as all you do is drive yourself mad. I'm just waiting for the police to take me out, giving them back part of the stolen goods. I think I told you in my last letter. They won't let me know if they're coming to take me out. Security reasons. They better hurry up, we don't want anyone finding it, do we? That was three weeks ago, they don't seem to be bothered. I suppose they are too busy at this moment. I'm only trying to do the right thing Martin, as I said in my last letter to you. Martin, I hope you get this letter. As from now on I won't be writing to you, but there's always Paul? I will drop you a line after I get sentenced, hopefully a few months time. All the best.

That really did seem to signal the end of our relationship, though I hoped it would resume sometime. Now Jones and the other three ringleaders, Reader, Perkins and Collins, were all pleading guilty. They would be sentenced after the trial of the other gang members who were pleading not guilty. The trial was looming and it made sense for Jones to stay quiet. Although I was tempted, I still wasn't intending to publish anything he had written because I feared it would prejudice the trial of the others. I wrote my thanks and mentioned that my father had died recently. Jones wrote back:

> Very sorry about your dad, it must be a great loss as dementia not a nice thing, so sad. Mind you, Martin, great age 88 isn't it? I bet you have some great times together over the years. I've just got my visits passed, about time or what Martin? Yes, Martin, I am trying to do the right thing, as to be truthful with you I can't work the police out. Strange or what, I won't go on about it as you know what I said in my last letter and thanks mate I do appreciate it that you will look into it.
>
> Since I've been here I haven't stopped looking at the news. My god, Martin, half of the people looking after this country are kiddy fiddlers. Can you believe it, all get bail destroying a child's life for ever, all are in a position of trust and it just gets pushed aside and forgot. I've drilled a hole in the wall. I'm the worst person on the planet. I won't go on, alright mate, as I wind myself up over shit, the world's going crazy as you see it before most people being a crime correspondent. Anyway, Martin, my tea is being served up now, the food is fantastic, served up, bone china on a silver tray. God bless, Danny Jones.

It was the fourth letter in which he had told me he was trying to do the right thing and show the police where he had buried his share of the Hatton Garden loot. And, again, he was urging me to look into the police refusal to take up his offer. I spoke to Sky's lawyer and he advised that to run the story was unlikely to be seen to prejudice the trial of the other gang members. I rang Scotland Yard and asked a press officer if Jones was telling the truth. The next day the chief press officer called me back and tried to warn me off. Without confirming anything, he said I might want to consider that even if it was true, whatever Jones was offering to give back may not be his own share. If any of the others felt it was theirs, they would be far from happy, Danny would be seen as a grass and could be in danger of physical harm, he said. If the police *were* trying to steer me away from the story, I thought, then the chances were, it was probably true. We weighed all this up and decided to run the report on air. After all, the first time Jones had asked for my help he said he wanted the public to know he was trying to do the right thing. I was sure some news organisations would have run the story straightaway.

My report about Danny Jones wanting to lead police to where he'd hidden his loot, including extracts from his prison letters, finally ran across Sky's television, website and digital platforms on 8 October, nearly six months after the heist. Other media repeated it. I didn't say where the stolen valuables were hidden. I couldn't, because Jones hadn't told me that much. A week later, a convoy of police vehicles, some with heavily-armed officers on board, collected him from his cell at Belmarsh and let him direct them through twenty-two miles of busy traffic to Edmonton Cemetery, not far from where he lived in north London. I wasn't invited and learned about it later. A police helicopter flew above the convoy all the way. Once inside the cemetery gates Jones clammed up.

Half-an-hour later, his solicitor Mark Davies was working at his desk when his receptionist buzzed through to say there were police officers to see him. He told me:

I said they haven't got an appointment, so find out what it's about.

And the receptionist said well, they want you to go with them and I said, no, I've got work to do. I thought I haven't committed a crime so they're not going to arrest me, though that's not a bar to being arrested as we all know. The long and short of it was the copper came into my office and said they'd got Danny in a secure location and needed me to go with them and have a word with him. It became clear he was going to show them where some of the property was, but he wouldn't do it unless I was there.

The officers took Davies in their green Jaguar to the cemetery where he said he was staggered by the sight that greeted him.

It was like a mafia funeral. There were six or eight high-value cars, not obvious police vehicles, all lined up inside the entrance and at least six machine guns dotted around the place. There was a helicopter overhead and I could see Danny sitting in the back of a car in chains, with two armed officers close by. They told him the security was so tight because they believed he had the means to finance an escape. He said, why would he turn a seven-year sentence into a fourteen?

A short distance from the main gate, Jones pointed to a memorial stone. It was in one of several rows of plaques marking the buried ashes of people who had been cremated. The name on the stone was Sidney John Hart, a relative of Jones's partner Valerie Hart. He told the police that under the stone they would find his share of the Hatton Garden loot. 'That's all I had,' a poker-faced Jones told them as they waited to remove the plaque where he'd hidden a plastic bag of jewels. Five minutes later he was put back in the car and the armed convoy, still with the helicopter overhead, drove south back to Belmarsh jail.

His solicitor, who was left standing among the graves with the Flying Squad officers and forensics team, said:

The reason Danny wanted me there was he didn't trust the police not to keep some of it for themselves. He's old-school, from a background of alleged Flying Squad dishonesty and he wanted me to ensure fair play. After he'd identified the grave there was a hitch, because the police hadn't got the necessary consent to enter the grave, so we had to sit there for four or five hours waiting for permission.

I wish I'd been there, with a camera crew.

'I hadn't taken my car because I didn't want to lose my space at work, where parking is a premium. It was a chilly day, and I was beginning to get cold,' Davies continued.

One of the officers had some gym kit in his car and offered me a fleece, but it was a medium and I'm a double XL. My abiding memory of that day was me sitting freezing on a bench in a graveyard wearing a fleece three sizes too small for me and waiting for the Church of England to sanction the breaking of holy ground. I didn't have anything to eat or anywhere to go to the toilet. I think the cops thought it was hilarious. After all, I am the enemy.

They might have been a bit more sympathetic towards him if they had known Davies's late father Arthur was a Metropolitan Police officer who, strangely enough, had arrested Danny Jones as a boy.

It was another six weeks before the whole saga of the cemetery search was revealed. It came during the second day of the trial of four men who were pleading not guilty to carrying out the Hatton

Garden raid. What the prosecutor revealed in court, for the first time, was the extraordinary game of double bluff that both Danny Jones and the police had been playing with each other. It turned out that Jones had hidden not one but *two* stashes in the cemetery, one bigger and more valuable than the other. In offering to show police the smaller of the two, he thought he could go back, when he was eventually freed, and dig up the bigger one. What *he* didn't know was that the police had already found it and, initially at least, must have thought that was all there was. That explained their long refusal to take him to the cemetery.

The valuables recovered from both graves consisted of gold, jewellery and single gemstones, wrapped up in plastic Sainsbury's bags. Together the two stashes were valued at around £500,000. What puzzled me was that the Flying Squad actually dug up the first stash on the day I broke the story of Jones's rejected offer to help them. Detective Superintendent Craig Turner, in charge of the investigation, insisted later the timing was pure coincidence. The Flying Squad had been planning to dig up the grave for some time and just happened to do it a few hours after they read my story. Turner refused to tell me how they found out about it. It still seems odd that they would have dithered at all when more than half-a-million pounds of stolen gems was at stake.

The four ringleaders, including Jones, had to await the outcome of the trial of the other gang members before learning what their sentences would be. One of those on trial was Carl Wood, a drinking pal of Danny's who described their thirty-year friendship and shared passion for keep-fit. In his evidence Wood described Danny as a sensitive and funny man who studied crime in books, films and on the internet. He also said Jones was an eccentric who slept in his mother's dressing gown and a fez hat like the one made famous by the comedian Tommy Cooper. After Wood was convicted, Jones sent me another letter. He complained about the bizarre description given of him in court, which was widely reported in the media, and then explained how he was recruited to the Hatton Garden gang by Basil, the real mastermind of the plot who was still on the run.

The Sun said I was an East End villain with a passion for women and daring crimes, and on the flip side of the story I sleep in a pink dressing gown which was my dead mother's and a Tommy Cooper hat. I can't be a super thief and a raving lunatic at the same time. I suppose it sells papers.

Basil was the brains as I was recruited by him, he let me in on the night of the burglary, he had keys and codes throughout the building. He said that no police wouldn't turn up as he had everything in control. He had inside help, he said the cameras wasn't working inside the building and the alarm system wasn't fit for a sweet shop. He said the safe deposit company was closing, as it wasn't making money. It was running a loss, that's why a certain person in the company, a trusted position, stuck the safe deposit up to be burgled.

That's all I know as Basil knew everything. We were just there under his guidance, where to drill, what to do and how to get in. I saw Basil about four times throughout. He came and went. I don't know nothing about him, where he lives, I wasn't interested. I can say that someone told me he was an ex policeman who got into security by the guy who introduced him to me. He said Basil knew about me from a close friend on the police force, as I was arrested for a similar raid in Bond Street in 2010. And that's how I was recruited for the Hatton Garden burglary.

As Basil said, we would be safe right from the start. If that ain't an inside job, Martin, I am Tommy Cooper. You don't need any brains to work it out.

The ringleaders, including Jones, were jailed for seven years. He didn't get any reduction on his sentence for showing police where he had buried at least some of his share of the loot. The final tally of what was stolen continued to change, up to £29 million at one stage, with most of it still missing. Trial Judge Christopher Kinch said the burglary stood 'in a class of its own in the scale of the ambition, the detail of the planning, the level of preparation and the organisation of the team carrying it out, and in terms of the value of the property stolen'. If Jones had once been looking for such kudos it was lost on him by the time he began his sentence, as he made clear in his final letter, three weeks later:

Martin, I'm pleased I'm off the double Cat A unit as it seems if I've come back to planet earth. Martin, I'm not writing any book or give anybody the say so about a film as everyone wants to get on the bandwagon. Let it die, it's all over. I'm not crying, I got caught, I will deal with it. I don't want anybody to feel sorry for me either. Everybody just get on with their lives and maybe this crime will fade away as it's become boring. As something else will take its place, another drama, terrorist, a rapist, paedophile and those corrupt politicians, not a hole in the wall.

I've got to wait ten months until the POCA [Proceeds of Crime Act hearing] comes up. I am also told they are keeping us in Belmarsh at least another twelve months as we have been put on hold as I thought we would have been made D cats by then and so did everybody else think the same. Never mind, they are going to make [it] difficult for us. It's a high profile case and the police did get egg on their faces. I will have a face to face with you, but I've got this POCA business to go through first as you must understand my situation, but I haven't spoke to anybody about films and books. I'm ok, I train in my cell twice a day, but I will be starting the prison gym shortly. It helps us. I've trained since a kid, raced across the Sahara desert, foot race, 160 miles racing the planet in 2006 like the Marathon Des Sables, run Hadrian's Wall 86 miles, Giants Causeway and many more adventures. Never smoked, drunk, always kept a clean life. Yes, one downfall, I was a thief and now at my age sitting in a prison cell. I feel like an old dinosaur as these places and the cons have changed from what I once knew 30 years ago. So the quicker I get out the better as I've got a job to go to working for Hilti drill centre. God bless mate, I will keep in touch.

His freedom had gone for a while, but at least he hadn't lost his sense of humour. Two years later, though, his sentence was almost doubled when he refused to pay back £6.6 million the police thought he had somehow kept. Jones said he had nothing left to give them. He served about seven years in the end, and the last I heard he was trying to settle back at home in north London. I still have his telephone number and he has mine, but to date, we've not spoken. Maybe I need to leave him to get on with his life, though I doubt that will be easy. With all that loot still missing he knows that all sorts of people will continue to show an interest in him: police, insurance investigators and, almost certainly, other criminals.

I'll be forever grateful for Danny's replies to my letters, especially as they led to police recovering some of the stolen jewels. I'll never forget the kindness he showed after the loss of my father, either. Most of the many letters I've written over the years to other prisoners have remained unanswered. The Yorkshire Ripper Peter Sutcliffe and Moors murderer Myra Hindley ignored me to the end, dying in jail without ever being tempted to write back to me. I'm still awaiting a response from House of Horrors killer Rose West, but I'm not hopeful she'll get in touch.

I had never heard of Danny Jones before he was nicked for the Hatton Garden raid, but he was well-known to other villains. Having the respect of your criminal peers is one thing, even welcomed by some, but becoming infamous for a notorious crime is not a good idea. It puts you firmly on the police radar and, if you wanted to go back to your old ways, you may find other criminals reluctant to work with you because of the attention you might draw. As we've heard, Bruce Reynolds said that being known as the mastermind of the Great Train Robbery became a millstone around his neck. When he came out of prison he couldn't get work, legal or illegal.

I'm not suggesting for a moment that Jones might return to crime – in fact, he said in his letters he planned to go straight – but in playing down the seriousness of the heist he may have been thinking of Reynolds's experience. By revealing Danny's correspondence with me I must have played a part in raising his profile, but I don't suppose either of us thought about the long-term effects. At the time, he was desperate to hand back his loot, or some of it at least, and I was after a good story. Danny, the police, me and my viewers, we all got what we wanted. It doesn't always work out like that.

Yes, it was a commercial burglary, attracting sentences much shorter than a robbery, but it's not difficult to see why it got so much publicity. So many old Flying Squad detectives were wheeled out to compare it with Valerio Viccei's raid on the Knightsbridge safe deposit vault near Harrods in 1987.

In an era of drugs gang warfare, rising teenage murders, escalating sex offences and an explosion in online fraud, the public saw the Hatton Garden raid as a crime caper, redolent of the much-loved Ealing comedy films of the 1950s and a poke in the eye of the Establishment. They were cheered on as loveable rogues. Goodness, the ageing lookout man apparently fell asleep on the job. At seventy-four, it must have been way past his bedtime. Such was the appetite for the details of the story and the characters involved, it inspired three movies and a major TV series soon afterwards.

It was crime as entertainment, up to a point. The reality is that most of the victims were small-time jewellery traders whose livelihoods were already under threat. They were being squeezed out of their tiny workshops by the new Crossrail transport link that was attracting new businesses and inevitable rising rents. Some long-established craftsmen were ruined by what they lost in the raid.

Some of the gang had serious previous convictions going back years. They probably got the sentences they deserved. One died inside and all but one are thought to be free. And most of the loot, according to the police, is still missing.

# CHAPTER 15

# THE TROLLS

*Although prosecutions have taken place against individual trolls
who have made a relatively small number of abusive comments
about their victims, no action ever seems to be taken
against those who target the McCanns*

– ANONYMOUS CAMPAIGNER

**D**epending on which way the wind is blowing, when you fly into Lisbon there are two ways to approach Humberto Delgado Airport. If you appreciate a good view, and you're lucky, the plane will carry you from the coast, up the gaping estuary of the River Tagus, across the 25 April suspension bridge and swoop low above the terracotta roofs of the old Alfama district in all its faded pastel glory. At the top of the vast Edward VII park, thirty seconds before you land, you will pass the five-storey concrete block of the Palácio da Justiça, which houses the Civil Court. It was there, in a crowded courtroom in 2009, that I watched Kate and Gerry McCann begin a long libel battle over claims they had played a part in their daughter Madeleine's mysterious disappearance two years earlier.

The McCanns sued author Gonçalo Amaral, the Portuguese detective who originally led the search for their daughter. He officially interrogated the McCanns as suspects before the case was closed, unsolved, in 2008. Soon after, Amaral retired and published his book, *The Truth of the Lie*. In it, he alleged that Madeleine, who was nearly four, died accidentally in the family's rented holiday apartment. He said her parents covered up her death and falsely claimed she'd been abducted.

The McCanns won the first round in their libel action and were awarded €500,000 damages against Amaral. But their victory was overturned in the Lisbon Court of Appeal. The appeal decision was supported by the Portuguese Supreme Court. The couple's ultimate defeat, in September 2022, came at the European Court of Human Rights in Strasbourg, where they had argued that the Portuguese courts had let them down by failing to protect their human right to be presumed innocent. The decision prompted hundreds of comments on the internet that criticised the couple, damned them and worse.

The parents had sued for libel because they believed Amaral's accusations against them would discourage anyone from looking for Madeleine, especially after the Portuguese police investigation fizzled out. But things had changed since then, they said. A new investigation, by Portuguese, German and British police, had been going for several years and had even identified a new suspect in their daughter's abduction.

What hadn't changed, though, was the level of vitriol that has been aimed at the McCanns almost from the day Madeleine vanished. A

Sky News report of the European Court decision, posted on You-Tube, attracted hundreds of comments, virtually all of them critical and many of them hateful. I was hardly surprised. And I don't suppose the parents were, either.

Kate and Gerry McCann have become, probably, the most vilified couple ever on social media, routinely subjected to accusations, threats and ridicule by anonymous internet trolls. No case has intrigued me, or occupied my time, as much as Madeleine's disappearance from Praia da Luz, a pretty seaside resort on the Algarve coast, in May 2007. The McCanns left her sleeping with her younger twin siblings Sean and Amelie, checking on the children every thirty minutes, while they dined with friends nearby. On the last check, she had vanished. This, more than anything, appears to have determined the public attitude towards them. People simply can't forgive the parents for leaving their daughters and son alone in an unlocked apartment. If their critics had their way, Madeleine's parents would have been charged with child neglect and may have spent time in Lisbon's old central prison. As they approached the Civil Court for the libel hearing each morning, the McCanns walked right past the jail's castellated wall. A sobering reminder, perhaps, of what might have been, though they fiercely denied they had abandoned their children.

Almost everyone I've met in Portugal, most UK police officers I ask and some of my family and friends, believe the McCanns played some part in their daughter's disappearance. That opinion flies in the face of the evidence, or lack of it. Two investigations, by the Portuguese police and the UK's Scotland Yard, ruled out the McCanns as suspects. A German prosecutor, who now leads the Madeleine investigation, says he has good evidence for her abduction against a convicted German sex offender. And it has nothing to do with her parents. But all of that has done little to curb the torrent of bile that is still poured on the couple on the internet. The trolling of the McCanns is a largely untold story. My efforts to tell it resulted in one of the couple's antagonisers killing herself.

Social media isn't exactly a new phenomenon. 'What hath God wrought?' asked the American inventor Samuel Morse, stealing a Biblical quotation for the first coded message he tapped out on his electronic telegraph system on 24 May 1844. Morse code, with dots and dashes signalling letters of the alphabet, became arguably the first social media platform. 'Telegraph operators could chat with each other by tapping on their keys. All the operators along the line could hear everything that was transmitted, and join in the unofficial banter, in effect occupying a single, shared chat room,' author Tom Standage wrote in his book *Writing on the Wall: Social Media – the First 2,000 Years*.

More than a century and a half after Morse came the first truly global networking sites, in which information could be shared instantly around the world. In 2004, Mark Zuckerberg launched Facebook. Two years later Jack Dorsey invented Twitter. Suddenly, anyone with a computer could publish whatever they wanted and hide behind false identities. Those platforms were manna from heaven for the growing number of people who were critical of Madeleine's parents when she went missing. Their criticism exploded into a relentless campaign of hatred, which found a home uncensored on social media. What hath God wrought, indeed.

I had referred to the McCann haters, as they became known, in numerous reports over the years. It wasn't until a group of sympathisers compiled a dossier of the abuse that I realised the extent of it. I felt rather embarrassed that I hadn't reported it more. It was 2014, seven years after Madeleine had vanished. The initial Portuguese police investigation, and a new inquiry by Scotland Yard, had found no direct evidence of anything that could explain what had happened to the little girl. But both forces had concluded that the McCanns had played no part in their daughter's disappearance. In most cases of missing children, the parents attract huge sympathy and sometimes a little criticism. In the McCanns' case, it was the reverse.

The dossier contained eighty pages of examples of internet abuse directed at the McCanns. The comments were posted on Twitter, Facebook and a number of online forums that appeared to have been created simply as platforms for more hatred towards the couple. The dossier was sent to authors Anthony Summers and Robbyn Swan, who were about to publish *Looking for Madeleine*, the most authoritative and definitive account of the Madeleine case. Summers said: 'There is a campaign of hatred against the parents. It is venomous and vitriolic, most of it done by cowards. We are taken aback by the extent of the sheer evil behind it.' The authors recorded details of the abuse in the book's paperback edition when it was published less than a year later. Before that, Swan introduced me to one of the McCann sympathisers. I also obtained a copy of the dossier and made plans for an extended news story.

The hateful comments included suggestions that the McCanns should be tortured and killed. One Twitter exchange, reproduced exactly as it appeared, went like this:

Is there Any. Terrorists want to murder the. #McCann parents id support it its gone on too long. #Goforit.

I'd supply the petrol.

I've got a box of Swan Vesta somewhere I think.

These 2 should burn in hell.

Another tweet read:

I'm in the mood for some water boarding, who's first K or G? #McCann lets sort this shit out.

One user responded:

I'd waterboard Kate and Gerry.

One post read:

We need some numbers for some assassins on taps.

Someone else wrote:

I hope the McCanns are living in total misery and later I want to see them smashed up the back of a bus or trampled by horses.

There were doctored photographs, including one of the parents' faces superimposed on the mugshots of the Moors murderers Ian Brady and Myra Hindley, who killed five children around Manchester in the early 1960s. Another pictured the couple alongside the serial killers Fred and Rose West. Another showed the McCanns walking hand-in-hand with Madeleine's brother and sister and a speech bubble exchange that read '*one down … two to go.*' Others showed the McCanns counting piles of cash, a dig at the money raised for Madeleine's Fund: Leaving No Stone Unturned Ltd, the official not-for-profit company set up to find their daughter and support the family. One picture manipulator had gone to some lengths to produce an image of a downcast Kate, in chains, with two green-and-yellow rubber Madeleine's Fund wristbands around her neck. Instead of 'Find Madeleine', the bands read 'Child Neglect'.

There was evidence, too, that Kate McCann was being stalked, with postings by people apparently in their hometown. One wrote: 'I was at the post office earlier, she wasn't in there. Saw her go in Peacocks then she vanished. Went looking.' Another wrote: 'Saw KM at the gym today, gave her a look of utter disgust, managed to hold my tongue though!'

The anonymous sympathisers who created the dossier said they had no connection with the McCann family. In email exchanges with me, one of those involved explained:

> We started out being concerned about people spreading misinformation about the case. We were concerned that if people believed the McCanns had harmed their child, then people would not come forward with information; information that might be the piece of the puzzle needed to find her. The rapid growth and reach of social media [Twitter and Facebook], however, changed our focus. We were now increasingly concerned for the physical welfare and safety of the McCanns, their children and their extended family.

The dossier was compiled after a Twitter user posted a photograph of the family. They were sitting together watching the Commonwealth Games in Glasgow. The picture clearly showed the twins, who were then nine years old. Although the youngsters had been widely photographed at the time of Madeleine's disappearance, their parents had, with media support, protected their identity as they grew older. 'We found it abhorrent that they compromised the safety and privacy of the McCann children, by posting a photo that would identify them to anyone wishing them harm,' said the sympathiser.

When I received it, the abuse dossier had only just been sent by its compilers to the Metropolitan Police. They hoped detectives would charge at least some of the McCann trolls and deter others. The portents were good. Only that month, a judge in London had jailed a man for eighteen weeks for bombarding Labour MP Stella Creasy with tweets in which he branded her a witch and threatened to rape her. The authors of the dossier pointed out that, apart from anything else, the McCanns were witnesses in an ongoing police investigation and ought to be protected from intimidation.

In a letter to the Scotland Yard commissioner, Sir Bernard Hogan-Howe, the compilers wrote:

> Over the past few years we have seen the tightening of legislation in combating stalking and harassment, and we have also seen some successful prosecutions against internet trolls, including those who have targeted people affected by tragedies. We are told that dedicated units have also been set up within the police to deal with this modern-day menace. However, although prosecutions have taken place against individual trolls who have made a relatively small number of abusive comments about their victims, no action ever seems to be taken against those who target the McCanns. This is

despite the indisputable magnitude of their activities, and the fact that they are an orchestrated and clearly identifiable group. Recently, some of them have started to tag @metpoliceuk in their abuse, thus demonstrating an astonishing level of boldness which may indicate a confidence that their activities will go unchecked.

The police response to the dossier compilers was this statement: 'In consultation with the Crown Prosecution Service and the McCann family, the material will now be assessed, and decisions made as to what further action, if any, should be undertaken.' A CPS spokesperson said: 'Police have alerted us to this information and an early discussion has taken place.' Sara Payne, the campaigning mother of murdered schoolgirl Sarah Payne, said: 'About time, they are certainly not the only victims, but they are the most abused. I hope this means this kind of disgusting abuse will finally be stopped.'

The people who write such messages on social media have become widely known as 'trolls'. The *Cambridge Dictionary* describes a troll as 'an imaginary, either very large or very small creature in traditional Scandinavian stories, that has magical powers and lives in mountains or caves'. It goes on to describe the modern version as 'someone who leaves an intentionally annoying and offensive message on the internet, in order to upset someone or to get attention or cause trouble'.

The former head of the Child Exploitation and Online Protection Centre (CEOP), Jim Gamble, described the thousands of online attacks as 'a legacy of bile'. It would always be there on the internet to confront Madeleine's siblings. He said:

If the Metropolitan Police haven't already begun an investigation into this, on the back of the complaints that they've received, I think they now need to pause, they need to take a long look at it. They need to reflect on the legislation that exists to deal with this under the Malicious Communications Act and Prevention of Harassment Act, and they need to look at the hardcore few who are being menacing, who are being malign, who are creating anxiety deliberately. I don't want to give this small, malicious group a larger audience than they have. I think the audience that some of them need is actually from the dock in court, so they can be held to account for the things which they have done, and that will send a strong message to many others. The internet is not anonymous. The police have the ability to identify the individuals that are doing this.

While the dossier compilers waited for a full response and possible action from the police, I set about trying to identify the McCann trolls. Almost all I looked at, typically, had adopted false identities or had made up bizarre names for their Twitter accounts, so it was difficult to confront them and ask them to justify their actions. I did, eventually, manage to identify several of them scattered around the country. While a colleague went to try to find two of them, I drove to Burton Overy, a pretty little Leicestershire village about fifteen miles from the home of the McCanns.

Divorcee Brenda Leyland, aged sixty-three, lived alone with her cat in a small, terraced cottage on Main Street. From there, she had been tweeting abusive messages about the McCanns under the Twitter name '@sweepyface'. She had posted, or retweeted, more than 400 tweets. In one tweet, she called for the couple to suffer 'for the rest of their miserable lives'. She was far from being one of the worst of the couple's abusers and at times had criticised the comments of others, but she had been relatively easy to identify. That's why I ended up on her doorstep, on a chilly Tuesday morning, the last day of September 2014.

For my planned report, I really needed an interview with one of the McCann abusers. Somebody such as Brenda Leyland. She may not have been entirely surprised to see me because, during my search of her tweets, I had clumsily added my name to her list of followers. From the way Twitter works, she would have received a message to say she was being followed by Sky News's crime correspondent. An open, upstairs window of her cottage suggested Leyland was at home. Rather than just knock on her door, my cameraman and I waited in our vehicle nearby, in the hope she would leave her house. It wasn't long before a woman arrived in a car to pick her up, and Leyland emerged from her front door. It seemed slightly less intrusive to approach her in the street, but I doubt it made any difference to the shock of being confronted by a television crew, especially in front of a friend.

She was just getting into the front passenger seat of her friend's car, when we walked up and I called out her name. The exchange that followed lasted forty-six seconds. The video is still available on the internet, via the Sky News website and YouTube. When I watch it back now, I'm struck by how unconcerned she seemed by our sudden appearance, given what was to happen a few days later. Leyland turned and looked at us as we approached, then closed the car door and walked towards us. I explained who we were. 'Oh,' she replied, without any hint of concern. She even gave me a brief smile. 'I'm just about to go out.'

As she shifted the strap of her handbag onto her right shoulder, I asked if I could talk to her about her Twitter account, her attacks on the McCanns and why she was trolling them so regularly. No, she said three times, as she responded to my rather quick-fire questions. She then headed back towards the car. She stopped and turned round: 'Look, I'm just going out with a friend, OK? Excuse me,' she said, before walking to the car. We followed her, with the camera rolling, and persisted: 'Why are you using your Twitter account to attack the McCanns?' She said: 'I'm entitled to do that,' then walked away again.

We had reached the vehicle when I asked her: 'You know you've been reported to the police, to Scotland Yard? They're considering a whole file of Twitter accounts...'

'That's fair enough,' she interrupted.

I kept going: '... and what supporters say is a campaign of abuse against the McCanns.'

She replied: 'OK, well, I'm going out now.' I said: 'The Crown Prosecution Service is considering it. Are you worried about that?'

'No,' she said, as she opened the door of the grey Honda and got in the passenger seat, gesticulating to her friend to get going. The engine coughed into life and the car pulled away.

I walked up Main Street and sat on a bench while I thought about what to do next. We had something in the can, but not really as much as I had hoped. Of course, Leyland might have refused to say anything, or may not even have been at home, so I was grateful for her few words. I wrote and recorded my 'piece-to-camera', where I explained part of the story as I looked directly into the lens. After a couple of hours, my cameraman and I were about to drive back to London, when the Honda returned. Leyland got out and walked to her cottage with her keys in her hand.

When I approached again, I expected her to be annoyed, but

she was friendly and, to my surprise, said: 'Come in, Martin.' She asked if I would like some tea. No journalist who has got over the 'doorstep' should ever refuse such an offer; the process of making, serving and drinking a cuppa simply extends the time you've got to get information from your subject. Leyland even introduced me to her cat and was keen to know about the four I had at home. Over the next thirty minutes, she said she did not want to give a formal interview on camera but explained her feelings towards the McCanns. Like so many others, she could not understand why they left their children alone in the holiday apartment. She said she had 'concerns' about the McCanns' fundraising, and she had used Twitter to express her feelings.

She hoped she hadn't written anything illegal. 'I have questions for the McCanns,' she told me. She admitted she used the Twitter name '@sweepyface' and said: 'I probably won't ever tweet again.' Before I departed, I said I hoped I hadn't ruined her day. She replied, seemingly jokingly, that I had ruined her life. I gave her a business card with my phone numbers and email address. I urged her to contact me if she wanted to. I left her feeling, I thought, concerned but not deeply worried about the report I was going to run.

The next day, Leyland called me and asked me if she would be identified in my report. I told her she would be seen and heard, but we would not name her or her village, a decision that had already been made by my bosses. I said I would keep her informed. I was aware of the likely impact on her of waiting for my report, which I was editing at Sky's headquarters in west London.

We spoke by phone again on Wednesday, the night before the broadcast, and although I didn't detect any particular concern, I asked her how she was feeling. She replied: 'Oh, I have thought about ending it all, but I'm feeling better. I've had a drink and spoken to my son.' I thought her words were no more than a throw-away remark and we said goodbye on friendly terms.

The report ran the next day, Thursday 2 October, from 6 a.m. and I was proud of it. I was disappointed that the McCanns had rejected the chance to give me their views. For the first time in a long time, I felt I had produced something that would make a difference, a welcome change from the crash-bang-wallop of daily news. I thought it was a worthy story that exposed wrongdoing, would prompt police action and perhaps even contribute to a debate on tightening the laws on internet abuse. How wrong I was about police action.

The next day, on BBC Radio 4's *Today* programme, Gerry McCann was asked about my report and Brenda Leyland's tweets. He said:

> I haven't read her tweets ... I think that is an issue, that our behaviour is modified by this. We do not have any significant presence on social media or online. And I've got grave concerns about our children, as they grow up and start to access the internet in an unsupervised capacity. There have been other instances, where people are threatening to kidnap our children. People are threatening violence against Kate and myself ... I'm glad to see the law around this area is being reviewed, but I do think we need to make examples of people who are causing damage.

Two days later, Brenda Leyland was found dead in a room at the Marriott Hotel, just outside Leicester. She had killed herself. I learned later she had deleted her Twitter account. I was in Cape Town when I heard the news of her death. I was there to cover the trial of a British man, Shrien Dewani, who was accused, and later acquitted, of arranging the murder of his bride Anni during their honeymoon in the South African city. I had just checked into my hotel when a colleague, whose family lived in Leyland's village, contacted me to tell me of rumours she had died. An hour or so later, one of my bosses at Sky News called to confirm the rumours were true.

I felt the same at that moment as I do today. I was and am devastated by her death and, as I told the police and the coroner later, the enormity of what happened will always be with me. I wished I had never done the story. No report is worth anyone's death, obviously. In the most awful way, it illustrated the potential impact of journalists' work and the responsibilities to truth and fairness that we all carry. In the following weeks, I was attacked on social media, threatened with violence, accused of murder and watched a growing Facebook campaign to get me fired. Anything I've reported on the Madeleine McCann case since has triggered a volley of internet abuse.

*Looking for Madeleine* co-author Robbyn Swan said recently:

I felt absolutely devastated when I learned that, after having been exposed for trolling the McCanns, Brenda Leyland had taken her own life. That does not, however, diminish the importance of exposing these stories of online abuse and intimidation. One must bear in mind that none of those who were vilifying the McCanns, or writing those things night after night after night, concerned themselves with what the implications might have been for the parties on the receiving end of their vitriol.

An inquest into Mrs Leyland's death was held at Leicester Coroner's Court five months later. It heard how she had suffered with mental illness and had attempted suicide before. Her younger son Ben, who lived in Los Angeles, said in a statement that his mother had 'panicked' after my encounter with her. Hours later she had rung him to say she had been tweeting about the McCanns, that I had called on her and Scotland Yard had been sent a report.

We discussed what action to take to avoid her name and picture appearing in the media. On October 2, I was aware the story had broken. I tried to contact my mother without success, I discussed with my dad and brothers going round to check she was OK. I got an email from mum on Wednesday saying she felt cheerier.

My mum has always struggled with depression and has undergone therapy and psychiatric treatment. I have been thinking a lot and have no doubt of the panic and fear in her voice, and think the Sky News report was the final straw.

Consultant psychiatrist Dr Kajetan Zakrzewski, who had once treated Mrs Leyland, said she had always been at risk of self-harm because of the state of her mental health.

The cause of her death was asphyxiation due to gas inhalation. Senior Coroner Catherine Mason recorded a suicide verdict. She said: 'I am satisfied that no one could have known what she was going to do and how she was going to do it.' She described Mrs Leyland as 'an intelligent and loving person.'

Sky News said in a statement after the inquest:

The team at Sky News followed its editorial guidelines and pursued a story in a responsible manner that we believed was firmly in the public interest.

Brenda Leyland's tragic death highlights the unforeseeable human impact that the stories we pursue can have, and Sky News would like to extend its sincere condolences to her family.

By then, Scotland Yard had passed the dossier to Leicestershire Police to investigate as the McCanns' local force. The Leicestershire detectives took their time. A year earlier, the CPS had issued guidelines around the use of social media, suggesting a high threshold was needed to prosecute abuse and underlining the right to freedom of expression. And there was this argument: could someone be a victim of trolling if they didn't use social media and the messages, however vile or threatening, had not been sent to them directly?

Louis Reynolds, social media and internet culture researcher at cross-party think tank Demos, was asked that question by *The Independent*. He told the online newspaper that while Brenda Leyland's comments were anti-social, he did not believe they would fall into the formal definition of 'trolling'. He said:

> This is kind of a further movement from what online trolling really is, because while this person was saying absolutely horrible things, they were just saying horrible things on the hashtag on this topic. The McCanns aren't on Twitter, so they were saying horrible things about the McCanns but not directly to them. The question is – that's anti-social behaviour, but is that trolling? I think the answer would probably, by the formal definition, be no it's not, it's just anti-social behaviour online.

Three months before my report was broadcast, a man had been jailed for posting a message on Facebook about Ann Maguire. She was a teacher who had been stabbed to death by one of her pupils at a school in Leeds a few days earlier. Jake Newsome wrote: 'Personally, I'm glad that teacher got stabbed up. Feel sorry for the kid. He should've p***** on her too.' It didn't matter to the prosecutor Sandra White, or the district judge David Kitson, that the message wasn't sent directly to Mrs Maguire, nor that she had obviously not read it. How could she? She was already dead. Newsome pleaded guilty to sending an offensive message. Sentencing him to six weeks in jail, the judge told him:

> You're entitled to express reasonable views, as are all of us. What none of us are entitled to do is abuse that freedom. What I find particularly offensive – that must have caused distress to all those who knew Mrs Maguire – were the derogatory remarks made saying that you were glad she had been killed. I can think of little more that can be upsetting or offensive. You clearly came from a troubled background, but this is so serious that nothing more [sic] than a custodial sentence can suffice.

Two years earlier, nineteen-year-old Matthew Woods from Chorley, Lancashire, was jailed for twelve weeks after admitting posting offensive Facebook messages about Madeleine McCann and toddler April Jones, who was abducted and murdered in Wales. One post read: 'Who in their right mind would abduct a ginger kid?' In another, he wrote: 'I woke up this morning in the back of a transit van with two beautiful little girls, I found April in a hopeless place.' He also wrote: 'Could have just started the greatest Facebook argument EVER. April fools, who wants Maddie? I love April Jones.'

Chairman of the Chorley magistrates' bench, Bill Hudson, told

Woods: 'The reason for the sentence is the seriousness of the offence, the public outrage that has been caused, and we felt there was no other sentence this court could have passed which conveys to you the abhorrence that many in society feel this crime should receive.' The court was told how Woods was arrested for his own protection when fifty people arrived at his home in protest at his comments. I don't know if anyone asked, but I'm pretty certain most or all of the protesters were angry at his comments about April, rather than Madeleine.

After seven months considering the McCann dossier, Leicestershire Police announced it would be taking no action against anyone. In a letter to the campaigners, Assistant Chief Constable Roger Bannister wrote: 'While finding that much of the material was extremely distasteful and unpleasant in nature, it was determined that none of the messages/postings constituted a prosecutable offence.' The campaigners were astounded and felt bitterly let down. I thought it a bizarre decision, but the force refused to explain more. And the trolling continued.

Two years later, ahead of the tenth anniversary of Madeleine's disappearance, trolls were targeting the McCanns' son Sean, posting on Facebook what appeared to be a recent photograph of him at school and attributing to him a sick comment criticising his parents. The photo had been uploaded to a Facebook page, which promoted the theory that Madeleine was dead and her body buried in the grounds of a house close to the Portuguese holiday apartment from where she had vanished.

A businessman obsessed with the McCann story, told me he 'and others' had created the Facebook page and it had attracted 140,000 UK followers. He also claimed he had written to Sean's school, threatening to reveal to the youngster, and other pupils, more details of his burial theory. I was told the school alerted police and reported the Facebook postings as malicious communications. No police action was taken.

The businessman said he had also written to the McCanns' lawyers, and Scotland Yard, urging the excavation of the plot where he believed Madeleine's body was buried. He told me that, five years earlier, he had travelled to Portugal and one night surveyed a private garden with a scanner which, he claimed, showed the likely presence of a child's remains. He even sent me scanner images. Several years later, he bombarded me with details of a completely different theory about Madeleine's disappearance.

Around the same time, a teenage girl posted a photograph of the McCann family having lunch in a restaurant several miles from their home. While the family was still eating, someone else posted a map of their location and asked: 'Anyone fancy a visit to Beefeater?' Others posted comments such as 'hope someone told the chef and he spat in their food' and 'I'd want to chuck my pint in their faces' and 'do the kids look pale and pinched – tell-tale signs?'

In a pooled television interview to mark the tenth anniversary, Kate McCann was asked about trolls. She said:

I think it has been shocking … that aspect of human nature that I hadn't really encountered before. Because I think it's so far from how you would behave, or people that you know would behave. It's been striking and quite hard really to get your head round. Because why would somebody write that? Why would somebody add to someone's upset – why would someone in a position of ignorance do something like that?

Former Home Secretary Alan Johnson said he couldn't understand why police refused to pursue the McCann trolls. He told me:

> We're all coming to terms with this not-so-new form of communication now and the dark side of it, or how we have to respond to it. You always come up with this argument: because of what it is, how can one country control it, how can one police force control it? And this argument between free speech and suppression, etc., I think that's a tough one. But what's not so tough is, here's the evidence of what was personally happening to the McCanns, who have come through this with so much dignity. The decision not to do anything with that is surprising, but Leicestershire Police would have to answer for that.

Johnson had a big interest in the Madeleine case. Two years after she vanished, and after Portuguese police closed their first investigation, he commissioned a scoping exercise to look for anything Portuguese detectives had missed. As a result, CEOP's Jim Gamble produced a secret report – it was delivered to Johnson's successor Theresa May – which led, eventually, to the ongoing Scotland Yard investigation. Much to Gamble's annoyance, the report was leaked to me. It shone a light on how the McCanns had fallen out with Leicestershire Police early on. It revealed the couple felt that the police family liaison officers appointed to help them would have been better employed as investigators, so they rejected them. The McCanns were frustrated by the role of UK police, especially their apparent inability to influence their Portuguese colleagues. Gamble's report concluded: 'Clearly, the McCanns have had a turbulent relationship with both Portuguese and UK law enforcement. They now openly acknowledge that there is a distinct lack of trust between all parties.'

The report also discussed the McCanns' hiring of several private investigators after the Portuguese investigation was shelved. The report said:

> It is clear that the McCanns and the private investigators working on their behalf have gathered a large amount of information during the course of their enquiries. This information does not appear to have been shared fully with the Leicestershire Constabulary or the Portuguese authorities ... It is imperative that they [private investigators] are encouraged and persuaded to share this information.

Relations got even worse than that. The couple sued the Leicestershire force because they felt it wasn't telling them enough about what was being done to find Madeleine. The force eventually agreed to tell them more. Is it too much to suggest that this poor relationship played a part in Leicestershire Police's decision not to pursue the McCann trolls? I put that thought to the force recently and got a rather blanket response: 'Due to operational reasons the force would not disclose detailed information relating to any investigation. Nor would we comment on the force's relationship with any victim of crime.' Ever since Madeleine's disappearance, her home police force showed little enthusiasm in talking to reporters about it. Nothing has changed.

The advent of social media has allowed everyone to be a publisher. It's a wonderful release for those worthy of an audience, but it's become a licence to offend and outrage for others who hide behind false identities and the right to freedom of expression.

While explicit sexual and horrific material is increasingly checked and removed, there appears to be no such monitoring of merely offensive comments or conspiracy theories. The McCanns know they and their family are targets of online attacks and believe the worst trolls should be exposed but, as far as I know, have never personally complained to the police.

The mainstream media follows social media intensely while big stories are running, particularly in pursuit of photographs and comments of those involved. Its content shapes our coverage and sometimes becomes the news itself. During the investigation into the disappearance of Nicola Bulley in Lancashire, the invasion of so-called TikTok detectives, live streaming their theories from the scene, was a distraction for the official police search and became a big part of the story. It prompted Lancashire Police to invoke powers to get rid of the amateur sleuths and hit back at criticism of their own investigators' initial lack of progress in finding Nicola.

As for the new suspect in the Madeleine case, he's a 45-year-old German drifter known as Christian B. Of course, I and millions of people know his full name, but under German privacy laws it can't be published. He is currently in a German jail serving seven years for the rape of an elderly American widow in 2005, in Praia da Luz, the village where Madeleine vanished two years later. He is a convicted paedophile and drug trafficker and, for several years, has been a suspect in Madeleine's abduction. There is no forensic evidence against him, nor are there any witnesses. The case against him is entirely circumstantial.

Apart from his previous convictions, Christian B was living in the area, his mobile phone was used nearby on the night, and he changed his car number plate the next day. And he is alleged, by an old friend of his, to have confessed to taking Madeleine. He denies any involvement in her disappearance. He told his lawyer Friedrich Fulscher, who told me, that he was having sex with a young woman in his camper van at the time, several miles away along the coast. German prosecutor Hans Christian Wolters, who believes Madeleine is dead, told me in January 2023: 'There will be no charge in the next months. Unfortunately, I'm not able to say how much time we still need to finish the investigation.'

# CHAPTER 16

# THE PRISONER

*It's the emptiness of never knowing when I'll be moved or where to.*
*It's the desperation of life itself, never seeing other cons, never seeing*
*a TV, having my family drift away. It's irreversible damage*

– Prisoner Charles Bronson

As I write, Prisoner A8076AG is awaiting the result of his latest parole hearing, an examination of his risk to the public after nearly half a century in jail. It was expected to be delivered in March 2023, as I was putting the finishing touches to this book. He hoped he had shown the Parole Board he was of no danger to anyone outside prison. With his reputation, that wasn't easy. His release would be great news for him but, because of the time it takes to edit, print and publish a book, not so great for me and my efforts to make this chapter up to date.

'I bet you can't believe I'm still in, can you? It's a fucking liberty, an absolute liberty, I'm seventy years old now Martin … I've never murdered anyone, I've never raped anyone. What am I in jail for?

People don't believe it. They think I'm a serial killer.' The words of Prisoner A8076AG Charles Bronson, one of the longest serving, delivered in a Cockney geezer growl. It was sent from his cell, in an audio message that he said later cost him a 28-day phone ban when the jail's governor heard the recording on Sky News.

I didn't feel too guilty, because Bronson wanted me to use it in the run-up to his latest parole hearing. He knew it would get him in trouble. Anyway, the prison sources insisted it wasn't a ban, just a mild punishment of having his in-cell calls monitored for a month. Apparently, Bronson breached prison rules by not seeking the governor's agreement that the message could be broadcast, a permission that is rarely granted. If he had asked, I think we both knew what the answer would have been. Bronson's had nearly forty-eight years of being told no, most often to the question: 'Can I be released yet?' He was unlikely to be troubled by a reprimand for misusing his in-cell phone.

In-cell phone? I was intrigued to learn that an increasing number of jails have landline phones installed in cells. It's a Ministry of Justice initiative, to make it easier for inmates to call their families in privacy. It beats queuing up to use the communal telephone in recreational areas where conversations can easily be overheard. In-cell phones also reduce the demand for smuggled mobile phones, which are valuable prison currency, fuel violence and, er ... aren't the most comfortable thing to hide during a strip search.

At the time of writing, there are an astonishing 140 jails in the UK. When Bronson wrote his book *The Good Prison Guide* in 2007, he'd been in thirty-three of them. You could add a few more since, and there may be others to come, though I wouldn't say that to the face of a man who is often described as 'Britain's most violent prisoner'. I, too, used to give him that dubious title. It's a bit tabloid, I know, but it readily identifies him in readers' minds and, without it, his newsworthiness over the years would have diminished or not have existed at all.

That hasn't stopped some of my colleagues from overstating his place in the crime world. One national newspaper called him, wrongly, a killer, and a *Daily Mail* writer who visited him described him as 'Britain's Hannibal Lecter – a man so savage that he's kept in a special cage'. Well, Bronson often is held in a cage, in the special secure unit of certain prisons. But, to my knowledge, he's never eaten anyone's liver with or without 'fava beans and a nice Chianti', as the fictional cannibal Lecter boasted in *The Silence of the Lambs*.

Bronson was first jailed in 1968, for causing criminal damage. In the following six years, he was in and out of prison regularly for similar crimes, until his conviction for armed robbery and carrying a firearm in 1974. They were hideous episodes: threatening a post office worker with a shotgun, beating up a garage attendant and inflicting grievous bodily harm on another victim. He got a seven-year sentence for the armed robbery and, apart from a couple of brief periods of freedom, he has been in jail or a secure mental hospital ever since, because of repeated acts of violence inside prison. These have included a bottle attack on a fellow inmate, another with a broken coffee jar, assaults on prison staff and kidnapping of other officials. Oh, and various rooftop protests.

He took a prison art teacher hostage and so terrorised him, at knifepoint, for two days in 1999, that his victim is still traumatised to this day. For that, Bronson was given a life sentence, though technically he was eligible for parole after only three years. I don't know if Bronson is the UK's most violent prisoner. He could be, and it certainly sounds like he is, but the Ministry of Justice doesn't keep a Top Ten. There's a lot of competition.

I've met, or at least crossed the path of, a lot of major criminals. I believe that all but a few deserved their jail sentence. Some, I thought, should have got more. But it's difficult to understand why Bronson has been incarcerated for so long. I think it's simply the inflexibility and lack of imagination of the prison system in the UK, a country that jails more people than any other in western Europe.

Bronson must feel that the authorities will keep him in jail for ever. The conundrum is this: does he keep getting locked up because he is violent, or is he violent because he keeps getting locked up? Is his violence inside prison the inevitable result of a system that appears to be unable, or unwilling, to encourage him towards eventual release? The convicted murderer Erwin James, who became a *Guardian* newspaper columnist, seemed to think so when he wrote: 'He is now being punished simply for being Charles Bronson.'

There really is a lot more to Bronson than the Neanderthal monster of the newspaper headlines. He's a talented artist, whose cartoon-ish drawings graphically depict the grim nature of prison life, the winner of two Koestler Awards for creative prison writing, a poet and an articulate man with a ready wit. He has the capacity, too, to send up his own depressing position with self-deprecating humour. A drawing he sent me, during the financial crisis in 2009, showed him in his cell, dangling from a noose attached to the blade of the Grim Reaper's scythe. In a speech bubble, he warns the Reaper: 'If you kill me, I'll be after your job. With this credit crunch you'll never get another job. Think about it, Reaper. I could well end up your worst ever nightmare.' The Reaper replies: 'What a nasty bastard.'

One authority figure who connected with Bronson, and helped him control his outbursts, was controversial psychiatrist Dr Bob Johnson. He treated dozens of Britain's most dangerous inmates in his role as a consultant at Parkhurst Prison on the Isle of Wight. Johnson said his unorthodox methods of encouraging his subjects to talk, rather than giving them control drugs, unlocked the root cause of their violence, which often stemmed from childhood trauma. When they understood where the violence came from, they behaved better.

Bronson had already spent time at Broadmoor and Ashworth secure hospitals when Johnson first examined him at Parkhurst in 1991, but the doctor found he had no major psychiatric disorder. What he did have, he decided, was an excess emotional dependence on his mother, and his outbursts were often triggered when his family were in any kind of trouble. Johnson concluded that Bronson was not as dangerous as the sixty murderers, including six serial killers, with whom he was also dealing at the time. Any physical harm done to Bronson's victims was much less than the damage inflicted by the others.

When Johnson stopped his work at Parkhurst, in the wake of political indifference and funding cuts in 1995, Bronson wrote him a moving letter. He sent me a copy. He wrote to the doctor, in capital letters as always:

A sad day to see you go! But I must admire your principles. It's a rare sight to see a doctor stand up to this system. I know it will be a bad blow for many, who will now be lost and have nothing more than a hell existence, a solitary survival, and all for trying to help themselves to be normal people … all will feel betrayed, all will feel bitter, some will return to violence as their last resort. But you know better than anybody, it's a sign of the times to put us in cages and forget us completely.

And then, in the same letter, Bronson gave his own insight into the causes of his violent behaviour. He blamed his constant transfer from one prison segregation unit to another without warning, the so-called magic roundabout, by a regime that seemingly doesn't know what to do with him. He was once shunted around jails fifty-eight times in four years.

He had, he wrote, worked hard, written and drawn and found peace in his life of isolation,

but in my last three years of multiple transfers it's gradually driven me to feel more persecuted. I was driven mad in the 1970s and I'm now experiencing the exact effects; lost, paranoid, confused, periods of depression, violent thoughts. As much as I've tried and put into changing my ways, the system seems destined to keep me isolated and on the move. Recently, I jumped on a doctor, I was overpowered, now I'm facing another court case, no doubt more years. But nobody asks why Bronson takes hostages. Well, the answer is Bob, I'm a very fucked up guy, desperate. It's the emptiness of never knowing when I'll be moved or where to. It's the desperation of life itself, never seeing other cons, never seeing a TV, having my family drift away. It's irreversible damage.

Johnson examined Bronson again in 2002, after the prison art teacher hostage incident. He found him suffering from post-traumatic stress disorder. His report said Bronson's mental health was damaged by the 'cruel and unusual' punishment of being confined to a single cell, twenty-three hours a day, being denied all social contact with other prisoners and having 'excessive restriction' placed on his family visits. A year later, after another examination of Bronson, Johnson wrote: 'It really is little short of disgraceful how little has been done to rehabilitate him ... surely, he should now be expecting to move on to conditions of more normal prison life, and eventually taking such steps as are necessary for his sensible, eventual release.'

Of course, there is the opposite, unsympathetic view of Bronson, from others who have also dealt directly with him. David Wilson, a criminologist, academic and former prison governor, who was at Woodhill jail during one of Bronson's earlier stays there, said he caused trouble and resisted any attempt to encourage him out of solitary confinement, because he didn't want a normal life inside jail. He said Bronson also knew he couldn't survive outside. In a newspaper article – yes, *The Guardian* again, where public opinion about Bronson is most often debated – Professor Wilson wrote, on the release of the biopic movie *Bronson* in 2009:

There has been no attempt to understand the film based on what is true and what is imagined, in much the same way that few wish to question what is true about Bronson, the various myths that have grown up around him and to which he has contributed, and all of which have undoubtedly added to his celebrity status.

Wilson said he once visited Bronson in his isolation cell and found him naked and covered in boot polish. The prisoner threatened to stab him with his moustache and told him to fuck off. To try to dissuade Bronson from attacking staff, Wilson said he would offer him books, a radio and exercise opportunities. Bronson then took hostage the librarian who delivered the books.

Wilson clearly hated the film, suggesting a prison governor character was based on himself but insisting he wasn't anything like the 'suave, detached, chain-smoking, balding, bespectacled and calculating' figure portrayed on screen. Also, Wilson was dismissive of Bronson's art. He thought it infantile.

I've not met Bronson, because my attempts to visit him have been rejected by whoever it is within the prison service who makes such decisions. Maybe they think it's for my own safety. I can't judge the difficulty faced by those whose job is to engage with him, but I disagree with Wilson about the art. Yes, the style is naïve, but the drawings are often compelling: vivid and detailed, with constant references to isolation, physical restraint, pain, madness and death. There are lots of naked men and tiny flying birds, usually with human faces. They may not reflect most prisoners' view of life inside, but they are a chilling insight into how Bronson views his own incarceration. And they are not without hope. Below a drawing of a naked figure sitting alone in a cell, with his head in his hands and a tiny devil figure lecturing him, Bronson wrote: 'God save our dreams, it's all we have left, one simple dream will bring you through all this misery.'

When I write to prisoners, I always enclose a return envelope, stamped and addressed to me. It saves them breaking into their meagre savings and buying their own. I add lots of paper, pens and coloured felt-tips for Bronson because I know he is a prolific artist. He once wrote back within a week and included dozens of drawings, one on each of the sheets I had enclosed. Some had a picture on both sides. He said he had created a book for me. Because they were becoming valuable, and often sold to raise charity funds, I sent them to Bronson's solicitor for him to decide what best to do with them.

I first wrote to Bronson on the advice of a friend and colleague, veteran Fleet Street crime reporter Jimmy Nicholson. Because he wore a black cape and claimed to have covered 'every trial since Barabbas, every siege since Troy', Jimmy was known as the Prince of Darkness. But he was an endearing and far-from-sinister figure, and he was the first to highlight Bronson's predicament. Jimmy had been in contact with Bronson for a while and had visited him during one of his stays in Wormwood Scrubs in west London. Jimmy was actually waiting to greet him on his last release in 1992, a period of freedom that ended after fifty-five days when Bronson was arrested for conspiracy to rob, possessing a firearm and GBH. It was Jimmy who took the striking photograph outside the Victorian twin towers of The Scrubs's main gate. It showed a slim, handsome Bronson, smartly dressed, doffing a dark fedora and grinning through his splendid, trademark handlebar moustache.

It was five years before that, during a previous release, that Welshman Michael Peterson changed his name to Charles Bronson, after the taciturn Hollywood film star of *Death Wish*, *The Magnificent Seven* and *The Great Escape*. It wasn't the actor's real name either, but copying it gave Bronson a more glamorous, tough-guy image and secured better billing for the amateur boxing bouts he fought during his occasional, early days of freedom.

Rugged features and an intimidating presence weren't the only things the prisoner had in common with the actor, whose gruff on-screen persona hid a surprising and similar sense of humour. The film director Michael Winner recalled how he and the actor were discussing the script of the first *Death Wish* movie. 'It's about a man whose wife and daughter are mugged and he goes out and shoots muggers,' said Winner. 'I'd like to do that,' said the actor. 'The film?' asked Winner, hopefully. The actor replied: 'No… Shoot muggers.' Perhaps the prisoner has since taken inspiration from something rather more serious his actor namesake once said: 'If my films have a lesson, it's that violence doesn't pay. My opinion is that violence only breeds violence.'

With his parole hearing looming, Bronson sent me another audio message arguing his case for freedom:

> They keep drumming it into the public that I'm a danger, but who am I a danger to? I've never been a danger to the public. I've been fighting them [the authorities] all my life, fighting for human rights, prisoners' rights, but it's cost me nearly fifty years of my life in boxes and cages. They cut you off from society, from your family, from your friends. I want to go home, I'm an artist born again, and I despise violence. I've been a model prisoner for ten years, but they still won't let me out.

He couldn't help signing off with humour: 'Between you and me, I can still do ninety-five press-ups in thirty seconds, so I'm still the guv'nor.'

People are intrigued by Bronson. It's difficult to square the tales of brutality with the fine detail of his art, the gruff expletives with the passages of eloquence, his despair with his humour. He's an enigma and so, too, is his situation. Why *has* he been locked up for so long when killers and rapists do their time and walk free?

Bronson attracts big audience figures. The majority of those who bother commenting publicly support his release. My TV and online report about his parole hearing, which included some of his audio message, was one of the most watched and read. I like to think it livened up our news bulletins for viewers who, for a long time, had been fed a constant diet of politics, war and climate change. In a rare hero-gram, my boss told me it was 'TV gold'.

A few years ago, Bronson changed his name again, to Salvador, after his hero the artist Salvador Dali. To the prison service and the parole board he is now known as Charles Salvador, but it was as Bronson he became notorious enough to have a major film based on his life and named after him. To those of us who write about him, and have some sympathy for him, he will always be Bronson. Whether he will always be a prisoner is another matter.

Psychiatrist Dr Bob Johnson is long retired, but he retains a keen interest in his former patient. His concern for Bronson hasn't diminished since the day they entered each other's lives. Johnson told me:

I first met Charlie, unaccompanied, on Friday 5 July 1991. It was highly irregular and should never have been allowed. Which is why I remember the date with such precision. I was totally new to prisons and their macho culture, having started work there only five days before. The cocky prison governor was playing a dastardly trick on me – let's get Charlie to bring the 'College Boy' down to earth – one punch from Charlie and my prison career would self-terminate, he thought. Except, I struck up a friendship with Charlie that's still going today.

If you talk to as many violent men as I have, then you'll find something quite astonishing: deep down they want to be friendly but have never been taught how. Of course, there's all the bluster, the threats and the trauma to get past first, though the Prison Service doesn't even start. So it was with Charlie. He was aggrieved – quite where, or how, was beyond him – it was my job to show him a way to escape all his earlier trials. Lock prisoners up, treat them appallingly and expect them to reform? You must be joking. Treat them as humans, for long enough, and they'll become more humane. It worked for me, as Charlie is happy to tell you. Will the government ever listen?

*Postscript: At his parole hearing in March 2023, Bronson put on a colourful performance. He swore, sighed loudly and told the panel: 'I've had more porridge than Goldilocks and the three bears and I'm sick of it.' He claimed he had changed his violent ways, had rehabilitated himself through his art and wanted to be free. He said he'd looked in the mirror and told himself: 'That's enough, pack it in.' He was awaiting the panel's decision, but he wasn't expecting to be released.*

# CHAPTER 17

# THE GORY DETAILS

*Index is increasingly concerned at the seemingly growing perception*
*within the British police that journalists are seen as unsavoury or*
*potentially disreputable individuals for officers to associate with*

– Ruth Smeeth, Index on Censorship

For all the long and unpredictable hours, the weekends and holidays interrupted by big breaking stories, the life of a crime reporter is rarely dull, sometimes grim and occasionally privileged. In 2017, in the twenty-four hours after the Manchester Arena bomb, I experienced all of that. I was reporting on a tragedy that had gripped the country, I heard stories of horror and bravery and, as the early evening sun shone on a huge gathering in Albert Square, I stood beside my colleague Kay Burley and listened to the stirring words of the poet Tony Walsh. At a vigil for the twenty-two bomb victims, he read his poem 'This is the Place', an exhilarating celebration of his home city.

With the line 'and there's hard times again in these streets of our city / but we won't take defeat and we don't want your pity', he captured the public mood of defiance. I mouthed a simple 'wow' to Kay. There were cheers and tears all around the square. Forever Manchester, the charity that had commissioned Walsh's poem five years earlier, later wrote of his performance: 'Two big fat fingers up to adversity'. Rock star Liam Gallagher said: 'The best thing I've ever heard come out of any Mancunian's mouth, ever.' At that moment, as a crime reporter, there was nowhere I would rather have been.

It's a cliché that the job gives journalists 'a ringside seat at the pageant of life', but it's true. We use it to fill TV and radio airwaves, newspapers and websites with news that is devoured by millions, holding the bad and powerful to account. We expose wrongdoing, sometimes enough to help change the law. Occasionally, we make mistakes, but we do much more good than bad. Yet, people everywhere have an ambivalent attitude towards my profession.

There's an old *Wizard of Id* cartoon, from some years ago, that captures that ambivalence brilliantly. Two young kids are walking along the road. First kid: 'What does your dad do?' Second kid, proudly: 'He's a reporter.' First kid: 'What does your dad *tell* people he does?' If people ask me what I do, I always tell them I'm a reporter. They never just say 'oh' and leave it at that. They always want to know more. But in polls of trusted professions we are often down near the bottom, along with politicians and car salesmen. As a crime reporter, I've experienced disdain from all directions.

In an Amsterdam court, I sat behind Patrick Adams, one of the brothers from the Adams family crime organisation, during a hearing in which he was fighting extradition to the UK. He'd been on the run with his wife Constance for two years. He was wanted, on a European Arrest Warrant, after a man was shot and seriously injured sitting in a car at a road junction in central London. I tried to interview Adams's Dutch lawyer Titia Korff the day before the hearing, but she told me he wouldn't let her talk to me. In court, she spent a long time trying to convince a panel of judges that Adams would not get a fair trial in Britain, because of people like me. She said he'd suffered years of media reporting, in which the family had been accused of involvement in armed robbery, drug trafficking and worse.

When the main judge asked Adams if he wanted to add anything I didn't expect him to speak, but he said he did and told him: 'There's a man sitting behind me, Mr Brunt, a reporter, who has written about me for twenty years. He accused me of killing a man called Kenneth Noye and burying him under the Millennium Dome.' Adams was clearly angry. He was referring to a *GQ* magazine article I wrote about Noye, the notorious killer we met in Chapter Thirteen. In the article, I had reported rumours that the Adams family, without actually naming them, had put it about in the underworld that Noye was dead, but I had concluded that he was still very much alive.

Over the years, I've written and said things far less damning of the Adams family than my newspaper colleagues. I felt Patrick Adams was singling me out just because I was the only UK reporter in court. If I hadn't called his lawyer the day before, he probably wouldn't have known I was there, sitting a couple of rows back. His words were a bit unsettling, but it suddenly got a lot worse. In a rather chilling moment, with his voice shaking, Adams told the judge: 'This man has ruined my children's lives.' It took several months, but Adams eventually lost his extradition battle, was sent back to the UK and was jailed for nine years after admitting causing grievous bodily harm.

His victim was a former associate Paul Tiernan, who Adams believed had turned informant. Adams claimed Tiernan had been about to shoot him, so he wrestled the weapon off him and fired in self-defence. Tiernan refused to give evidence against Adams, claiming he didn't recognise his attacker. The original attempted murder charge against Adams was watered down to GBH, to which he pleaded guilty. I spoke to Tiernan by phone after the sentencing: 'I've never been a grass, never been a police informant. I would never do anything like that,' he said. 'I've been that man's best friend for thirty years and someone has just whispered something stupid in his ear, and it turned out like this. I'm OK, but I don't want that word "grass" hanging over my head. It is not true.'

In my world you probably couldn't get two figures further apart than Patrick Adams and the new commissioner of the Metropolitan Police, Sir Mark Rowley, but they appear to share a disparaging view of the media. I've known Sir Mark for many years, during his previous roles at the Met and Surrey Police, but when he came out of retirement in 2022 and emerged as the front-runner for the top job at Scotland Yard, I genned up a bit more on him. My research included reading *The Sleep of Reason*, the crime thriller he co-authored with a journalist after he quit the Met in 2018. I didn't expect to enjoy it, but it's a great read. The story is about a right-wing terror attack in London and is infused with the authority you would expect from a former head of counter-terror policing. But the book doesn't half slag off the media.

As early as Chapter Two, the authors have a TV news crew driver arguing with a security man about access to a crime scene, a senior woman detective ignoring journalists' shouted questions, and 'a bulbous crime reporter … who had doorstepped her repeatedly …

the last person she wanted to speak to now'. Perhaps it's pure co-incidence that, moments later in the narrative, a rat 'saunters' across the detective's path. A group of journalists are later described as a 'horde', and the book's heroine foresees a media storm ahead 'with all its speculation, blame games and half-truths'.

A couple of pages on, the officer decides to speak to the victims' families because 'the last thing she needed was a victim's uncle going rogue and whining to the press about the police'. Further in, the book describes a 'pack' of journalists lounging on the pavement in Downing Street and swapping notes, so they all have the same story. Then, a really cheap shot: the No. 10 cat is 'licking its bottom contemptuously on the doorstep, its rear end facing the journalists. A media critic.' That was attributed to the character of an assistant commissioner, which just happens to be the role Rowley had before his initial retirement.

Maybe I was overreacting, but I wondered if this was what Rowley really felt about the media. He could hardly blame those sentiments, albeit fictionalised, on his co-author David Derbyshire, who is a journalist himself. I put all this to Rowley as we chatted after an interview to mark his return to the Met. He laughed off my concerns. He said it was pure fiction. They were the character's feelings about journalists, not his own. I still felt he had gone along with a common ploy of authors: to make journalists the bad guys. He pointed out that the book was just as disparaging of its politi-cal characters, which is true. Despite that, Amber Rudd, a former Home Secretary with whom he had once worked closely, gave the book a good review. So did I.

There was a serious point to my questioning of the commission-er, though, because his appointment came at a time when crime reporters were still feeling the effects of the phone-hacking scandal, the Leveson Inquiry into press ethics and the collapsed trials of journalists who paid officials for stories. All those episodes had damaged the traditional, close relationship between crime reporters and their police contacts. Meetings in pubs and restaurants had been banned for more than a decade. Regular, official get-togethers with detectives had effectively stopped. We weren't getting along like we used to.

As a senior officer in charge of a high-profile case, Adrian Harper said he saw the media at its best and worst. He was a detective superintendent when he investigated the random stabbing of a young pregnant mother, Abigail Witchalls. She was left for dead in a country lane at Little Bookham, a pretty Surrey village, in 2005. There were no witnesses, CCTV footage or forensic evidence. The victim had managed to give scant details of her attacker: white man, earring, blue car. Police also had a report of a couple in a blue car, speeding away, who could be potential witnesses.

Harper said:

I made a quick media appeal with those basic facts about a couple in a blue car. I wouldn't normally show my hand so early, but we had nothing else to go on. Within an hour, a couple went into a police station and said it could be them. We were able to rule them out by lunchtime. Without the media's immediate help I could have been side-tracked for weeks, looking for that couple as suspects.

Harper and I grew up in the same area of Cambridgeshire. I was at school with one of his brothers and our sisters were friends. My father and his were teacher colleagues. When I turned up at the scene of the stabbing decades later, we were delighted to see each other, but Harper didn't do me any special favours. He told me he always thought it important to have a good, professional relationship with the media. He saw what he felt was the bad side of journalism a few days later, soon after he arrested a suspect. He got ready to show Abigail, still critically ill in hospital, twelve photographs, including one of the suspect. It was, unusually, a picture identity parade.

Harper, now chief executive to Kent's police and crime commissioner, recalled:

> I had everything sorted and about to go, when a *Sun* reporter rang to say he had a photograph of the suspect, and he was going to publish it. It was a mugshot that had clearly been leaked from a police source. I didn't have time to get an injunction because we still didn't know if Abigail would survive. I asked the reporter to hold off publication until after the ID parade. If he had used it before the parade, it would have compromised my investigation, for legal reasons.

The reporter, Jamie Pyatt, told me later the officer did not need to ask him to hold off publishing the photograph because he would never want to compromise an investigation. Abigail didn't pick out the suspect anyway, and he was eliminated. A later suspect committed suicide, and prosecutors said the young man would have been charged over the stabbing.

Ten years on, Harper gave evidence when Jamie Pyatt, with other journalists, was on trial during the cash-for-stories investigation Operation Elveden. The reporter admitted paying a police officer £10,000 over nine years for tip-offs, including the photograph, but argued it wasn't a crime. Pyatt was cleared of encouraging the officer to leak information. The jury accepted Pyatt's defence that he was simply doing his job and his actions were in the public interest. The officer, PC Simon Quinn, pleaded guilty and was jailed for eighteen months. All the journalists were acquitted at trial or by the Appeal Court, as explained earlier in the book.

One of Harper's senior officers at the time of the stabbing was Mark Rowley, who would occasionally visit the scene and talk to the journalists covering the story. Seventeen years later, after writing his book and becoming the new Met commissioner, Rowley held a welcome briefing with crime reporters. He said he wanted to re-establish good relations with us. In a mood of genuine enthusiasm, he said: 'We tried drinking together, that didn't work, we've tried the Mexican stand-off and that didn't work. There must be a compromise somewhere in the middle.' In his first month in the new job I interviewed the commissioner three times, which was three more times than I did his predecessor, Dame Cressida Dick, in her final year in office. None of it was over a bottle of wine, but it was a promising start. If Sir Mark ever finds time to write a second novel, perhaps his hero will be an old hack who's been around the block a few times. I'm not counting on it.

His book's disparaging view of the media may have reflected the secret treatment we were being subjected to by chief constables. Around the time of Rowley's appointment, we discovered that, in a warning about the dangers of corruption, all police forces had been encouraged to consider journalists in the same group as extremists. The College of Policing, which sets standards and training, was advising forces to make all officers tell their bosses if they knew any journalists, in the same way they were required to reveal any link with extremists.

When the secret policy was discovered, it prompted a fierce response from journalists and liberty groups. Ruth Smeeth, the chief executive of Index on Censorship, said:

Index is increasingly concerned at the seemingly growing perception within the British police that journalists are seen as unsavoury or potentially disreputable individuals for officers to associate with. Freedom of the media is a bedrock of our democracy and the tendency to see reporters as a threat, rather than an asset, is something we are more used to seeing with our work in authoritarian regimes around the world, rather than advanced democracies.

The *Daily Mail*'s crime editor Rebecca Camber, chair of the Crime Reporters Association, and the Society of Editors executive director Dawn Alford, wrote to the College of Policing on our behalf:

The media fulfils a vital role in keeping the public informed about the work of the police and, alongside bringing offenders to justice and helping keep communities safe, media scrutiny promotes transparency and aids understanding of how police forces across the UK operate. The inclusion of journalists within a 'notifiable associations' list in counter-corruption guidance gives the wrongful impression that reporters seek to corrupt or deceive, and equates the profession with the wrongdoing and dishonesty that journalists work to uncover.

The College of Policing said, in response, that it recognised journalists' important role in holding police to account and publicising appeals for help, but the public expected forces to have policies to protect sensitive information. That included officers being asked to declare any conflicts of interest, to be open and transparent and mitigate any risks. It added: 'The guidance given to police forces should not impede healthy relationships between the police and the media. We are working with the National Police Chiefs' Council and others to review the guidance, and will listen very carefully to any issues raised by the media.'

And so they should. Every day police up and down the country urge the media to publish appeals asking for the public's help in finding killers, rapists, burglars, muggers, thieves and fugitives. They expect news organisations to carry warnings of terror threats, publicise safety campaigns and celebrate police successes. They arrange press conferences and would look stupid if none of us turned up. Sometimes, they set up interviews with victims who they believe are the real perpetrators of the crime, to see how they react under the twin spotlights of live TV cameras and reporters' delving questions. In at least one case, detectives even directed those media questions to help confirm their suspicions.

When Oxford student Rachel McLean vanished in 1991, police suspicion fell, as it often does, on someone she knew and the last person to see her alive, in both cases her boyfriend John Tanner. He suggested that Rachel had disappeared after meeting a stranger. Without a body or any other tangible evidence, detectives arranged for Tanner, officially the grieving lover, to appear at a press conference. They briefed journalists to ask him specific questions that they couldn't ask themselves. Dutifully, a reporter asked him directly: 'Did you kill Rachel?' Tanner showed a lack of emotion, even smirking before he replied: 'I did not kill her. I don't know what happened to her. In my heart of hearts I know she is still alive.' His manner and body language convinced police he was their man and, when his girlfriend's body was discovered below the floor of her home, he confessed to strangling her. In court, Tanner pleaded not guilty to murder, but he was convicted. It was a vindication of the detectives' unusual methods and the media's support for them.

The disappearance of schoolgirl Shannon Matthews, in 2008, was another high-profile investigation in which the pressure of live press conferences fuelled police suspicions and helped expose the truth of what really happened. On camera, her mum Karen showed little upset, spoke without hesitation and, although she said the things expected of a grieving mother, appeared unconcerned at the prospect that Shannon was dead. And no wonder, because she knew her daughter was alive. Nine-year-old Shannon had been kidnapped by Michael Donovan, the uncle of Karen's boyfriend. Karen hatched the plot with Donovan to hide Shannon away, then 'find' her and claim a reward of £50,000. It was nine months after the disappearance, in Portugal, of three-year-old Madeleine McCann, a mystery that got huge publicity. The shameless pair even approached the Madeleine's Fund campaign group for cash to help them search for Shannon.

The case also demonstrated sharply the contrasting attitudes to journalists. The Matthews family lived on the deprived Moorside estate in Dewsbury, west Yorkshire, the sort of place where nosey southern strangers like me aren't readily welcomed. Against our expectations, the initial reception we London journalists got from neighbours was one of the warmest I've ever had in my years of traipsing through the broken lives of crime victims. Use my toilet? No problem. Tea? Milk and sugar? Of course, come and drink it in my kitchen. Shelter from the rain, phone charging or just a natter, it was all on offer. People could not have been more helpful. They recognised we were there to broadcast appeals, including mum Karen's pleas, and help bring home one of their own, safe and sound. That all changed when police found Shannon, drugged and hidden under a bed in Donovan's flat, twenty-four days later.

Suddenly, as the kidnap plot unravelled, we were intruders into the residents' collective dismay and anger. They must have felt we were projecting the dysfunction of the Matthews family onto everyone who lived on the estate. With the key suspects arrested, and not available to be lynched, we became the target of abuse, accused of being parasites and revelling in their horror. We read the warning signs and left town. Karen Matthews and Michael Donovan were later jailed for eight years, but I never went back. The bitterness lingered and, eleven years later, Karen was recognised and attacked by a woman in a fish-and-chip shop 200 miles from Dewsbury. At times, we journalists felt we weren't far from being given similar treatment.

Reporters used to develop a thick skin early in their careers on local papers. The big test was being sent to call on the family of a child who had died suddenly, usually in a road accident or at school. It was a dreaded assignment known, rather cynically, as the death knock. Sometimes you were welcomed in by tearful parents who wanted to tell the world about their lovely child. If you were really lucky, they gave you a photograph, your report made the front page and you won plaudits from the editor. More usually, though, you were told a polite no thank you. Sometimes you were sworn at, castigated for your lack of feeling, even chased by the family dog back down the garden path where you hoped you had remembered to leave the gate open.

What it taught you was empathy – not just 'I know how you must be feeling', because you absolutely don't have any idea what they are going through – and how to deal with people in the worst situation, when to persist and when to leave. Since those days, on football riots, bomb blasts and murders from Cardiff to Kuala Lumpur, I've been called every name: bloodsucker, scum, pariah and worse. Sometimes I feel I deserve it. I understand that it's never personal and that I'm an easy target for their anger because they don't know me, there's no one else around and, hey, everyone blames the media anyway, don't they? I also know that the same people who hurl abuse at me go home and turn on the TV news, and the next day read a paper to find out what's going on. I wonder where they think the news comes from.

# CHAPTER 18

# THE COURTROOM

*Our fascination with true crime and violent crime
is not just normal, but necessary*
– CRIMINOLOGIST DAVID WILSON

I wouldn't have written this book, or stayed in my job so long, if it wasn't for the public's abiding fascination with crime, real or fictitious. It's what's made you keep turning the pages to reach this point. I hope. Which is very near the end of this book, but for those of you who consider your appetite for such stories to be unlimited, there is another place where you can immerse yourselves in tales about the human capacity for violence and greed, at first hand, with all the main characters either appearing or featured in one room.

In the capital city of London it's the Central Criminal Court of England and Wales, though there are smaller versions within a few miles of most people. Many of you will know the Central Criminal Court better by its nickname, the Old Bailey, and recognise the golden scales of justice statue on top of its roof. Old Bailey is actually the name of the street on which the court has stood since 1902. Before that, earlier versions of the court complex were located nearby for more than 400 years. Unlike other London attractions, such as the Chamber of Horrors in Madame Tussaud's wax museum, or the gory London Dungeon, the spectacle inside the Old Bailey is real and free, though the queues can be just as long when there's a big trial on.

Its pale Portland stone exterior and landmark dome are steeped in history, surviving the bombs of the Blitz in the Second World War and those of Irish Republican Army terrorists in 1973. It's proved tougher, too, than all the prisoners who have passed through its cells and those who stood in the dock of Court Number One as a judge donned his black cap and sent them off to face the hangman's noose. The death penalty may be long abolished, but the daily list of cases posted outside the court does not get any less gruesome. Each of the Old Bailey's eighteen courts often has a chilling tale to tell, though you may have to wait patiently in the public gallery for the details to emerge, as proceedings can sometimes be drawn out.

When I began writing this book and looking for a place to start my research, I wandered into the Bailey on a random day. It was Wednesday 27 June 2018. The court schedule was listed, by defendants' names, in a glass cabinet on the street near the main door. The word *alleged* should be added to each, of course. Here's a selection of what was coming up:

Members of a banned far-right group planning to kill an MP with a Roman sword.

Man arrested outside Buckingham Palace with four-foot samurai sword and shouting 'Allahu Akbar'.

Two men planning to join terror group IS and murder Prime Minister Theresa May in Downing Street.

Website designer killed his date who fell off a motorboat.

City worker who slashed a colleague during a nightclub row leaving wounds needing thirty stitches.

Doctor accused of 118 sexual offences.

Woman who filmed her boyfriend being murdered and uploaded footage to Snapchat.

Man who doused his girlfriend in petrol and tried to set light to her.

Four men up for murdering a friend of the rapper Dizzee Rascal.

Four men accused of shooting a bouncer at a Newcastle nightclub.

Two men who attacked a rival drug dealer, smashed his car with baseball bats and stabbed him thirteen times.

Group said to have smuggled Albanians into the UK in inflatable boats.

So there, in one building on one day, it was possible to go and hear tales of murder, attempted murder, terrorism, GBH, people trafficking and sexual assault. Some of them were pre-trial hearings, but often in the early stages of such cases many of the facts are routinely discussed in open court in front of visitors to the public gallery, even if the media is not allowed to report the details until the trial, which may be many months ahead.

The grimmest stories usually end up being reported in newspapers and on television and radio, but not as much as they once were. News agency reporter David St George, working from a dingy office in the bowels of the Bailey, used to make a good living filing copy to London's three evening papers and the bulging pages of national dailies.

Sadly, media coverage of court proceedings across the country has been dwindling for several years now. It's largely because of the parlous state of the newspaper industry, whose editors argue, partly due to a drop in advertising revenues, that they have no money to send their own reporters and can barely afford to pay a news agency to cover it for them. The same goes for council meetings, a vital example of democracy at work but another area that is now poorly reported by the media.

Our national newspapers have reduced their court reporting in favour of chronicling the behaviour of the latest 'stars' of reality TV shows or, in more recent years, the tedious and repetitive machinations of the pre- and post-Brexit political debate. Coverage of the coronavirus pandemic cut editorial space for court reports, and later the stories themselves dried up when some courts around the country closed completely during the lockdown.

Even in comparatively normal times, though, the world's most famous court does not always run smoothly. I'd heard a rumour about a long trial in which two jurors had been excused from continuing for personal reasons and the judge was worried about losing more as the hearing dragged on. A trial can't continue with fewer than nine of its original twelve jurors. It was a corruption case with seven defendants and allegations of bribes, prostitutes and boozy nights used to secure contracts for the £3 billion extension to London Underground's Jubilee Line. In a quotation to rival anything I've heard from the lips of the most theatrical barristers, prosecutor Patrick Upward QC told the jury that the tube train network had been betrayed 'for a harlot's caresses, a few pieces of silver and the brush of a barmaid's skirt'.

Not that we could report his words at the time: the case carried a blanket reporting ban. There were other linked trials yet to be heard that risked being prejudiced by any publicity of the first. Few of us had paid much interest, until a third disgruntled juror, fed up with loss of earnings, went on strike. How bad could things be? When we got into court to see for ourselves it was pretty dire. The trial had originally been estimated to last no longer than eight months but had already dragged on by then for two years. It had become Britain's longest-running, dogged with delays as defendants and lawyers in turn went sick, two with scarlet fever, and like the striker, jurors complained they were suffering financial hardship. One was almost certain to miss her wedding day, another said he had spent so long away from home his wife was convinced he was having an affair.

The trial was abandoned on the advice of the Director of Public Prosecutions and the Attorney General, both in agreement that the remaining jurors would struggle to remember the evidence. Six of the defendants were formally acquitted (one had pleaded guilty) and the inspector of the Crown Prosecution Service began an investigation to see what lessons could be learned from the trial's collapse. It was a case that was barely reported until its dramatic end, when the press benches suddenly filled up.

No reporter, me included, ever got a seat at Kingston Crown Court in Surrey, because whoever designed the building in the late 1990s forgot, or didn't bother, to allocate space for the press. To this day we have to sit in the public gallery, which is fine unless you happen to be stuck beside the defendant's angry and aggressive mate who hates the media. I covered a murder trial once at Huntingdon Crown Court, in Cambridgeshire, not far from where, as a young boy, I used to do a paper round. The court clearly didn't have many important cases because I didn't even know it existed. Staff were rather surprised to see a reporter at all. A large, colourful diagram on the wall offered visitors a helpful 'who's who' guide to what went on inside a courtroom, with written explanations of everybody from the judge to the jurors. There was no mention of a court reporter. I felt as rare as the swallowtail butterflies that we sometimes saw on school trips to the Fens. And much less appreciated.

Because it plays host to the most serious cases, I spend more time at the Old Bailey than any other court building. It has an overwhelming sense of the past, especially inside the older courtrooms where some of the most notorious criminals in history have gripped the brass rail of the dock as they learned their fate: wife killer Dr Hawley Crippen, nightclub hostess Ruth Ellis, who was the last woman in Britain to hang, gangster twins Reggie and Ronnie Kray and serial killer Peter Sutcliffe, known as the Yorkshire Ripper. But you don't have to travel to London. There are hundreds of criminal courts in Britain, and you can walk into any of them and hear stories of dreadful, true crime.

Stories like the murder of father-of-three Anthony Williams, which was reported in his local media, didn't get a mention in the national press. His horrific killing, in a largely middle-class market town, illustrated so much about drugs, gangs, violence, revenge and the cheapness of life, but it wasn't unusual enough to make national news.

Williams, a drug user, had allegedly robbed a dealer in London and was back at home when his victim and another young man caught a train and went looking for revenge. They tricked their way into Williams's flat and stabbed him many times, stopping others who were there from intervening. His attackers did little to cover their tracks and were arrested, carrying both the murder weapon and a gun, as they waited for a train back to London.

The sheer nonchalance with which the pair took an away-day train ride from London to kill in front of witnesses, and thought they could get away with it, must have shocked readers of the *West Sussex County Times*. Or maybe it didn't. Maybe they were horrified, not that it happened, but only that it happened in their lovely, quiet town, rather than on the dangerous streets of south London they might view from a speeding commuter train. Sales of that local paper have fallen like many others, but I bet that anyone who saw the story read it to the very end.

Most people can indulge their fascination with the grisly details of true crime, safe in the knowledge that it's something that happens to other people, like the hundreds I joined one Friday afternoon queuing outside Madame Tussaud's. I wanted to discover if the wax museum's famous Chamber of Horrors was as frightening and popular as I remembered it as a kid. It hadn't always had a good review, according to a book I bought in the museum's gift shop. In *Madame Tussaud: Her Life and Legacy*, author Geri Walton quotes *Punch* magazine from 1850: 'Good Madame Tussaud, devoting art to homicide, turns to the pleasantness of profit for the abomination of blood.' I imagine that review encouraged more visitors, rather like the warnings at the start of TV programmes that show sex and violence.

The Good Madame's Chamber had been part of the museum since the early 1800s and remained open for another 200 years. It was closed 'permanently' in 2016, after parents complained the exhibits were terrifying their children and amid a feeling that a celebration of murder was in rather bad taste. It was replaced with the family-friendly Sherlock Holmes Experience. That decision must have had a lot to do with the $1 billion global box office success of two Hollywood *Sherlock Holmes* movies and a critically acclaimed BBC TV series, to say nothing of the museum's close proximity to the fictional Holmes's 221B Baker Street address.

The museum, however, had so many requests to bring back the Chamber that it did so in 2022, on the eve of Hallowe'en, with a warning at its dingy basement entrance that 'anyone under sixteen, with a heart condition, pregnant or plain scared' should avoid it and take the stairs to the next attraction. When I went, I didn't see anyone turn back. The museum's main exhibits were still overwhelmingly showbiz and pop music orientated, but it was in the Chamber of Horrors that visitors appeared most captivated and lingered longest. It was macabre and creepy, but was it frightening? Not really, except when I was first into the prisons section and a guide lurched out of the darkness with a loud 'welcome'. He then introduced me to serial killer Dennis Nilsen standing unsmiling behind the bars of his cell.

The bloody severed heads on spikes, from the streets of Paris, were a reminder that Marie Tussaud established her early career by making grim wax death masks of some of the principals guillotined during the French Revolution. The modern wax figures were more animated, if a little melodramatic. There were recorded screams and shadows to accompany Jack the Ripper and swirling fumes around the half-submerged body of one of acid bath murderer John Haigh's victims. The filmed reconstruction of the hanging of wife killer Dr Hawley Crippen was chilling and realistic, with a voiceover intoning 'may the Lord have mercy on your soul' before the actor plunged through the gallows trapdoor.

David Wilson, emeritus professor of criminology at Birmingham City University, insists public fascination with true crime is hardly surprising. He said:

> People consume those stories because they recognise in them something about themselves as individuals, their families, their communities, the society which they're living in and they're bringing their children up in. Our fascination with true crime and violent crime is not just normal, but necessary. Knowing when and in what circumstances someone will use violence helps society, and us as individuals, evolve by eradicating the circumstances in which violence is most likely to happen. Continuing to remember these perpetrators and what they did, not only allows us to see patterns of victimisation over time but also social and cultural change and, sadly, sometimes continuity.

Wilson believes interest in crime is also driven by a sense of justice. He moderated a series of live discussions on miscarriages of justice with US defence lawyers Dean Strang and Jerry Buting, which sold out in UK theatres, including the London Palladium.

> Every single night, people would come with questions that wanted

to discuss the minutiae of miscarriages of justice, the technique in terms of interviewing suspects, the disadvantages of how evidence gets misrepresented, the forensics behind how two men were convicted. It was fascinating, their knowledge, because people really do want to have justice. They can see themselves in those circumstances in which that person gets wrongly accused of a murder and goes to prison.

He has a theory, too, on the generally accepted fact that more women than men have an interest in true crime. They read more true crime books than men, who tend to be drawn to books on the violence of war. It seems odd that women, the less aggressive gender and much more likely to be the victims rather than the perpetrators of violence, are more inclined to dwell on the facts of it.

That disproportionate number is consistent over a long period of time. I think it has some evolutionary psychological significance, because it's quite clear that women have had to understand male violence as an adaptive survival strategy for millennia. Whatever the current zeitgeist might be about a fascination for true crime, the zeitgeist is only part of what's inherent in our DNA, which is that as human beings we should be interested in this, but as women, their gender has to be interested in this because that allows them to survive.

Consultant forensic psychologist Kerry Daynes agreed, up to a point. She explained:

It is certainly the case that women's interest in the true crime genre is driven by a survival instinct, however, I find the evolutionary explanation too simplistic. After all, young men are at the greatest risk of becoming victims of violent crime, so why don't they make up the majority of the true crime audience? The answer, I think, lies in the fact that the media, in all its forms, is far more likely to focus on cases where a female is the victim – particularly where that woman is young, white, middle-class and conventionally attractive and/or has been subject to exceptionally brutal or sexualised assault by a stranger (the 'beautiful women killed in interesting ways' trope, as I refer to it).

On top of this distorted media diet, women live with the reality of a high level of street harassment from men. Society responds by bombarding us with constant safety advice, firmly placing the onus on women, rather than the perpetrators, to change their behaviour if they want to avoid victimisation. No wonder, then, that women are disproportionately fearful of serious violent crime, based on faulty assumptions. The true crime genre functions to simultaneously heighten women's anxieties and yet deliver a sense of control – women consume it in the belief that learning about 'offender' and 'victim' behaviours will allow them to respond effectively if they ever find themselves in a similarly dangerous situation.

More men than women are the victims of homicide. But the numbers of UK women killed by men, or where a man is the prime suspect, are startling. According to the blog *Counting Dead Women*, figures gleaned from media reports revealed that in 2021 the figure was at least 144, many of them at the hands of their partners or former partners. If Professor Wilson is correct in thinking that women can learn from studying male violence, then maybe there are lessons here for crime reporters as well. This one, at least. When I reported the murders of Steve Wright, the Suffolk Strangler, in 2006, like most other journalists I described his five victims as prostitutes. I got an angry letter from a viewer pointing out that it was unfair to label his victims as prostitutes. I was told: 'They might be sex workers, but they are, first and foremost, troubled and vulnerable women; poor, mentally ill, victims of abuse, drug addicts or alcoholics, all desperate for money. Nobody chooses to become a prostitute.'

Author Howard Sounes has written eleven non-fiction books, all with biography at their core, including three about true crime. His first, *Fred & Rose*, which is about the Cromwell Street murders in Gloucester, doesn't shy away from the grisly details of what Fred and Rose West did to their victims, and the book has been reprinted forty times since its publication in 1995. Most of Sounes's readers are female. He said:

When readers started to contact me as they do, to say either I love your book or I hate your book, they were almost always women. Their attitude seems to be a curious one, a sort of paradox. They say: 'Oh my God, this story is so terrible, it kept me up all night, how can people do such terrible things?' And then they'll say they couldn't put it down and when they review it online, they give it five stars. They write things like 'oooh, I went to bed all curled up with *Fred & Rose*' followed by an exclamation mark.

As a man I'm unlikely to be the victim of a serial killer, but if you're a young woman, you know that in the back of your mind you do stand that risk and I think that must be what fascinates them. Also, it partly titillates some to be frank. It's a bit like a sort of fun thing, right? It's safe to read about it, but it's something that's connected to you.

On the same day I toured Madame Tussaud's I joined a different crowd of visitors at another grim exhibition entitled 'Executions – 700 years of Public Punishment in London'. There was more of a connection between the two than I had thought. Some of those executed during the nineteenth century became more infamous in death by appearing as exhibits in touring waxwork museums. For authenticity, some donated their clothes to Madame Tussaud, though she would have had to pay for them because traditionally they became the property of the executioner, according to the exhibition's guidebook.

Visitors to the Executions exhibition, held at the Museum of London in Docklands, walked around mostly in silence, perhaps stunned by the gory nature of officially sanctioned violent death, the hanging, the quartering, the beheading, the burning and worse. Who knew that in February 1531 cook Richard Roose was boiled to death near Smithfield market for poisoning two people? He used the porridge he made for the household of the Bishop of Rochester. The guidebook explained how he was dipped up and down in the boiling water until he was dead.

Almost all the visitors at that exhibition were adults, most of them women and a few were accompanying children who looked slightly below the recommended age of twelve. It was the school half-term, though what sort of holiday treat the exhibition was rather baffled me. I overheard the odd whispered conversation, including one woman to her male companion as they read of Richard Roose's fate: 'I hope that was quick, but I don't suppose it was.' Another woman was fanning herself as she gazed at one of the more vivid beheading sketches. I couldn't tell if it was from shock or the effects of the overheated building on the mild autumn day.

The museum's social history curator Beverley Cook said public execution was a subject the museum felt it had to confront because for so long it was an undeniable feature of life in the capital. Even those who didn't join the crowds were much aware of what was happening. And it wasn't just a feature of the very distant past. From 1863 you could go by underground tube train to watch an execution. She said:

> Not everyone went for the same reason. The mob would go for the crime opportunities, to pick pockets and so on, some because they were curious to see particularly gruesome murderers they may have read about or followed their trial and others who wanted to confront death in a funny sort of way. A lot of people wanted to see justice being done.

I asked Cook if she believed people would attend a public execution in Britain today and her answer was unequivocal.

> Oh absolutely, I think that's borne out by the fact so many people watch them online. I suppose to actually physically go and see a public execution, if it was in this country, I think people might feel a bit embarrassed about doing that, but it wouldn't stop them maybe looking at it online, as they did with the ISIS beheadings.

In 2014 and 2015 the terror group posted a number of videoed beheadings of hostages on the internet. Cook said: 'There were more people watching public executions online than there ever were in London, because obviously it's a global audience.'

When Professor Wilson asked his 450 first-year criminology degree students how many of them had watched a beheading video on the internet, all of them raised their hand. He has never watched one and neither have I. I don't need to see it to know it's wrong, and I feel that to watch a beheading even now would be such an invasion of the victim's privacy and dignity. I can't imagine I would have joined the crowds at Tyburn or Smithfield.

I once walked unannounced into a television edit suite and caused panic among five cameraman colleagues who were crowded around a screen, watching one of the earliest beheading videos. Someone hit the off-button and they rushed out, clearly embarrassed. It was as though I had caught young boys watching pornography. I recently asked one of the cameramen who was there why he had wanted to watch it. 'It was partly curiosity,' he said,

> I had never seen one before. As cameramen in war zones we see terrible things and it was probably something to do with proving to myself that I can stomach more than I think. To seek it out is probably quite debasing, but I didn't feel bad about it.

The owner of a crime museum in Gloucestershire, who already had a reputation for showing graphic images, put the beheading videos on display in 2015 and invited me along. I went and did a report, without filming or viewing the videos, and felt sure that as soon as it was broadcast the police or his local council would rush round and try to close the building down. Nothing happened, and many years later you can still watch them at the Crime Through Time Museum at Littledean in the Forest of Dean. As he set up the video display in a discreet corner of the town's beautiful former jail, owner Andy Jones said:

> I'm sure I will be criticised for showing such graphic images, but people have a right to see the true horror of what Islamic State is doing. It's especially important we don't sanitise it, because the government and the police keep warning us that these atrocities are very likely to be committed on the streets of the UK.

Jones may have got away with bad taste, but he couldn't resist closure during the coronavirus pandemic. The museum soon reopened however, and the last time I checked it was thriving. That other house of horrors, the Old Bailey, just about stayed open through the health lockdown but with only a few courts in action. Judges worked from home and we reporters became used to covering cases on video link. By the start of 2023 it was getting back to normal, slowly. A clerk at the Bailey told me that at one stage there were 190 murder trials waiting to be heard, a shocking example of justice delayed for the defendants and their victims' families.

One case that did manage to get on was the sentencing of 25-year-old Ben Oliver, for the manslaughter due to diminished responsibility of his grandfather David Oliver. The hearing was of huge significance because, for the first time in 100 years, cameras were let inside a courtroom. They had been banned in all courts after the publication of a snatched photograph of wife killer Dr Crippen standing in the dock. We and other news media were allowed to broadcast, live, Judge Sarah Munro QC handing down Oliver's sentence and her reasons for it. It was probably the biggest change

I'd seen in the world of crime reporting and the judge's words were more enthralling than I had expected.

It was a complicated case. Oliver had stabbed his grandfather in a frenzy after learning of unproven sex abuse allegations against the 74-year-old. The young killer had suffered years of school bullying, depression and suicidal thoughts. He was diagnosed with autism spectrum disorder. The judge described him as 'irreparably damaged' but also said he was 'a dangerous offender.' The TV viewer really did get a sense of how the judge had to balance justice and fairness, something that would have been lost in my normally distilled version of what I witness and then describe second hand as a court reporter.

The broadcast shed light, too, on a judicial system that is often difficult to understand. It was a victory for democracy and transparency, though there are other areas where justice is increasingly carried out behind closed doors. The Old Bailey broadcast was an extraordinary development, but filming was severely limited. All viewers saw and heard was the judge, in close-up, though there are calls for more general live coverage of trials. There were many people involved in making that first live broadcast happen on the day, from the engineers running cables around the building to the director sitting in our studio eleven miles away. What it hadn't needed was me. Throughout the broadcast, my seat in court was empty. Courts have always been a big part of a crime reporter's life. I wondered if, like those swallowtail butterflies, I really did now belong to an endangered species.

# CHAPTER 19

# THE COPPERS

*Expect to be tested. You will see the absolute worst of humanity and a cruelty to others that will break your heart. So, make sure you are seen as the best of people in this role. You will be the rescuers of many at their darkest times*

– FORMER CHIEF CONSTABLE SIR DAVE THOMPSON

It's over ten years since Lord Leveson published his report into the culture, practices and ethics of the press and dramatically changed the relationship between police and reporters. His brief was to look at media relations with police *and* politicians, but nothing much has changed in the way hacks and MPs interact. They still go drinking together, meet for lunches and swap gossip and information. In a breach of what his Lordship intended, my political reporter colleagues still get exclusive stories from those elected public servants. Lucky them.

Leveson ushered in new privacy concerns that were difficult to argue with: when police ask us to join them on early morning raids, we are no longer invited inside the premises to film suspects being arrested and their homes searched. That had always felt rather intrusive, given that under British law a person is presumed innocent until proved guilty. Even before Leveson, some forces had insisted that if a camera crew did want to follow the hit squad in, then I had to get the suspect's permission to be there. You can probably imagine how many said yes. Other police teams were more helpful and if a suspect asked who we were, the detective's answer was often a vague 'they're with us'.

Much of the media have stopped naming suspects before they are charged, too, unless the name has been published first elsewhere. Police press officers were adamant they would not confirm the names of anyone who was simply arrested. In the past, we could usually get such confirmation from them, unattributably. The first real test of the new post-Leveson mood came soon after his report, with the arrest of entertainer Rolf Harris, in 2013, for indecent assaults on young girls. He was questioned and released on bail. We all found out pretty quickly what was going on, but it took three months for *The Sun* to publish his name. Harris was eventually jailed for more than five years for indecent assaults on four females, one aged seven or eight.

Other celebrities, such as singer Cliff Richard and radio presenter Paul Gambaccini, were wrongly suspected of sex abuse. Their names leaked and were published while they were being investigated and, although they were never charged and were completely exonerated, they felt their reputations would never recover. They and others are still campaigning for a change in the law, to ban the media from naming anyone being investigated for sex crimes. I can imagine that trying to shake off the stigma of sex abuse allegations must be difficult. Discovering the name of an anonymous suspect in a high-profile case, though, is still a big challenge for crime reporters. News editors want to know the identity, as do my own friends and family who know that I might know. I still feel some kudos in providing the answer, even if I can't publish it.

An academic study by Marianne Colbran, a visiting fellow at the London School of Economics, five years after Leveson, said that the clampdown on police contact with reporters had led journalists to look for crime stories elsewhere, including social media. She was referring, specifically, to the Metropolitan Police's media relations, but Leveson's damning of the 'self-serving cosiness' between reporters and their police contacts was taken on board by all forces. We certainly looked for stories elsewhere, but the fact is we always had done. No crime reporter can afford to rely on police contacts alone. There are plenty of other sources: lawyers, politicians, probation officers, prison warders, trade unionists, taxi drivers, viewers, criminals and other journalists. I'm not sure it needed an academic to identify social media as a journalistic source of information. We had been plundering Facebook and Twitter for stories ever since they were created. Relying on what members of the public post, though, has always been a bit of a lottery.

Twitter was launched in 2006 and it was four years later that it suddenly became a prime source of information for me, as I tried to cover a dramatic, breaking crime story. The police would give us only the barest detail, so I had to resort to Twitter postings from witnesses as the drama unfolded. It was a quiet news day when the first hint of the crime popped up on Twitter: 'There's something happened in Sunningdale. Undercover police shooting someone, I think. A30 closed.' There were other tweets that added a little more detail and then a photograph of what looked like a body on the road, behind a white van with its rear door open. In another picture, you could see an armed policeman. A new tweet mentioned two bodies. Thames Valley Police press officers would tell us nothing, but clearly there was something big going on.

What made the story more compelling was the location: Sunningdale, a leafy village of swish golf courses and movie star mansions a few miles from the Queen's own favourite home, Windsor Castle. I sat in the studio discussing the 'incident' for the best part of an hour, until the police confirmed they had stopped a van, found a body inside it and were hunting suspects who were on the run. Everything I reported, initially, was based on, and attributed to, the growing number of tweets. They didn't tell the whole story, but it didn't matter. It was enough to inform our viewers that a major armed police operation was underway. We were persuaded to report the story by the sheer volume of tweets, all describing much the same scene. I took a gamble, and it paid off. I don't recall any great outcry from viewers. What was important was to explain the source of the information and be honest about what we didn't know.

It felt like a seminal moment. It seemed the world had changed, as I had to trust the witness accounts of people I hadn't even spoken to, some of them anonymous. A couple of them, who we were able to identify, were contacted and persuaded to give live interviews down the phone, again a risky business that could have backfired spectacularly. In the end, most of their observations proved to be pretty accurate, though there was only ever one dead body, not two. Businessman Shaleem Amar had been attacked with hammers at his rented luxury mansion, in what police believed was a business row over money. When armed officers intercepted the gang's van, they found 33-year-old Amar dying in the back of it. Four men were later jailed for kidnap, torture and murder.

Concern over the use of information supplied by so-called 'citizen journalists' – basically, the public reporting news – was suddenly swept away. We were already developing an appetite for user-generated content (UGC), usually camera phone footage, and learning what we could and couldn't trust. Today, we all use words and pictures from anywhere and anyone, as long as we can verify it somehow. Contrast that episode with a drama, seven years later, when Twitter wasn't so reliable.

It concerned Oxford Circus Underground Station, one of central London's busiest, which stands in the middle of Oxford Street and Regent Street shopping area. Two men had some sort of row on one of the platforms in November 2017. It was not long after deadly terror attacks in the capital and Manchester. Many shoppers witnessed a rapid evacuation of the station and mistook it for another terror attack, a fear fuelled by misinformed tweeters. They included pop star Olly Murs. He was caught in the panic as he shopped for presents in a department store half a mile away. He posted a series of dramatic messages to his 8.4 million Twitter followers, including: 'Fuck everyone get out of @Selfridges now, gun shots!! I'm inside.' He said he and other shoppers were hiding in one of the store's offices.

Forty-two minutes later, the Metropolitan Police, with its paltry 1.1 million followers, tweeted:

We have not located any trace of suspects, evidence of shots fired or casualties. Officers still on scene. If you are in a building stay there, if you are on the street in #OxfordStreet leave

the area. Officers continue to search the area. More updates as
soon as we have them

Armed police swamped Oxford Street and part of the West End was
evacuated. When police later confirmed no shots had been fired,
Murs was widely mocked for spreading fear, though months later he
suggested he had been correct and there may have been a cover-up.

Scotland Yard's media chief, Ed Stearns, tried to play down the dis-
pute, insisting that the influence Murs may have had on worsening
the panic had been overblown. Stearns had some advice for celebrities with millions of social media followers: 'One hundred percent,
anyone with a large following, if they're in an incident, probably the
most effective tweet they can put out is follow @MetPoliceUK for
latest information and retweet what we're putting out.'

Stearns must have taken it for granted that the public would trust
the police. Perhaps they might in matters of public safety, but the
changes in the relationship between the public and the police, especially the Metropolitan force, is an issue that has overshadowed my
reporting in recent years. Fundamentally, that relationship has been
damaged by a deterioration in two things: culture and performance.

There have always been badly behaved police officers. An extreme example was serial killer Dennis Nilsen, who murdered at
least six men and teenage boys and hid their dismembered bodies
around his north London home. He was a Metropolitan officer for
nearly a year in 1973 but resigned before his killing spree. Nilsen
was a constable at a time of widespread corruption among Scotland
Yard officers. When the reforming commissioner, Sir Robert Mark,
began in his job in 1972 he promised 'to arrest more criminals than
we employ'.

Twenty-five years later, I listened as one of his successors, Sir Paul Condon, said he had 250 corrupt officers he couldn't sack because of an inadequate disciplinary system. It wasn't just the Met. Condon's contemporary, West Midlands Chief Constable Ted Crew, complained that he, too, couldn't get rid of officers 'who wouldn't be employed by Sainsbury's'. At the start of the new millennium, another Met commissioner, Sir John Stevens, told us he was getting to grips with corruption within the ranks, with dozens of officers being prosecuted. The problem persists and threatens the proposition that policing works only with the consent of the public. Taxpayers need to have confidence in the integrity of police officers who, after all, have enormous powers over us all.

Those powers have seldom been more abused than they were by PC Wayne Couzens, a diplomatic protection officer in London, when he abducted, raped and murdered marketing executive Sarah Everard. Although he was off-duty and driving a hire car, he used his police warrant card to stop her as she was walking home alone one March night in 2021. He used the handcuffs he carried to restrain her, after falsely arresting her for allegedly breaching Covid pandemic lockdown laws. Couzens strangled his 33-year-old victim with his police belt. The Couzens case brought a spotlight down again on police vetting procedures. It was revealed that in a previous job with the Civil Nuclear Constabulary, his interest in violent pornography and the discomfort he caused female colleagues had earned him the nickname 'The Rapist'. After he was jailed for life without parole, the Met issued advice to any woman suspicious about a man confronting them and claiming to be a plain-clothed police officer. They were told: 'Wave down a bus.' The press and the public leapt on that ludicrous response. It was widely thought to have contributed to the departure of Commissioner Dame Cressida Dick, the first woman to hold the post, six months later. She quit after losing the confidence of London's Mayor Sadiq Khan.

Although Couzens had no previous convictions, his case prompted Freedom of Information requests from journalists about serving police officers with a criminal past. The Met admitted to 150, with the list of crimes including assault, criminal damage, firearms offences and theft. Some officers had been convicted before their recruitment, others while they were serving in the force. Committing a crime did not mean automatic dismissal for a police officer, though that was an issue that was to come under much more controversy later. *The Sun* went on to make another FOI request, to find out what the situation was in all forty-three of Britain's police forces. It discovered that, nationally, the figure was 354 serving officers with criminal convictions. Sixteen forces, though, refused to give out the information.

Other episodes of appalling police behaviour were revealed in the wake of the Couzens case, again mostly in London. Two officers were jailed for taking and sharing photographs of the bodies of two murdered sisters. Two more policemen based at Charing Cross Police Station were fired for sharing private racist, sexist and misogynistic texts in a chat group on the encrypted WhatsApp messaging service. A constable and a former colleague were jailed for three months for sharing similar messages in a chat group with Couzens, offences that came to light when Couzens was arrested and his mobile phone examined.

The three of them joked about shooting children and disabled people with their electronic Taser guns. They also messaged about raping a female colleague, as well as making racist and homophobic comments. When the two officers appeared in court, they described it all as 'banter' but were convicted of sending grossly offensive messages under the Communications Act, a law drawn up in 2003 when social media was in its infancy and long before WhatsApp existed. Judge Sarah Turnock said: 'The persons to whom these messages relate will undoubtedly [have] been caused great distress by knowing police officers find it funny to joke about them in such a deeply offensive manner ... Significant harm has undoubtedly been caused to public confidence in policing as a result of these offences.'

One of the officers said he had no expectation the messages would or could be read by anyone outside the texting group, a point picked up after the trial by law academic Professor Andrew Tettenborn. The professor accepted the messages were unpleasant, but he questioned the whole prosecution of the two officers. A few days later, I was intrigued to read an article he wrote in the online magazine *Spiked*:

> This policing of private speech should worry us all. Imagine if the two policemen sentenced this week had said exactly the same things to each other in a pub. Or imagine they had merely conversed on the street. The idea that they might be hauled before the courts and imprisoned, simply for sharing offensive comments among themselves, seems absurd. The fact that they spoke on WhatsApp should not turn their conversation into a crime. More alarming still is that the powers-that-be clearly see no problem in this.

A prosecuting barrister I know well told me that he and colleagues believed that public confidence in the police had fallen so much, jurors were not so trusting of police evidence as they once were. He sensed that more trials were ending in acquittals because of this, though that wasn't backed up by statistics. According to the latest data compiled by the Ministry of Justice and His Majesty's Courts and Tribunal Service, acquittal rates have stayed much the same. The data was obtained by Cheryl Thomas KC, professor of judicial studies at University College London. She said: 'The jury acquittal rate has remained stable at around 26 per cent over these three years – despite the fall in prosecutions during Covid. There's no indication of any real change in recent years.' While it's possible the prosecutor's concerns may be reflected in the next set of statistics, it's impossible to know how juries actually arrive at their verdicts. Their deliberations are strictly secret, and no one is allowed to ask about them.

In one magistrates' court, I watched a detective get convicted over a road-rage clash with a female motorist. I stumbled across the case while I was waiting for another, a valuable lesson in staying alert. It's easy to fall asleep after a couple of hours in a stuffy court-room. The two drivers confronted one another over a parking space in a south London street. Trainee Detective Constable Ajitpal Lotay claimed the woman had been abusive to him and had called him either a 'prick or a Paki'. She claimed Lotay had flashed his warrant card at her and threatened to 'call his team and get my car removed'. The chief magistrate, Paul Goldspring, admitted: 'This amounts to a one-word-against-another case.' There were no witnesses and the magistrate had to rely purely on the evidence of the two motorists. He chose to believe the woman, acknowledging that for Lotay his verdict meant 'potentially the end of his career'. The days when a police officer's word was to be believed without question seemed an awfully long time ago. Of course, as it was a magistrates' court, there was no jury involved, but as it was a chief magistrate deciding, on the evidence of the two people involved, that he believed the motorist and not the policeman, it was even more illuminating.

In the wake of the Wayne Couzens case, I had to analyse a lot of official reports as police forces were put under an intense spotlight. In a ten-year review of policing in England and Wales, the outgoing chief inspector of constabulary, Sir Tom Winsor, said public confidence was damaged and needed to be restored. His State of Policing 2021 report took some wading through because it was 200 pages long. He praised advances in the investigation of some crimes, such as domestic abuse, but criticised a woeful response to fraud. He also pointed out that a chronically low provision of mental health treatment was putting an unfair burden on police officers who increasingly had to deal with sufferers. He said the current forty-three regional forces should be scrapped in favour of a single system and called for more police funding: 'The public must decide how much threat, harm and risk they are prepared to tolerate.' Sir Tom also highlighted how as many as 850,000 children were susceptible to danger online, including the threat from predatory paedophiles. 'Would the public tolerate low funding of those sorts of crime if they knew that figure?' he said. 'We used to say that children were unsafe out at night, now they are more unsafe in their own bedrooms.'

Prevention, said Winsor, was the cheapest way of cutting crime. He was pointing out the obvious, but he clearly felt it needed to be said. The prevention of crime and disorder was the first of nine principles of policing, defined by Sir Robert Peel, the reforming Home Secretary who established the Metropolitan Police Service in 1829. At the same time as Winsor's report, the independent think tank the Police Foundation called for the setting up of a Crime Prevention

Agency to help solve 'a crisis of confidence in policing'. Its report was a mere 192 pages long. It urged for more neighbourhood policing and better training. Most controversially, the Foundation suggested a renewable licence-to-practise for all police officers, like doctors, but that idea was fiercely rejected by the Police Federation, which represents junior ranks.

More and more reports kept landing on my desk. The Home Office released shocking figures showing how few crimes ended up with anyone being charged: less than 7 per cent for house burglaries, 4 per cent for theft and only 1 per cent for car theft. Winsor's successor as chief inspector of constabulary, Andy Cooke, said in a follow-up report: 'The current low charge rates for these crimes are unacceptable and unsustainable – there needs to be a concerted drive to address this issue because it directly affects the public's confidence in the police's ability to keep them safe.'

All this was happening at a time when the government, after years of public spending cuts and falling police numbers, was funding the hiring of an extra 20,000 officers to be in place by the spring of 2023. Police were hit with more FOI requests, one which revealed that of the 15,000 trainee officers recruited so far, 1,837 of them had already quit because of dissatisfaction over pay, conditions or job expectations. Zoë Billingham, a former inspector of constabulary, said the recruitment process was being rushed and questioned the motives of some applicants. She told BBC Radio 4's *Today* programme:

Are people coming into policing with their eyes open or is there a glorified sort of box-set view of what policing is? I despair when I see police recruitment adverts focusing on the helicopters, the fast cars, the dogs, the guns. Actually, the day-to-day job of policing is very often dealing with some of the most vulnerable members of our community who are in crisis and who need care and compassion.

Billingham agreed with police who felt overwhelmed by their workload. She said if the public expected a better service, it may have to pay more in taxes to ensure their communities were safe.

Tom Fontyn may be just the sort of police recruit Billingham hoped was signing up. When I first met him, he was working in a cafe. After three years, and a variety of other jobs in local shops and bars, he decided it was time to get a career. When I saw him again in 2022, he had completed his fifteen weeks' training with Sussex Police and had just, rather nervously he admitted, made his first arrest.

> We are taught to respect people, treat them like you would your mum and dad, or your brother. Just being human is the really important thing. I want to help people. If you are called to deal with someone really struggling, and you're the only person they see that day, in the time you are with them you can try and make a good impact on them, maybe guide them, even change their views on the police.

His thoughts echoed the words of another policeman I knew, someone at the other end of the police hierarchy. Sir Dave Thompson, the outgoing chief constable of West Midlands Police, gave a speech to all his new recruits in which he urged them:

> Expect to be tested. You will see the absolute worst of humanity and a cruelty to others that will break your heart. So, make sure you are seen as the best of people in this role. You will be the rescuers of

many at their darkest times. Don't judge those you serve. So many of them lack the opportunity you have had. Your friendship and service to those in need is unconditional. Never become jaded or think the public are not behind you. The British public are in their character reserved and silent in their quiet support. Saving thanks for the big moments but always knowing you stand between them and the dark.

At the age of twenty-seven, Tom Fontyn failed his first police interview and was rejected. He was told there was a lot of demand for the new jobs on offer, but he was encouraged to apply again and was accepted. The troubled time policing was going through, it seemed, wasn't deterring new recruits. It certainly hadn't put off Tom. He said: 'Whenever the police mess up, it's always straight on the news, but people like Wayne Couzens are just individuals, they don't represent policing.'

However, those who had once thought that being a police officer was a job for life have been quitting in greater numbers than ever before. I was told about Detective Sergeant Tom Hurley, who resigned after sixteen years with the Metropolitan Police, leaving behind what must have been an exciting career in which he had worked on counter-terror, homicide, fraud and cybercrime. He wrote on the LinkedIn social media site:

These unique roles in policing have all afforded me the opportunity to achieve some amazing things, with an incredible team of people that always went above and beyond (working every hour of the day and night, forgoing sleep and cancelling plans with family and friends) to put the most dangerous offenders in prison for a very long time, and deliver justice and hopefully some comfort to the families of the victims. I enjoyed (almost) every minute.

But he'd had enough, he explained: 'I miss my role … [and] the people, but not the place, nor the politicisation of policing and the constant media bashing.' There can hardly be a more police-orientated family than Tom Hurley's. His father, grandfather, great uncle and two uncles were all police officers. His grandmother worked for the police as a civilian. Two cousins are still detectives.

His father Kevin Hurley, a 69-year-old retired detective chief superintendent, told me that he understood how his son had become disillusioned.

I'm mortified but relieved about Tom leaving and delighted he's gone into a job doubling his pay. He's working much shorter hours and without the worry of complaints, gender identification, saying the wrong thing, having to be politically correct in the office and seeing people, for diversity reasons, being leapfrogged for promotion over his head. What finally made him go was the constant criticism of his mission, being a police officer, the lack of focus from leadership on catching bad people and the sense of a lack of support from the senior officers. When he resigned, his chief inspector sent him three texts: can you help me find your replacement, don't forget to hand in your kit and good luck in your new job. In that order. When he had his end-of-service interview, which they all have, a senior officer asked Tom if he could help him with his own CV because he wanted to get out as well. There's a much used saying among cops now: TJF, the job's fucked.

It would be easy to dismiss Kevin Hurley as an out-of-date, politically incorrect, old-fashioned cop, but he still cares passionately about law and order, enough to have been voted in as the first police and crime commissioner in Surrey. There, before he lost out in the next election, he promoted a zero-tolerance policing approach to tackle low-level crime in the belief it would help reduce more serious offending. Although he sympathised over his son's resignation from the Metropolitan Police, he tried to re-join himself when he applied to become the commissioner in 2022. He was hardly surprised, though, that he was rejected without an interview for the job that eventually went to Sir Mark Rowley. 'Like the rest of my family, I have too much to say which has always held me back from promotion, although I got the same grade as Mark Rowley on the strategic command course for senior leaders,' he joked. It's Hurley's humour and honesty that has kept the two of us in touch for many years.

I first met Hurley, a long-serving volunteer army reserve paratrooper, in the middle of a football hooligan riot in Toulouse, south-west France, during the 1998 World Cup. His army background was being put to good use. A stocky figure, he was dressed in a rugby shirt and big, baggy shorts and was warning rampaging England fans to shut up and behave, or they would be arrested. Rioting could get 'our' team thrown out of the tournament, he told them. He carried a megaphone to help get his message across. He'd been brought in to lead the British police squad helping the French deal with hooliganism, what's known in football circles around the world as 'the English disease'. Hurley was chosen for the job because of his experience in crowd control and his fluent French. He said he had got to know his French counterparts at a pre-World Cup tournament in Morocco, where they had bonded over boozy nights in gangster bars. Kevin wasn't your average cop.

Twenty-four years on, he told me:

> I really wanted the commissioner's job because I knew exactly what was wrong with the Met and policing in general. The culture, the behaviour, has gone bad for a minority because there are not enough good leaders, the inspectors, chief inspectors and superintendents who manage teams of officers. You can trace that back to the early 1990s when those ranks were stripped of overtime payments. It meant a lot of good detectives didn't want to climb the ranks and lose their overtime, so you ended up with others, over-promoted officers who couldn't discipline or inspire their teams. That's why we got Couzens, the Charing Cross text messaging group and so on.

In his application to be the new Met commissioner, Hurley wrote: 'The Met is in an accelerating decline. You now have the choice. Appoint someone who is the norm, has likely been part of that. Or try someone different. I am that.'

In appointing Sir Mark Rowley in 2022, the Home Secretary and the Mayor of London did choose someone who had been 'part of that', though he had left the force in 2018 after four years in charge of specialist operations, including counter-terror. At his retirement party, Rowley told me he needed a rest and, with his family's support, was going travelling alone in south-east Asia where he expected to study yoga. I don't know if he was seeking inner peace, conscious-ness expansion or a guiding light, but if he was, even then, plotting his return, the force he took over was very different from the one he left. Rocked by the recent staff scandals, the force was also failing in tackling crime and had just been put into special measures by the chief inspector of constabulary. The police watchdog had found the force had failed to record 69,000 crimes and was providing a poor service to victims. The sanction meant the force would be subject to enhanced monitoring and support for the foreseeable future.

When Sir Mark returned, four years after his retirement, the Home Secretary warned him he had to 'get the basics right', turn the force around and lead the charge for better policing across the UK. He told me during one interview that his friends thought he was crazy to want the job. On the other hand, things could hardly get worse. When, within a month, a report found racism, misogyny and homophobia in his force, he took it on the chin, but, although he didn't say so, it hadn't been on his watch. He promised more trust, less crime and high standards, a mantra he joked should be tattooed on his forehead. Rowley, like his predecessors, vowed to get rid of hundreds of corrupt or badly behaved officers. He also launched a blitz on burglars, robbers and drug suppliers and warned courts to expect a wave of prosecutions. In his first four months, he gave media interviews all over the place, conscious no doubt of his predecessor's much-criticised defensiveness. On his first day back I stood beside him, admiring the view from the eight-floor balcony of Scotland Yard. 'Impressive, isn't it?' he said. 'Yes,' I agreed, 'and it's all yours.' He smiled. I didn't add: 'For better or worse.'

At the start of 2023, Rowley said he was optimistic about the future of policing because of the 'extraordinary people' under his command. He paid tribute to them in a New Year statement on his LinkedIn profile page, where he quoted Theodore Roosevelt, who, before he became the 26th President of the United States, was the police commissioner of New York:

It is not the critic who counts; not the man who points out how the strong man stumbles, or where the doer of deeds could have done them better. The credit belongs to the man who is actually in the arena, whose face is marred by dust and sweat and blood; who strives valiantly; who errs, who comes short again and again, because there is no effort without error and shortcoming.

I wasn't sure who, through Roosevelt, the commissioner was having a dig at. But I didn't take it personally.

The new year was barely a fortnight old when Rowley's optimism took a severe bashing. PC David Carrick, an officer who carried a gun to guard Parliament and foreign embassies, pleaded guilty in court to a catalogue of sex attacks on vulnerable women during his twenty-year career with the Metropolitan Police. His crimes included twenty-four rapes. He treated his victims as sex slaves, regularly humiliated them and locked some in a tiny understairs cupboard. Carrick told them: 'You'll be safe with me, I'm a police officer.' He also warned them that if they reported his behaviour, their word would never be believed over his because he was a policeman. Even when he *was* reported, no action was taken. Police had nine opportunities to stop him before he was finally arrested.

I have rarely spent such a busy week as I did covering the Carrick fallout. Like sex killer PC Wayne Couzens two years earlier, the Carrick case provoked widespread horror and condemnation and prompted similar, obvious questions: how could he have ever become a cop, why wasn't he stopped, what did his colleagues know of his behaviour? The answers were due to be delivered in a number of upcoming reports. And, more fundamentally, what has gone so wrong with British policing? Once again, there were calls for a dramatic overhaul to ensure tougher vetting, more whistle-blowers and a fast-track system for sacking bad officers. What it needed, police, politicians, the media and the public agreed, was a change in police culture and standards. Every staff member in the forty-three regional forces in England and Wales, a figure of 227,000, was to be checked for any complaint against them, of misogyny or predatory behaviour, that hadn't been properly investigated. It was a huge undertaking, as if police weren't busy enough, but in the prevailing mood few argued against it.

The Metropolitan Police, by far the country's biggest force, is always at the forefront of British policing issues. It handles the most controversial investigations, it has the biggest successes and the worst failures. In the past few years, the force has lurched from one crisis to another. It's become the lightning rod for policing failings.

It has survived troubled times before – corruption scandals, the Macpherson Report and the phone-hacking investigation – though it hasn't always learned the lessons.

The Met solves extraordinary cases. It has great detective stories to tell, but it's not very good at selling them because its press officers have sometimes exhibited a bunker mentality, too used to explaining the mistakes and not exploring the good things their colleagues do.

Crime reporters will hold the Met to account, of course, but we are not looking to bash it up all the time. I, for one, would rather be telling viewers about extraordinary detective work. The brand name of its iconic headquarters Scotland Yard is soiled, yet it is still tasked with showing the way forward in restoring public confidence and trust in policing.

# EPILOGUE

When mother-of-two Nicola Bulley disappeared without a trace from a Lancashire riverbank, her family and friends expected her to turn up within hours. When she didn't, the country was gripped by a new mystery: did she somehow go into the water and drown, as the police thought, or had she disappeared for some other unexplained reason, as her family desperately hoped? To add to the riddle, the experienced leader of an independent search team suggested a 'third party' was involved. He wanted to know if Nicola had any enemies or stalkers, implying she may have been abducted or killed. Conspiracy theories were already rife; when it emerged that a witness had told police about a suspicious 'tatty red van' parked up near where she began her walk, it simply added to the intrigue.

It was a crime story in all but name. It certainly felt like one, and everyone treated it as such: the police who assembled a team of forty detectives, news chiefs who assigned crime reporters to the case, and the public who provided a huge audience for TV, newspaper and online media reports. The Nicola Bulley story encapsulated many of the themes I have explored in this book, not least the public's fascination with crime.

The media attention was such that it prompted complaints from other families whose loved ones had gone missing and, despite police appeals, had attracted nothing like the coverage. The news agenda is driven by several things – timing, space, taste and so on – but people are always engaged by a mystery. Nicola seemed to have vanished into thin air.

Part of her appeal was how ordinary she appeared: a mum who had just dropped off her two young daughters at school before taking the family dog Willow for a walk through the idyllic countryside. As she strolled near the River Wyre in the village of St Michael's on Wyre, she used her mobile phone to dial in to a work conference call. The phone was later found on a bench, still connected to the call. Nicola was nowhere to be seen.

She was an attractive, hard-working woman who was used to juggling several demands at once. Often dressed in an anorak and bobble hat, she had posted many selfies on previous walks near the spot where she was last seen. They showed a happy 45-year-old with a captivating smile. People could relate to Nicola. She was a white, blonde, middle-class woman. They identified with her. They wanted to know all about her and find out what had happened to her.

In the UK, on average, one person is reported missing every ninety seconds, according to the charity Missing People. It's an astonishing figure. It means that on Friday 27 January 2023, Nicola may have been one of nearly 1,000 people across the country whose whereabouts someone was sufficiently worried about to raise an alarm. I'm not aware of any of the others making national news.

Most missing people turn up or are found within forty-eight hours. Almost all, 97 per cent, return within a week. The search for Nicola went on and on.

Developments in the case regularly achieved some of the highest viewing figures on Sky. The search was constantly front-page news in national papers, which, because of dwindling sales, cannot afford to misjudge their readers' interests. Feature writers joined their news reporter colleagues in the media blitz. At the same time, tens of thousands of people had died in the Turkish and Syrian earthquake, but while that tragedy attracted huge interest and sympathy, it didn't resonate on such a personal level as Nicola's story. People couldn't imagine being buried alive by tumbling buildings in a poverty-stricken town 2,000 miles away, but they could see themselves doing the school drop-off, taking the dog for a walk, strolling along a country path on a chilly morning...

Victims of crime are usually doing something mundane, simply going about their everyday business like the rest of us, when horror strikes. Maybe we dwell on their misfortune because we feel lucky it wasn't us. Madeleine McCann vanished from a holiday apartment on the sort of package trip millions of us have taken, but without such a tragic ending. When schoolgirl Sarah Payne ran innocently from a Sussex cornfield into the clutches of a murdering paedophile, in their minds people could place their own children at the scene and give thanks the same thing didn't happen to them.

When I first read about the way in which serial killers Fred and Rose West cruised the streets in their car, stopping to pick up female teenage hitchhikers in the 1970s, I immediately thought of how many lifts my own sister accepted from strangers as she thumbed her way to and from university.

We all share a basic morbid curiosity about bad things, especially someone else's troubles. Who doesn't glance across from the safety of their own car as they crawl past the scene of a motorway crash? But how many of us would admit to an appetite for the bloodiest details of the goriest crimes? Well, apparently, if we have such an interest, we should acknowledge it, because it's not a sign of abnormal tastes. It's human nature, a necessary defence mechanism, according to psychologists. Knowing who commits such crimes, how and why, can actually help us protect ourselves from similar threats. That especially applies to women, who are far more likely to be the victims rather than the perpetrators of violence. That may be why they are much bigger consumers than men of true crime books, documentaries and podcasts.

Criminal psychologist Amanda Vicary explains that it's women in particular who study the details to learn defence tactics:

It's all related to survival, right? If you know how to escape when you're kidnapped, if you know what red flags to look for in a new romantic partner, all of these things could prevent you from being kidnapped or killed yourself. My studies show that women are really drawn to these elements and drawn to them more than men are, and it's likely because we women fear being the victim of a crime. And so this heightened fear of crime draws us … to learn what went wrong, to try to keep it from happening to us.

Stoking a fear of crime was something that once severely troubled news policy chiefs at the BBC. They issued guidelines on sensational reporting, urged editors to limit crime coverage and banned the showing and description of horrific details. The corporation scrapped the post of national crime correspondent, a role shared since by its home affairs reporters. I'm not sure its concerns lasted, because it gave prominent coverage to the grim details of the crimes of rogue cops Wayne Couzens and David Carrick.

Until the recent upsurge in true crime productions, I'd never thought much about the reasons for people's fascination with crime. I cover the stories and just assume viewers and readers are as interested as I am. But something must have made me choose crime over, say, politics, transport or health reporting. The truth is, I can't get as curious about a sudden Cabinet reshuffle, a planned high-speed rail link or a new cancer drug as I can about a diamond heist, a serial killer or a super conman.

The exposure of fraudster Mark Acklom got a huge response from those entranced by the astonishing stories he spun. How could his victims have fallen for his lies? How could Carolyn Woods, the woman he wooed and promised to marry, have possibly believed he was a Swiss banker, a multi-millionaire and an MI6 spy, whose absences were explained by his secret training missions to Iraq? When he told her he'd been shot, she went to his hospital, but he insisted, for security reasons, on meeting her in the car park. He appeared with an expertly bandaged head and part of an intravenous drip dangling down the front of his medical gown.

Woods very eloquently described to me how plausible she found Acklom. It's not difficult to understand that, subconsciously, she wanted to believe him and, like the best fraudsters, he exploited that desire. I'm sure many of those who followed my reporting of Acklom did so in the hope of learning how to recognise such characters and avoid the same pitfalls.

The disappearance of Nicola Bulley also demonstrated how

the public love to play detective. I was bombarded with theories about what might have happened to her, whether she was alive or dead. People sent me their research into her personal finances, interpretations of her friends' comments, analysis of her family's body language. It was no surprise. Armchair detectives are fed on an increasingly concentrated diet of TV crime dramas and documentaries. Viewers are regularly urged to consider the evidence of unsolved cases.

My colleagues in our regional bureau very quickly established a good relationship with Nicola's family. They did the first interview with her parents and sister and then did one with her partner. I covered the story twice from the scene and a week into the search I got a text from one of Nicola's best friends, saying: 'You're all so lovely! Thank you so much. I cannot say the BIGGEST thank you to you all, for keeping the story alive as the search continues!' We were all stunned when, as police announced after three weeks that a body retrieved from the river had been identified as Nicola's, a senior officer read out, live on television, a statement from her family that included the line: 'We tried last night to take in what we had been told in the day, only to have Sky News and ITV making contact with us, directly, when we expressly asked for privacy.'

I've no idea what was said and done by my colleagues or rivals, but the criticism shone a harsh light on a dilemma I mention elsewhere. The work of a journalist covering the story of a missing person is naturally intrusive. Some families welcome our enquiries, others merely tolerate us. They must value our initial interest because we are the conduit for their pleas for the public's help, but I doubt that any of them pause to consider where the relationship might lead. As the story grows, so does our intrusion. Sometimes we build up a close, even warm relationship. We encourage relatives to share their feelings and, occasionally, they reveal quite intimate thoughts. What, then, should we do when the worst news is broken to them? Ignore them, drop all contact and be accused of cynicism now 'the story' is over? It seems far more human and understandable to maintain brief contact and simply pass on condolences. It's a fine judgement.

Nicola's case also highlighted a wider concern: a lack of confidence in the police, something that was troubling forces everywhere. It didn't matter that Lancashire Police had recently been given a general 'good' rating in an efficiency inspection. All over the country, British policing was being hammered for poor standards and performance. Serving officers were being convicted of murder and rape and misogynistic behaviour, violence was on the rise, detection rates of burglary and theft had plummeted. It had become easy to lose faith in the experts.

When Lancashire Police couldn't find Nicola after ten days, her frustrated family brought in a private search team. Like the parents of Madeleine McCann, there was a danger they, too, were falling out with the very people whose job it was to help them. The area was also invaded by amateur sleuths, some streaming their own thoughts live on social media as they scoured the riverbank for clues that they thought the police had missed.

Faced with increasing criticism, police felt forced into making an extraordinary disclosure to counter 'false information, accusations and rumours'. They revealed that Nicola had been graded as high risk of harm when she vanished because of alcohol problems and struggles with the menopause. The force may have regained some public understanding of the focus of its investigation, but it did so at great cost to Nicola and her family's privacy and it did nothing to boost confidence in police attitudes to women. For the foreseeable future, perhaps, all high-profile operations will be viewed through the prism of a failing police service.

When it comes to my reporting, I can't always avoid the horror. Sometimes it's necessary to delve deeply into it if I want to convince an audience I know what I'm talking about. The morning I spent with two Scotland Yard detectives in the occult crime unit in Pretoria, where they were investigating the sacrificial murder of a little boy, was one of the most uncomfortable experiences I've ever had. I've described some of the crime scene photographs we saw elsewhere in this book but not all of them, because the worst were almost beyond imagination.

In the preface I wrote about another boy, decapitated by his own father in another ritualistic killing. I still have a photograph of the bloody scene, though I could never broadcast it and wouldn't want to. Yet I'm sure there are many who would like to see it. I have to acknowledge there is a desire among some people for the things others recoil at.

The psychologists and criminologists may be right that, even if we aren't consciously aware of it, each one of us has a basic instinct for gore. Alongside the desire to learn how criminals operate to protect ourselves from similar attacks, the need to ensure those in power are held to account, the flirtations with apparently lavish and exciting lifestyles and the drive to see justice done, this simple, genetic fascination is no doubt what drives so many people to consume the details of the crimes I report on. But I work in the mainstream media. It can cater for people's appetites only up to a point and, though reporters may once have dwelt on the grimmer aspects of violent crime, that point is shifting in favour of a more sensitive audience. There are other places to go to satisfy such cravings.

Soon after Covid lockdown restrictions were lifted, Andy Jones reopened his astonishing Crime Through Time museum in Gloucestershire. I asked him if there had been any renewed attempt to shut down his exhibition of ISIS beheading videos. He said he'd had several complaints. Police came in and looked around, but they took no action. I still found it difficult to believe that Jones had installed the videos in the first place, and that visitors had actually wanted to watch them. Outside the building he posted plenty of notices about the content inside, but for years visitors have known to expect uncensored exhibits. I hesitate to call them attractions. Jones makes it clear the place is not suitable for children. He also produces advertising flyers declaring it 'the UK's most infamous and politically incorrect black museum'. I can't decide if he wrote that as a warning to keep out or an inducement to enter.

# ACKNOWLEDGEMENTS

For a long time, people have been telling me I should write a book. I hope they were right. More importantly, I hope they bought it. Many friends, colleagues, acquaintances, relatives and complete strangers have contributed in some way to what's here.

I'm especially grateful to those I interviewed for the book and their names are recorded where I've quoted them. Others agreed to read various passages and comment as the writing progressed. A few more simply encouraged me to keep going or urged me on with the odd 'isn't that bloody book finished yet?'

Thanks also, in alphabetical order, to: Paula Sousa Baquero, Shekhar Bhatia, Sam Bordbar, Andrew Brunt, Rebecca Camber, Carolyn Castledine, Simon Howson-Green, Clive Jackson, Mark Loebell, Jordan Milne, Ken Millett, Henry Milner, Will O'Reilly, Geoff Paterson, Stephen Rayner, Toby Sculthorp, Mike Sullivan, Tony Summers, Robbyn Swan, Tot Taylor, Craig Turner, John Twomey, Ashley White, Carolyn Woods and Stephen Wright. And to those who chose to stay anonymous.

Thanks to my fellow hacks, especially the crime reporters, whose daily chronicling of grim events I've plundered gratefully. Along the road, I've often had great help, too, from photographers. I miss the inspiration and fun of Geoff Garvey and Jimmy 'The Prince of Darkness' Nicholson. They both taught me a lot.

At Sky News, thanks to Jonathan Levy and John Ryley, and especially to John O'Loan who lured me onto the telly in the first place. I owe a big debt to all the camera operators, engineers, news editors, video editors, producers, directors, assistants, floor managers, archivists, runners and make-up artists. Especially the make-up artists. Ryan Ward and his colleagues in technical support have kept me plugged in and connected.

Thanks to many press officers, mostly those at the Metropolitan Police, the National Crime Agency, the Home Office, the Ministry of Justice, the Crown Prosecution Service, the NPCC, the IOPC, HMICFRS and Crimestoppers.

My agent Andrew Gordon at David Higham Associates showed enthusiasm from the start and offered crucial advice. At Biteback, Olivia Beattie, James Stephens and editor Ryan Norman made the book happen.

I wrote about a few of these characters first in *GQ* magazine, where its former deputy editor Bill Prince showed me that I was capable of writing more than 300 words.

Thanks to my parents who instilled in me confidence, an enquiring mind and a sense of right and wrong: everything you need to be a crime reporter, or a police officer. Or a villain. I *think* they were happy with my choice.

And special thanks to Eve, my partner, for her amazing faith and support. Her unsung editing skills made this a better book.

## ACKNOWLEDGEMENTS

Apologies if I've forgotten anyone or misremembered names, places or events. As Laurie Lee said: 'Some of the facts may be distorted by time.' The mistakes and omissions are all mine. I probably *should* have written this a long time ago.

# INDEX